101 REASONS TO QUIT BELIEVING IN THE MORMON GOD(S)

(From a Mormon's Perspective)

101 REASONS TO QUIT BELIEVING IN THE MORMON GOD(S)

(From a Mormon's Perspective)

Richard Nemelka

PearlPublishing.net

**101 Reasons to Quit Believing in the Mormon God(s)
(From a Mormon's Perspective)**

Text copyright © 2016 Richard S. Nemelka
Cover design copyright © 2018 Pearl Publishing, LLC

All rights reserved. No part of this book may be used or reproduced in any manner whatsoever without written permission of the author or publisher, except by a reviewer who may quote brief passages.

October 2018
Second Edition

SOFTCOVER
ISBN 978-0-9826175-5-7

Pearl Publishing, LLC
2587 Southside Blvd., Melba, ID 83641
www.pearlpublishing.net—1.888.499.9666

TABLE OF CONTENTS

Table of Contents v
Explanation of Abbreviations ix
Introduction xi

REASONS

1 – God Hasn't Answered My Prayers 1
2 – Too Much Ambiguity in Answers to Prayer 4
3 – Reliance Upon Faith is Not Enough 8
4 – Lack of Personal Experiences in Knowing God 11
5 – Difficulty in Finding God Through Scriptures............................... 13
6 – Lack of Proof of God's Existence 16
7 – God Doesn't Seem to Care Anymore 19
8 – God's Lack of Concern for Mankind's Suffering 24
9 – God is an Absentee God 26
10 – God Changes His Involvement with Mankind 29
11 – God is not the Same Yesterday, Today, and Forever 31
12 – God is not Fair 34
13 – God is a Jealous God 37
14 – God is a God of Confusion 39
15 – God Makes Mistakes 43
16 – God is a God of War and Violence 46
17 – The Mormon God Discriminates Based on Nationality 51
18 – The Mormon God Discriminates Based on Religion 54
19 – The Mormon God Discriminates Based on Race 59
20 – The Mormon God Discriminates Based on Gender 61

v

21 – The Mormon God Changes His Revealed Word 64
22 – God, The Father Once Being a Man 67
23 – Doctrine of Man Becoming a God 71
24 – Only Some of Us Can Become Gods 73
25 – Christ as a Spirit Son Being a God 76
26 – Questions About the Holy Ghost 78
27 – Becoming a God Without Gaining a Physical Body 80
28 – Problems With Joseph Smith's First Vision 82
29 – Absence of Plain and Precious Truths Restored 85
30 – Problems with the Book of Mormon God 87
31 – The Confusing Godhead in the Book of Mormon 89
32 – Gods with Too Many Names 94
33 – Lack of Evidence Supporting the Book of Mormon 97
34 – The Book of Mormon's Murder of Laban 101
35 – God's Destruction of Cities in the Book of Mormon 103
36 – Lack of DNA in Authenticating the Book of Mormon 106
37 – Book of Mormon's Lanugage is Lost 110
38 – Joseph Smith, the Real Author of the Book of Mormon 114
39 – God Wouldn't Have Authored the Book of Mormon 116
40 – Lack of Gold Plates 119
41 – Questions about the D&C God 122
42 – A Confusing Exception to the Gospel Plan 125
43 – The Three Degrees of Glory Controversy 127
44 – Issues with the Doctrine and Covenants' Revelations 129
45 – The Word of Wisdom Problems 132
46 – Doctrine and Covenants Section 132 (Polygamy) 135
47 – Doctrine of Multiple Wives in Heaven 138
48 – The New Jerusalem and Independence, Missouri 140
49 – Necessity of Temples and Temple Work 143

50 – The Temple Creation Ceremony Inconsistencies 146
51 – Problems with Temple Signs and Tokens 151
52 – Taking One's Life 153
53 – Baptisms for the Dead Questions 156
54 – Endowments for the Dead Confusion 159
55 – Celestial Marriage Problems 161
56 – Questions About Mormon Rituals 163
57 – Adam and Eve Discrepancies 167
58 – Mankind's Lack of Opportunity to Have the Gospel 169
59 – Lack of Revelations Since Joseph Smith 171
60 – Problems with the Pearl of Great Price God 173
61 – The Book of Abraham Problems 176
62 – Incorrect Translation of the Papyri 178
63 – Changes for Blacks and the Priesthood 182
64 – Existence of Kolob and the Throne of God 185
65 – God Creating Other Worlds Without Number 188
66 – God's Centillion Spirit Children 191
67 – God's Firstborn, Second Born, etc. 193
68 – The Absence of a Heavenly Mother 196
69 – War in Heaven Inconsistencies 198
70 – Perfect God Loses One Third of His Children 201
71 – Satan, Lucifer, or the Devil Problems 203
72 – Questions About the Pre-Existence 206
73 – Ambiguity of the Creators of the Earth 208
74 – Problems with Man Being the First Flesh on Earth 210
75 – Non-Belief in Dinosaurs 212
76 – A Vengeful Old Testament God 214
77 – Noah and the Flood Inconsistencies 217
78 – Moses and the passover Killings 219

79 – Two Sets of Commandments Given to Moses 221
80 – Joshua and the Invasion of the Promised Land 224
81 – Job and the Bet Between God and Satan 226
82 – Differences in Same Verses of Scripture 228
83 – New Testament Book of Revelation Difficulties 234
84 – New Testament Records Not Preserved 237
85 – New Testament Not Written at the Time it Happened 240
86 – The God in Joseph Smith's Translation of the Bible 242
87 – Differences in the New Testament Gospels 244
88 – Miracles Then, But None Now 247
89 – Visions Then, But None Now 250
90 – Christ's Alleged Perfect Life 252
91 – Is the Atonement Really Necessary? 255
92 – This Life Should Not Determine Eternity 258
93 – Confusion in the Second Coming 260
94 – Joseph Smith's Second Coming Confusion 264
95 – Battle of Gog and Magog Confusion 266
96 – Millennium Inconsistencies 268
97 – Judgments of God Issues 270
98 – Death and the Spirit World Questions 273
99 – Necessity of Missionaries in the Spirit World 277
100 – God's Language Used to Communicate with Man 282
101 – Still No Answer to Prayers 284

EXPLANATION OF ABBREVIATIONS

As Mormons, we believe in four (4) books of scripture or revelations from God. They are: (1) the Bible (King James Version) containing the Old and New Testaments; (2) *The Book of Mormon* (an alleged religious history of the early inhabitants of the Americas); (3) *The Doctrine and Covenants* (revelations and visions given to Joseph Smith and others); and (4) *The Pearl of Great Price* (revelations and translations given to Joseph Smith). Joseph Smith also wrote *History of the Church* and an *Inspired Translation* of the Old and New Testament.

All of the above books are referenced numerous times in *101 Reasons* and therefore have often been abbreviated as follows:

> King James Version .... KJV
> Old Testament .... OT
> New Testament .... NT
> Book of Mormon .... *BOM*
> Doctrine and Covenants .... *D&C*
> Pearl of Great Price .... *PGP*
> History of the Church.......................... *HC*
> Joseph Smith's Translation .... *JST*
> (Also referred to as the *Inspired Translation*.)

INTRODUCTION

God, the Eternal Father, his son, Jesus Christ, and the Holy Ghost are the three (3) distinct and separate Gods of Mormon theology. This "Godhead" sets Mormonism apart from other Christian religions. At the beginning of the 2012 Republican Party presidential race, two Mormon candidates (Mitt Romney and Jon Huntsman, Jr.) both received some negative criticism concerning their beliefs in God and Jesus Christ. Matt Slick, president and founder of CARM, called the Mormon religion a "cult," based upon its belief in many Gods (Slick). This opposition is not surprising, considering that the Mormon "Gods" are very different from the "God" or "Gods" believed in by other religions.

For most of recorded history, man has been attempting to find "God," examining thousands of paths (both spiritual and intellectual), trying to obtain this knowledge. Apparently, many believe they have found their "God," based on the fact that over ninety percent (90%) of the world's population believe in some type of God, Gods, or a Supreme Being. Further, as mentioned in the *Dictionary of Gods and Goddesses* by Michael Jordan, there are over 2,500 entries of deities derived from various cultures in the past and the present (viii). I am one of these searchers, attempting to find answers to questions about Deity, especially the Gods of the Mormon religion.

Finding God is a personal quest—one that an individual has to make for him or herself. I was raised a Mormon, but have had numerous questions about the Mormon God(s) in whom myself, Mitt Romney, and Jon Huntsman, Jr. were taught to believe. I thought I believed in them. However, over the past ten (10) years, through enormous reading, pondering, and examination, I have encountered 101 reasons why I should quit believing in the God or Gods of the Mormon religion. Many of these reasons I have struggled with for fifty (50) years, but have never found satisfactory answers.

There are many well-educated Mormons who have achieved substantial success in business, politics, science, education, sports, and other endeavors. The General Authorities of the Mormon Church, which includes the Prophet, First Presidency, and the Twelve Apostles, are also well-educated and intelligent people. All of these men were taught to believe in the Mormon God or Gods; and perhaps they have either had a Divine Intervention in their lives, where God has answered their prayers or appeared to them, or the *101 Reasons* discussed herein have not affected them the same way that they have me.

This is hard for me to understand; but then (as indicated herein), there are way too many things that I do not understand. I have tried to explain the *101 Reasons* in plain and simple language that almost everyone, including myself, can understand. Hopefully, the Reasons elaborated herein are worthy of the reader's examination and consideration. Some Reasons may be more relevant or worthy of examination than others. I have only discussed those that I personally have struggled with throughout the years.

I could have added "Problems With..." or "Questions About..." at the front of each title of every Reason, but that would have been too repetitive. I ask the reader to accept the premise that each "Reason" is a problem or question that I have had about the topic of that "Reason." The order of the *101 Reasons* is not based on any priority or particular importance of the topic, simply on my attempt to have some sort of continuity in the discussion of the various topics.

REASON 1
GOD HASN'T ANSWERED MY PRAYERS

As a Mormon, I was taught to pray to God the Father in the name of His Son, Jesus Christ, and to read the scriptures which included the *Bible,* the *Book of Mormon,* the *Doctrine and Covenants,* and the *Pearl of Great Price.* I was also taught to participate in fasting, family and individual prayers, weekly family home evenings, and to attend weekly Church meetings. I was expected to have a Temple Recommend, to go to the Temple and participate in those ceremonies at least once a month, and to participate in other Church functions or activities whenever possible. I did this for the first sixty (60) years of my life.

One religious principle I was encouraged to follow was to ask God the Father, in prayer, when I needed an answer to an important question or issue. I was taught to follow the Prophet Joseph Smith's example when he followed the exhortation in James 1:5 in the Bible that states: "If any of you lack wisdom, let him ask of God, that giveth to all men liberally, and upbraideth not; and it shall be given him." Joseph Smith prayed at the age of fourteen (14) in a grove of trees near Palmyra, New York in 1820 and recorded his first vision in the *HC,* 1:5. It states:

> When the light rested upon me I saw two personages, whose brightness and glory defy all description, standing above me in the air. One of them spake unto me, calling me by name, and said—pointing to the other—"THIS IS MY BELOVED SON, HEAR HIM."

Joseph Smith proclaimed to the world that this was the real God, the Eternal Father, with His Son, Jesus Christ, who was also the real God of this earth.

As a member of the Mormon Church, I have wanted to know whether the God I was taught to believe in was the real God, and whether what I had been taught about God was in fact true. After high school, I followed my father's desire and wishes and attended Brigham Young University, a college established by the Mormon Church, where students are further educated (including in the theology of the Mormon religion). During the four years of my college education, I took many religion classes and read numerous religious books, again praying to receive an answer as to the existence of God; but again, nothing came.

After graduating from BYU in 1966, I passed up an opportunity to try and play professional basketball in order to serve a two-year mission for the Mormon Church in New Zealand. While serving my mission, I was fortunate to be the Assistant to the President of the mission for one year. During that time, I had numerous opportunities to be taught by the Mission President and also by the two General Authorities assigned to the South Pacific: Elder Paul H. Dunn and Elder Thomas S. Monson, who became the 16th Prophet and President of the Mormon Church. I prayed on a daily basis for two years. Still, I did not receive a direct answer that God existed and that the Mormon God that I believed in was in fact that God. I did have various religious experiences in the mission field that others claimed were answers to prayers; but I was never sure.

During the first sixty (60) years of my life, I have literally prayed hundreds of times to God, just as Joseph Smith did, to find these answers. I have prayed almost daily for many years. However, I never received a direct answer to any of my prayers and could not understand why. Many people told me that I just wasn't spiritual enough to receive answers. So I worked on that by reading all of the scriptures many times, fasting, working in the temple, and praying more often. I was a very active member of the Mormon Church, attended Church every Sunday, held a temple recommend, married in the Temple, held many positions in the Priesthood (such as Elders' Quorum President and High Priests' Group Leader), and served in many other capacities in the Church (including Gospel Doctrine teacher for many years, Scoutmaster for the Boy Scouts, and advisor to many Young Men organizations). Nevertheless, I still did not receive any answers to my prayers.

I read many books written by General Authorities about prayer and receiving answers. Then I decided to pray harder and longer—sometimes for hours, often while driving for long distances, pleading for an answer; but again, no luck. Others suggested that perhaps I had received an answer but just did not recognize it. They described all of the ways that they believed indicated to them that they had received an answer to *their* prayers. However, it did not make sense to *me* to have to rely upon someone else's description of an answer to a prayer. If God existed, then I would know when *my* prayer was answered; and not just because the circumstances fit into someone else's definition of what constituted an answer to a prayer.

I asked myself many times why I could not receive an answer to my prayer like Oliver Cowdery—a scribe and witness for the *Book of Mormon*—did to his. In *Doctrine and Covenants* 6:20–23 we read:

> Behold, thou art Oliver, and I have spoken unto thee because of thy desires; ...Behold, I am Jesus Christ, the Son of God. ...verily, I say unto you, if you desire a further witness, cast your mind upon the night that you cried unto me in your heart, that you might know concerning the truth of these things. Did I not speak peace to your mind concerning the matter? What greater witness can you have than from God?

For some unknown reason, I was never fortunate enough to have received such an answer.

My continual quest for an answer to my prayers about God's existence continued for another fifty years after returning from my mission in New Zealand, but without success. Why wouldn't God answer my prayers? Why was it so hard to just find out if God existed?

REASON 2
TOO MUCH AMBIGUITY IN ANSWERS TO PRAYER

It has been confusing to me as to whether a person actually received an answer to his or her prayer. The Mormon religion teaches that a person may receive an answer to their prayer through the power of the Holy Ghost, which can be manifested by the person feeling a swelling or burning in their bosom when they are praying or asking for an answer. This concept of how God lets us know if something is right is found in *D&C*, 9:7–9, where the Lord talks to Oliver Cowdery in regard to his attempt to translate the gold plates:

> Behold, you have not understood; you have supposed that I would give it unto you, when you took no thought save it was to ask me. But, behold, I say unto you that you must study it out in your mind; then you must ask me if it be right, and if it is right I will cause that your bosom shall burn within you; therefore, you shall feel that it is right. But if it be not right you shall have no such feelings, but you shall have a stupor of thought that shall cause you to forget the thing which is wrong;

The first time I had a similar experience was when my brother, Mark, died of a heart attack at the age of 23, while playing softball in a church tournament. I was 21 years old (in the summer of 1965). After I returned home from basketball practice and learned of his death, I went to the Cottonwood Hospital in Murray, Utah. I saw my brother's lifeless body lying on a bed, still in his softball uniform. My Dad, who was apparently still in shock, walked over to my brother and slightly slapped him on the face to show me that my brother was actually dead. This was my first experience of the death of a close loved one. I was devastated and did not know what to think or do. I excused myself from the room to be alone and offered a prayer, asking God why my brother had been taken at such a young age. A calm and peaceful feeling came over me; and I felt that my brother still lived and that I would see him again in another life. Was this an answer from God or not?

Other members of the Mormon Church have had similar experiences of feeling this alleged "manifestation of the Spirit," as they have been taught to understand it to be. One such experience was shared with me by a close friend, who was also serving a mission for the LDS Church in New Zealand from 1966–68. He wanted to know if the *Book of Mormon* was true; so he read it and prayed about it.

Not only missionaries, but also members of the Mormon Church, are taught to read the *Book of Mormon* and ask God whether the book is true. This is pursuant to the promise made in Moroni 10:4 of the *Book of Mormon* which states:

> And when ye shall receive these things, I would exhort you that ye would ask God, the Eternal Father, in the name of Christ, if these things are not true; and if ye shall ask with a sincere heart, with real intent, having faith in Christ, he will manifest the truth of it unto you, by the power of the Holy Ghost.

One morning, as my friend was praying after reading some chapters in the *Book of Mormon*, he asked if the book was true. While praying, he felt this swelling and burning in his bosom; and from then on, he believed that the *Book of Mormon* was true and from God.

Many other members of the Mormon Church, especially converts, have expressed similar experiences of having their prayers answered by this feeling in their bosom. However, some have had additional experiences in their lives that have caused them to question whether these feelings were really from God through the Holy Ghost, or just from their own consciousness. One such story was told to me by a close acquaintance. After having been married for over four years and going through some very difficult times, my friend decided that it would be best to get a divorce. He had been married in the Mormon Temple for "time and all eternity," so this was a major decision. For that reason, he fasted and prayed for an answer. He believed that he received an answer, because he felt this same feeling in his bosom and also felt at peace with his decision to get a divorce. When he discussed his decision with his Bishop and then the Stake President, he was advised that the answer that he had received from his fasting and prayers did not come from God, but rather from Satan. Obviously, this caused a great amount of confusion in his mind, because all of the previous feelings that he had experienced were similar and in accordance with what he had been taught as to how to know if you had received an answer to your prayers.

Another experience from another friend adds to the confusion. He was also married in the temple for "time and all eternity." His wife had an affair. He forgave her and they tried to work it out. However, eventually, she wanted a divorce. She fasted and prayed about her decision and told him that she had received an answer to her prayers and had felt this same swelling and burning in her bosom and that the Holy Ghost had manifested to her that she should get a divorce. Amid all of the heartache and confusion, my friend sought counsel and advice from a General Authority with whom he had become acquainted. Because of his confusion, he wanted to know if in fact his wife had indeed received a spiritual confirmation that they should get divorced. The General Authority talked with the wife and then told my friend that his wife had most likely answered her own prayer and that her spiritual experience probably did not come from God.

So are our experiences spiritual and from God? Or are they the product of our own desires and conscious thoughts? Does God really answer prayers? If He does, why are they arbitrary or ambiguous? Many behavioral counselors recommend a book by David D. Burns, M.D. titled *Feeling Good*. In his book, Dr. Burns discusses cognitive therapy, which is based on the premise that "your feelings result from the messages you give yourself." In other words, your thoughts create your feelings (xviii). In Chapter 3, Dr. Burns discusses his premise that "you feel the way you think." He states:

> Your feelings are created by your thoughts and not the actual events. All experiences must be processed through your brain and given a conscious meaning before you experience any emotional responses (30).

Dr. Burns mentions that cognitive therapy isn't a new idea, but has been around for centuries. He references the Greek philosopher, Epictetus, who stated that people are disturbed "not by things, but by the views we take of them" (xviii). Then he references the book of Proverbs (23:7), where it states: "For as he thinketh in his heart, so is he," and finally Shakespeare, who stated, "For there is nothing either good or bad, but thinking makes it so" (Hamlet, Act 2, Scene 2).

When we apply this premise to the alleged spiritual experiences that we have, then perhaps it becomes less confusing. Do we create the feelings in our bosoms and was the General Authority in the previous story correct in his assessment that a person can answer their own prayers? Can we rely upon these alleged "spiritual experiences" to satisfactorily answer our initial question as to whether God exists or not?

Many of us, as members of the Mormon Church, have read the Bible (both Old and New Testaments), the *Book of Mormon*, the *Doctrine and Covenants* , and the *Pearl of Great Price* numerous times, plus many other LDS Church books, while fasting and praying. Did we receive an answer from God upon which we could rely as to the truthfulness of the scriptures or as to who was the real God? Or did we just answer our own prayers? I have been trying for decades to obtain an understanding of God and who He is; but I have never received any direct answers to my queries. In fact, I now have more unanswered questions than before.

REASON 3
RELIANCE UPON FAITH
IS NOT ENOUGH

Members of the Mormon Church are taught from birth through the teachings of Joseph Smith to believe in the Godhead based upon faith. In fact, the principal of "faith" has been the answer given by almost every leader in the Mormon Church when they have been asked a question for which they did not have the answer. They have usually said, "You just have to have faith."

Non-members of the Mormon Church are aware of the fact that Mormons rely upon "faith," because they don't have answers to a lot of the tough questions. In the musical comedy *The Book of Mormon*, there is a song titled "I Believe," where it states some of the beliefs of the Mormon Church that are out of sync with mainstream religious beliefs. Some of these include the following:

1. God lives on or next to a planet called Kolob!
2. Jesus has his own planet too!
3. We can have our own planet!
4. The Garden of Eden is in Jackson County, Missouri!
5. President Russell M. Nelson speaks directly to God!
6. In 1978, God changed His mind about black people!

The lyrics of the song then state, "I am a Mormon! And a Mormon Just Believes!" Therefore, do we just have to "believe"? Can't we find just a few answers to our many questions? Besides, what exactly is "faith"?

Joseph Smith taught the Elders of the early Mormon Church about faith in a pamphlet that has been titled *Lectures on Faith*, but was referred to by Joseph Smith as "Lectures on Theology" (*HC*, 2:176). It is interesting to note that when the Mormon Church first published it in the *Doctrine and Covenants of the Church of the Latter Day Saints* in 1835, it consisted of two parts: the first contained the *Lectures on Faith* and the second consisted of selected revelations and inspired declarations received prior to that time. This continued until 1921 (Dahl and Tate 3–7). Presently, the Mormon Church's *Doctrine and Covenants* does not have the *Lectures on Faith* in it.

The first, second, and fifth of the seven lectures are informative and helpful to our discussion herein.

The first lecture discusses faith. It states that "faith is the assurance which men have of the existence of things which they have not seen; and the principle of action in all intelligent beings" (*D&C, 1844* 6). Simply put, it means that we can only have a belief of ideas that we cannot experience through our senses. Further, we would not perform any physical or mental act if we did not believe said act would accomplish something. Therefore, unless God visits us or speaks to us like He did to Joseph Smith, we can only have faith that He exists, based upon all that we have learned or experienced. Then why would God state in the scriptures (i.e., 3 Nephi 14:7–8) that we can ask and receive said assurance that He exists, and then not make it easy to receive or know that you have received that assurance?

The second lecture discusses God, which is the "object on which [faith] rests" (*D&C, 1844* 13). It describes God as "omnipotent, omnipresent, and omniscient, without beginning of days or end of life" and that God began conversing with man (Adam) "face to face" from the time of Adam's creation (*D&C, 1844* 13, 17). This first conversation between God and Adam was the beginning of man's knowledge of God's existence. That knowledge continued after Adam and Eve were cast out of the Garden of Eden and separated from God by a veil. We know this because they continued to call upon God, heard His voice, and then were visited by an angel sent to them (Dahl and Tate 43). Nevertheless, you and I have not heard His voice or been visited by an angel!

The fifth lecture teaches about the Godhead being three separate personages. It is interesting to note that even in this explanation of the Godhead (which is probably the most specific as compared to the Bible, the *BOM*, the First Vision, or the *D&C*) it only describes God the Father as a personage of spirit. It also describes the Holy Ghost as a personage of spirit, but describes God the Son as a personage of tabernacle (flesh and bone). Notwithstanding this discrepancy, it does clarify somewhat who and what God is, but it is also confusing because it refers to God talking with Adam, despite the fact that Mormons are taught that it was Jehovah, or a pre-mortal Jesus Christ, who was conversing with Adam, and not God the Father. However, the identification of which God was Jehovah in Mormon theology changed over time, especially from 1830 to 1916, which only added to the confusion. (See Reasons 30 and 31 herein, and "The Development of the Mormon Jehovah Doctrine," by Boyd Kirkland.)

However, the *Lectures on Faith* do not explain why we cannot find answers to relevant and important questions about God's existence and this life through evidence and facts, rather than relying on faith for everything. How are we supposed to know that the God we were taught to believe in is in fact real and the correct God to worship? Reliance upon only faith—rather than on some form of knowledge (either personal or spiritual)—is hard to accept. This is because so many of the scriptures admonish us to *know* God and teach us to believe that he *does* answer our prayers, or at least will allow us to have some experience in order to verify our faith. I have not had any of these kinds of experiences, despite years of reading and pondering everything that we have received from the "God" of the Mormon religion. "Have faith" should not be the only proposal available to us in our attempt to find God.

REASON 4
LACK OF PERSONAL EXPERIENCES IN KNOWING GOD

Although Joseph Smith claims to have seen both God and Jesus Christ in person in 1820, there does not seem to be any other verified experiences since then, in the almost-200 years, where any other individual in the Mormon faith has actually seen God or Jesus Christ. Why not? The most common answer to this question is that no other man or woman has been "righteous enough" to have had the experience. Logically though, this answer does not make sense.

First of all, Joseph Smith was only 14 years of age when the purported "vision" took place. Therefore, he had not lived long enough after the age of accountability (8 years old) to have shown whether or not he was "righteous enough" to have had the personal experience of seeing God. Secondly, why haven't other 14-year-olds, who haven't had time to become unrighteous, had the same experience of seeing God? Thirdly, according to the Mormon religion, our purpose here upon the Earth is to gain knowledge about God and live in accordance with His commandments. How can we do that if it is so very difficult to even find out if God actually exists?

In 3 Nephi of the *Book of Mormon*, Jesus Christ appears in person just after his death in Jerusalem to the surviving inhabitants in the land of Bountiful, which is believed by many Mormons to be somewhere in Central America. After Jesus Christ's personal visit, the inhabitants "became an exceedingly fair and delightsome people" (4 Nephi 10), and

> there was no contention in the land. ...no envyings, nor strifes, nor tumults, nor whoredoms, nor lyings, nor murders, nor any manner of lasciviousness; and surely there could not be a happier people among all the people who had been created by the hand of God (4 Nephi 1:15–16).

This state of prosperity and righteousness lasted for almost 200 years; but then the inhabitants began to be lifted up by pride and became iniquitous. Therefore, the question begs to be answered,

"Why wouldn't Jesus Christ appear again to these current inhabitants so that they would be reinforced in their belief in God and once again enjoy prosperity and happiness? Why wouldn't God or Jesus Christ continue to make appearances to God's spiritual children here upon Earth, so they would know for sure that He exists and how He wants them to live their lives?" The same could be said in regard to any of the last 200 years since Joseph Smith saw and talked with God and Jesus Christ. Moreover, why wouldn't they appear in the present world so people today would know that they existed? With over 7 billion people living upon Earth today, surely a visit from God or Jesus Christ to someone or some group, that was verifiable, would be beneficial to all of us.

I have never asked to see God or Jesus Christ and would be the first to admit my lack of worthiness to be so blessed. Surely though there have been other people who have lived upon Earth just as righteous as Joseph Smith, who deserved a visit, which could have been recorded and shared with the rest of us. If not a visit from God, then perhaps a visit from an Angel or an ancient Prophet should have occurred to someone other than Joseph Smith. Numerous visitations were made to Joseph Smith by Angels and ancient Prophets while he was still in his twenties. Wouldn't others also benefit from a personal appearance; and wouldn't it have benefitted the spread of the Gospel of Jesus Christ if many others had the same experiences as Joseph Smith? Wouldn't it be easier to believe in a God whom was more available to his children?

If not being allowed to experience a personal visitation from God or Jesus Christ, then perhaps another kind of manifestation verifying that God exists should be available to people, and not be a complicated process. As I mentioned in Reason 1, I have not had such an experience, although many of my friends believe they have. Nevertheless, all of those experiences lacked any other verification other than that person's feelings, which we explored in Reason 2. It seems as though there should be a simple way to have a verifiable personal experience with God (or some other heavenly being) that is not based solely upon how we feel, but rather based upon facts or our senses. If God exists and He wants us to know that He exists, then it should be a personal experience that everyone can have if they are sincere in their desire to know.

REASON 5
DIFFICULTY IN FINDING GOD THROUGH SCRIPTURES

With no personal success through prayer in finding God, I have tried through reading all of the alleged "Words of God"; to wit, the Bible, *Book of Mormon, Doctrine and Covenants, and Pearl of Great Price.* I have read the Bible, cover-to-cover, six (6) times and different books or chapters hundreds of times. I have read the *Book of Mormon*, cover-to-cover, over twenty-five (25) times, as well as different books or chapters therein, hundreds of times. I have read the *D&C* and *PGP* over nine (9) times each, cover-to-cover, and different chapters or sections even more numerous times. Further, as a Gospel Doctrine teacher, I have taught the *Book of Mormon*, Bible, and the *D&C*, along with Church History, for many years. Also read were the seven (7) volumes of the *History of the Church* and hundreds of other popular LDS Church books and publications.

Despite all of the reading and studying, I still did not find God. Was it because it is so difficult to understand what truth is and what is fiction in the various alleged scriptures? For example, how can an intelligent, truth-seeking individual accept the story of Noah and the Ark that is found in the Bible and referred to in the *Book of Mormon*? (See Genesis 7 and Alma 10:22.) How did Noah get billions of different species in an ark smaller than a football field? Moreover, why is there no physical evidence of an earthly flood?

Would God murder hundreds of innocent children just to force the Pharaoh to let the children of Israel leave Egypt, when He simply could have caused a deep sleep or other phenomenon to assist the departure? (See Exodus 12 and 1 Nephi 17.) Would God murder innocent men, women, and children just because others refused to repent? (See Joshua 6 and 3 Nephi 8 and 9.) There are far too many other examples of the same in both the Bible and the *Book of Mormon*. Can one rely upon the Bible to find God? Is it really the "Word of God?" Some, including myself, are not sure that it is. The King James Version of the New Testament of the Bible, accepted by Mormons as the official version, was translated by a group of scholars in the early seventeenth century who based their rendition on previously written Greek texts. The main Greek text relied upon by these same scholars was produced and published by a Dutch scholar named Desiderius Erasmus in approximately 1516 C.E. According to Bart D. Ehrman in *Misquoting Jesus*, Erasmus went to Basel, Switzerland in July 1515 in search of suitable manuscripts that he could use as the basis of his text; but he did not uncover a great wealth of manuscripts (78–81). He relied heavily on just one twelfth-century manuscript for the Gospels, and another, also of the twelfth century, for the book of Acts and the Epistles. Erasmus's editions (he made five, all based on the first rather hastily assembled one) became the standard form of the Greek text published by Western European printers for more than 300 years.

It should be noted here that it is a well-known fact and accepted by all Bible scholars that we do not have today, nor did they have when the King James Version was translated, any of the originals of any of the books of the New Testament. The only texts or manuscripts available were copies that were made, in most instances, centuries after the events actually happened.

Throughout his books, *Misquoting Jesus* and *Jesus Interrupted*, Mr. Ehrman gives numerous examples of approximately 250,000 changes and errors (both intentional and unintentional) that are in present-day Bibles, including the King James Version, when compared to the existing ancient Greek manuscripts. There would probably even be more errors if present-day Bibles were compared to the alleged original books of the New Testament.

In regards to the Old Testament, we also do not have any of the original texts or manuscripts either. We do have a few fragments from the 2nd century B.C. and a complete manuscript from the 4th century C.E. We also now have the Dead Sea Scrolls that were discovered in 1947. These scrolls produced fragments of almost all of the books of the Old Testament and two scrolls of the Book of Isaiah, one complete and one around 75 percent complete. These manuscripts generally date from between 150 B.C. to 70 C.E.

Mr. Ehrman said it best in regards to the New Testament (which could also be said of the Old Testament):

> We don't have the original manuscripts or even copies of the originals...what we have are copies made centuries later. And these copies differ from one another in so many places we don't even know how many differences there are. Possibly it is easiest to put it in comparative terms: there are more differences among

our manuscripts than there are words in the New Testament...This was a human book from beginning to end...If one wants to insist that God inspired the very words of scripture, what would be the point if we don't have the very words of scripture...it would have been no more difficult for God to preserve the words of scripture than it would have been for him to inspire them in the first place. If he wanted his people to have his words, surely he would have given them to them (and possibly even given them the words in a language they could understand, rather that Greek and Hebrew). The fact that we don't have the words surely must show that he did not preserve them for us. And if he didn't perform that miracle, there seemed to be no reason to think that he performed the earlier miracle of inspiring those words. (*Misquoting Jesus* 10–12.)

These problems with the authenticity of the scriptures make it difficult to find God through the scriptures or to believe in the Mormon theology that God *can* be found there.

REASON 6
LACK OF PROOF OF GOD'S EXISTENCE

"Does God exist?" is a question that has been asked and debated for centuries and received numerous different answers. My question is somewhat simpler and is, "Why isn't there any tangible and verifiable proof of God's existence?" It would seem to be easy to establish the existence of God, especially with today's technology and the apparent ability of God to manifest His existence to mankind.

In order for this to happen, God could reveal himself to mankind as He did to the Nephites in 3 Nephi 12. One giant appearance of God in the skies, and then God descending to the Earth to proclaim Himself to mankind, would be sufficient. This could take place at any singular place on the Earth because it would be broadcasted all over the world at the time that it occurred. It could be verified by hundreds of media outlets and authenticated easily by our modern technology.

I remember in the 1977 movie *Oh, God!* (starring George Burns and John Denver) that no one would believe John Denver that God existed, even after George Burns appeared in court and testified as "God." That kind of appearance is not what I am suggesting. Everyone sees the sun come up in the morning and the moon come out at night, so no one would miss a manifestation in the sky. Of course, there would be skeptics saying that it was a man-created event, just like those who claim we didn't land on the moon. However, if the event was witnessed by almost everyone on Earth simultaneously, and verified by everyone witnessing the event, then it would be very hard to deny.

Nevertheless, there are those religious people who would want to remind me of the scripture in Matthew 12:38–39 that states:

> Then certain of the scribes and of the Pharisees answered, saying, Master, we would see a sign from thee. But he answered and said unto them, An evil and adulterous generation seeketh after a sign;

I am not suggesting a sign, but an actual appearance of God Himself to mankind, just like happened in the *Book of Mormon* when Jesus Christ appeared to the Nephites. In fact, the real question is, "Why hasn't an appearance of God occurred like Jesus Christ's appearance?" Look what happened after Christ appeared to the Nephites for over two hundred years thereafter, as recorded in 4 Nephi 1:15 and 16:

> And it came to pass that there was no contention in the land, because of the love of God which did dwell in the hearts of people. And there were no envyings, nor strifes, nor tumults, nor whoredoms, nor lying, nor murders, nor any manner of lasciviousness; and surely there could not be a happier people among all the people who had been created by the hand of God.

So if God did appear in this time period, when it could be recorded and manifested to all of mankind, wouldn't that be beneficial to everyone in establishing proof that God does exist, cares for us, and wants us to be happy?

Many others would argue that God would not appear today, because there is too much evil and wickedness. Those responsible for this wickedness would have to be destroyed first, like God did to all of the cities and inhabitants prior to Christ's appearance to the Nephites. Maybe that wouldn't be such a bad idea; but then we're talking about the Second Coming of Christ. What I don't understand is why, when it would have been an enormous benefit to mankind, was there not an appearance of Christ in other places in the world, like occurred in the *Book of Mormon* times? Although the *Book of Mormon* does state that Christ went "to other sheep" after His appearance to the Nephites (see 3 Nephi 16:1), we don't have a record of that event/s. Another appearance of Christ to mankind could have been recorded like the *Book of Mormon* event; and those records could be available for mankind to verify and authenticate. Yet we can't even verify the *Book of Mormon* story.

Then there is the argument that mankind needs to develop faith in God without being shown the truth of God's existence. I just don't buy that argument. It doesn't explain Jesus Christ's appearance to the Apostles in Jerusalem after His death, or His appearance to the Nephites in the Americas (as recorded in the *Book of Mormon*) after His crucifixion, or the alleged appearance of God and Jesus Christ to Joseph Smith in 1820. If the purpose of life is to understand and follow God's commandments, why make it so hard for everyone to even know whether God exists or to know about His commandments? Just one global appearance would solve the problem and we would all know that God exists because we would have witnessed the appearance! This lack of proof of God's existence continues to be troublesome for me.

REASON 7
GOD DOESN'T SEEM TO CARE ANYMORE

There are many stories in the Bible where God seemed to care and did something about the suffering of his children upon Earth. God intervened and performed many miracles through Moses to help the Israelites leave Egypt. In Exodus 12:12, after Moses had performed other miracles, God killed the firstborn of all man and beast in Egypt so that the Israelites would be allowed to leave by the Pharaoh. Then in Exodus 14:27–28, after the Pharaoh had let the Israelites go, he then led his army (including 600 chariots) after the Israelites. Moses was instructed by God to part the Red Sea and then returned it to its strength when the Egyptians continued their chase. All the chariots, horseman, and host of the Pharaoh were killed by the Red Sea. God then fed the Israelites manna in the wilderness (Exodus 16:14–15) and fought the Israelite battles to allow them to settle in the "Promised Land" (see the Book of Joshua). God continued to fight the Israelite's battles and helped them prosper as told in the stories of David, Isaiah, Ezekiel, Daniel, and others in the Old Testament. However, all of that occurred approximately 2500 to 3500 years ago.

The *Book of Mormon* also tells of many stories where God cared about and fought for His children on Earth. In Omni 1:12–13, around 150 B.C., God warned King Mosiah to flee out of the land of Nephi and then led them to the land of Zarahemla. In Mosiah, Chapter 27, God sends an Angel to Alma the Younger. He is "born again" and converts thousands. In Alma 62:50, the Nephites remember that God had delivered them from death, bonds, prisons, all manner of afflictions, and from their enemies. Later prophets (Nephi and Lehi) are encircled by fire caused by God and rescued from prison (Helaman 5:27–29). In 3 Nephi, just prior to Christ's appearance to the *Book of Mormon* people, God destroys numerous cities and kills thousands so that the more righteous would be the only ones left (described in more detail in Reason 35).

Since the time of Christ though, it appears that God has not cared what happens to his children upon the Earth. History is full of genocides, massacres, plagues, and great suffering and misery. In none of these instances did God intervene. Where was God during the past

2000 years? Where are the written stories of God's intervention into the misery and suffering of mankind during the last two centuries?

Following are some of the atrocities that have occurred since the death of Jesus Christ where the Mormon God or Godhead chose not to intervene:

> 1. During the Roman Empire from Christ to Constantine in the 3rd century, the Christians were stoned, killed, and fed to dogs. Emperors including Nero, Marcus Aurelius, and others murdered thousands of Christians (Gibbon).
>
> 2. Attila the Hun and the barbarian nation of the Huns, from 434 to 453 A.D., invaded the Roman Empire. There were so many murders and bloodlettings that the dead could not be numbered. They took captives, destroyed or captured more than a hundred cities (including Constantinople), and slew the monks and maidens in great numbers (Callinicus).
>
> 3. In thirty years of genocide, from 774 to 804 A.D., two thirds of the Saxons were killed. In 777 A.D., Charlemagne, a devout Christian, after conquering the Saxon rebels, gave them a choice between baptism and execution. When they refused to convert, he had 4500 of them beheaded in one morning (Manchester).
>
> 4. It is estimated that Europe was "Christianized" at a cost of about 8–10 million lives. From 414 A.D. through 1648 A.D., there were large-scale organized exterminations of Jews. Examples are: (a) in 1349 A.D., in more than 350 towns in Germany, all Jews were murdered, mostly burned alive (in this one year, more Jews were killed than Christians in 200 years combined of ancient Roman persecution of Christians); (b) in 1648 A.D., the Chmielnicki massacres took place; and (c) in Poland, about 200,000 Jews were slain. This list goes on and on, century after century, right into the kilns of Auschwitz (Deschner).

5. Christianity was responsible for the genocide of 60 million Indians in the Americas by the end of the 16th century alone. When the Christians were exhausted from war, God supposedly saw fit to send the Indians smallpox. A total of maybe more than 150 million Indians (of both Americas) were destroyed in the period of 1500 to 1900, two thirds by smallpox and other epidemics, and some 50 million killed directly by violence, bad treatment, and slavery (Aguilar).

6. Throughout the period of Tsarist Russia, the people were indoctrinated by their churches into believing the Jews were responsible for the death of Jesus. This blind and extreme intolerance and hatred directed towards Jews was no more unexpected than that in Roman Catholic and Protestant countries. Thousands were mistreated or killed. Persecutions in Ukraine resulted in the deaths of at least tens of thousands of Jews. The 1917 Russian Revolution brought with it more hatred and death of the Jews. In the Russian Civil War that followed, between 70,000 and 250,000 people were murdered in what were known as the Petlyura Pogroms (Hakeem).

7. From 1894 to 1923, the Ottoman Empire conducted a policy of genocide of the Christian population living within its extensive territory. The Sultan, Abdul Hamid, first put forth an official governmental policy of genocide against the Armenians of the Ottoman Empire in 1894. Systematic massacres took place between 1894–96, when Abdul savagely killed 300,000 Armenians throughout the provinces. Massacres continued; and in 1909, government troops killed (in the town of Adana alone) over 20,000 Christian Armenians ("Abdul Hamid").

8. From 1930 to 1940, according to historians working after the Soviet Union's dissolution, the total victims dying from Stalin's purges and massacres ranged from

approximately 4 million to nearly 10 million, not including those who died in famines (Wheatcroft).

9. Over six million Jewish men, women, and children were murdered in the Holocaust by Hitler and the Nazis from 1939–1945 (Wheatcroft).

10. From 1949 to 1987 in China, Mao was responsible for about 40 million total deaths. The Great Leap Forward created a famine that killed some 30 of the 40 million. If we confine our indictment to deliberate killings, then Mao was directly responsible for the other 10 million deaths (Ontario Consultants).

11. The great challenge for Christianity in Sudan, especially in the southern part of the country, is closely linked to the civil war between Sudan's North and South. This war has raged intermittently since 1955, making it possibly the longest civil conflict in the world. It continues unabated, mostly outside the focus of diplomacy or the attention of international media, taking a huge and terrible human toll. Over two million people have died as a result of the war and related causes, such as war-induced famine. About five million people have been displaced, while half a million more have fled across an international border. Tens of thousands of women and children have been abducted and subjected to slavery. By all accounts, it appears to be the worst humanitarian disaster in the world today (Deng 13–21).

12. The 1994 Genocide: an estimated 800,000 Rwandans were killed during ethnic and religious violence over the brief span of 100 days, between April and June 1994. (The most detailed discussion of the role of religion in the Rwandan genocide is Timothy Longman's *Christianity and Genocide in Rwanda*.)

13. From 1995 to 1999, over 200,000 Muslims were murdered by Serbian Orthodox Christians in

Bosnia. Over 50,000 Muslim women and girls were raped (Ontario Consultants, *ReligiousTolerance.org*).

From all of these examples, there has been an apparent lack of concern or caring by God or the Godhead. The above genocides and atrocities demonstrate a failure of God to intervene in anyway whatsoever, like He supposedly did in the Bible and the *Book of Mormon*. Why God has been so uncaring since the death of Christ is a mystery to me. There were many, many instances in history, as mentioned above, where a caring God could have saved the lives of millions and allowed them the chance to experience more life upon the Earth.

REASON 8
GOD'S LACK OF CONCERN FOR MANKIND'S SUFFERING

In Reason 7, we discussed many of the atrocities that have occurred upon Earth since the time of Christ, and the fact that God did nothing about them. Therefore, I concluded that He just didn't seem to care anymore. In Reason 8, I would like to examine God's lack of concern for all of the suffering that we presently find in the world on a daily basis, such as hunger, disease, and death.

Here are examples of some of the suffering that is taking place in the world today and in the past decade:

1. <u>Hunger and Malnutrition</u>.

Children are the most visible victims of [mal]nutrition. Children who are poorly nourished suffer up to 160 days of illness each year. Poor nutrition plays a role in at least half of the 10.9 million child deaths each year. [Mal]nutrition magnifies the effect of every disease, including measles and malaria. The estimated proportions of deaths, in which undernutrition is an underlying cause are roughly similar for diarrhea (61%), malaria (57%), pneumonia (52%), and measles (45%) (Black 2003, Bryce 2005). Malnutrition can also be caused by diseases, such as the diseases that cause diarrhea, by reducing the body's ability to convert food into usable nutrients (World Hunger Education Service).

2. <u>Diseases Causing Death</u>. Those who suffer the most from diseases that cause death are again children and people living in the underdeveloped countries. In *Wikipedia*, under "List of causes of death by rate," there is a comparison of deaths from diseases between undeveloped and developed countries. Aids, diarrhea, childhood diseases, malaria, and measles are in the top ten causes of death in underdeveloped countries, but not in the top ten causes of death in developed countries. There were almost ten million deaths from these five diseases in the year 2002. From 2013–2016 thousands of deaths occurred each month from the Ebola virus and other diseases in Africa (*Wikipedia*, "Ebola virus disease").

3. <u>Continual Terrorism and Religious Wars</u>. The 9-11 terrorist attack of the Twin Towers in New York; the terrorist wars in Iraq and Afghanistan; the continual alleged religious wars in Syria, Egypt, and Palestine; and terrorist attacks in the Middle East all cause thousands of deaths each year. The Israelite people today continue to fight their neighbors for survival.

What revelations have been given to the current Mormon Prophet, Russell M. Nelson, regarding the above health problems and conflicts in the world? The answer is obvious: none! Why hasn't God revealed to his Prophet here upon Earth information that would be useful in solving some of the suffering going on in the world? The *Doctrine and Covenants* is full of revelations from God given to his Prophet for such mundane issues as where missionaries should go, when missionaries should go to the Indians, what land to buy, calling Emma Smith as a scribe to Joseph, etc., etc., etc! What a wonderful act by God it would be, to reveal to his Prophet today something that would be useful to eliminate some of the suffering going on in the world. This would be a God in whom to believe.

REASON 9
GOD IS AN ABSENTEE GOD

One concern I have about the God that Mormons have been taught to believe in, is that the God of the Mormon religion is an absentee God. If God created the Earth and all of mankind, then I would think that He would be extremely involved in what was transpiring with mankind throughout all of history. However, even if we accept the belief that Jehovah, or Jesus Christ, is "one with the Father," and His (Jehovah's) appearances and dealings with mankind are on behalf of God, the Father/Elohim, they are still so infrequent as to suggest that we believe in an absentee God.

If we are the literal spiritual offspring of God the Father, and Jesus Christ is our elder brother, then it seems that there should be more involvement between God the Father and His children upon Earth. However, this has not been the case. God the Father/Elohim terminated speaking directly to man after Adam and Eve were banned from the Garden of Eden. In the Mormon temple ceremony, after the banishment of Adam and Eve, it is alleged that they were visited by Lucifer (Satan) and then Peter, James, and John, who eventually banished Satan from the Earth. It appears thereafter that almost all communications with mankind have been from Jehovah/Jesus Christ.

There are a few instances where God the Father/Elohim was involved and spoke, but only a few. They were the following times:

1. when Elohim spoke at the baptism of Jesus (Matthew 3:17) (although some people doubt that it was God the Father who spoke, but rather Jehovah or Jesus Christ speaking to himself as another member of the Godhead);
2. at the transfiguration (Matthew 17:5);
3. prior to the appearance of Christ to the Nephites (3 Nephi 11:7); and
4. during Joseph Smith's First Vision (*HC*, 1:4–6).

The only time that Elohim visited mankind, or appeared on the Earth in a vision, was when He appeared to Joseph Smith in his First Vision. There are other instances in the scriptures where it is alluded to, by stating that

Jesus Christ was seen "on the right hand of God" (*D&C*, 76:23); but no description of God was given. Therefore, it seems that Elohim has in fact been an absentee God.

We can acknowledge the Mormon religion's position that all of Jehovah's dealings and communications with mankind were essentially the dealings and communications of God the Father, since they both are of the same mind, wisdom, glory, power, and fullness. Therefore, anything done by one would be the same as being done by the other. Therefore, for purposes of this discussion, we will assume that Jesus Christ as Jehovah (or the God of the Old Testament and of the *Book of Mormon*) is the God of the Mormon religion that has personally dealt with mankind. As a member of the Godhead, it would be the same as if God the Father or Elohim had dealt with us. This is according to the teachings of the Mormon religion: that Jehovah, or the God of the Old Testament, is in reality Jesus Christ acting for and in behalf of God the Father or Elohim (McConkie 392).

So who has Jehovah dealt with upon Earth on behalf of Elohim and Himself? The only Christian records that speak of the same are the Bible, the *Book of Mormon*, the *Doctrine and Covenants*, and the *Pearl of Great Price*. However, these four books of scripture indicate that Jehovah's communications with mankind were limited to a small group of people called the "House of Israel" or the "chosen people of God." Researching the records of the Chinese people, which go back thousands of years before Christ, we find no personal communications or dealings between Elohim or Jehovah with this large section of the human race. The same is true of the people living in India, Russia, and most of the rest of the world.

In fact, it would be safe to state that Elohim and Jehovah have only been involved with less than ten percent of the people who have lived upon Earth. By only having alleged prophets in the House of Israel, or with the chosen descendents of Abraham pursuant to God's covenant, and limiting communications with them, Elohim and Jehovah have in fact been absentee Gods to ninety percent of Elohim's spiritual children who have lived upon Earth. Would God limit his word, teachings, and involvement to such a limited number? Would God be that unconcerned about ninety percent of His children and not speak to them? Wouldn't God communicate with most of his children if He was communicating with *some* of them? Nevertheless, we have no evidence that Elohim or Jehovah did. Therefore, it appears that the God that I was taught to believe in was an absentee God to the majority of mankind, since a short time after the creation of man.

Accepting the proposition that the scriptures represent Jehovah's communications and dealings with the "House of Israel," even these communications and dealings have been sporadic. The Bible seems to indicate that from approximately 500 B.C.-which was when the last prophet, Malachi, recorded his writings in the Bible-until the birth of Christ, Jehovah was absent from communicating or dealing with the House of Israel in that area of the world. However, the *BOM* does indicate that Jehovah was communicating with the prophets in the Americas during this time period until 420 A.D. For approximately 1400 years we have absolutely no recorded writings of Jehovah or Elohim communicating or dealing with the "House of Israel' until the First Vision of Joseph Smith. The question remains unanswered as to why God would discontinue speaking to his Prophets or to mankind for hundreds of years, and discontinue sending heavenly messengers to said Prophets?

REASON 10
GOD CHANGES HIS INVOLVEMENT WITH MANKIND

In Reasons 8 and 9, we discussed God's lack of concern with mankind and that He is mainly an absentee God. In this Reason (10), we will discuss the differences in God's involvement with mankind as mentioned in the Old Testament and *Book of Mormon*, compared with the time period from 400 A.D. to 1820, and from 1845 to the present.

In regard to said time periods, there is only one difference: we have no written evidence or revelations indicating that God has been involved with mankind from 400 A.D. to 1820 A.D., or from 1845 to the present, which is approximately 1600 years total. Why is that? As mentioned in other Reasons, God took an active part in the Israelite history found in the Old Testament and in the 1000 years covered by the *Book of Mormon*. Then, in the space of 25 years, from 1820–1845, God was extremely active in his involvement with Joseph Smith and the early Mormon Church, as is recorded in the *Doctrine and Covenants*. There were numerous appearances of Jesus Christ, ancient apostles and prophets, angels, and other heavenly beings. Additionally, there were over 100 different revelations given by the Lord to mankind through his prophet (Joseph Smith). Why did God change in his involvement with mankind? Why not be more involved today due to all of the problems going on in the world?

Again, there are questions upon questions, with no answers. The argument could be made again that we do not know God's purposes, and as Mormons we should "just believe" without any factual evidence. But why was factual evidence given so abundantly in the Bible, *Book of Mormon*, and the early history of the Mormon Church? What's fair about that (see Reason 12)? It wouldn't be that hard for God to just give some factual evidence today to let us know that He may care or be concerned. For example, God could let us know through his modern-day prophet, Russell M. Nelson, where the exact location was for the ruins of the ancient City of Zarahemla that played such a pivotal role in the *Book of Mormon* and then we could excavate those ruins.

There would likely be ruins, because the city was rebuilt in approximately 38 A.D. and lasted for over 400 years. Additionally, the

Nephites at that time built their cities with stone and cement (Helaman 3:7–11). We could send modern-day archeologists, both from the Mormon Church and from independent sources, to examine and verify the authenticity of the ancient city of Zarahemla. If we were lucky, we would not only find the ruins, but also artifacts such as pottery, swords, etc, and murals showing horses and chariots to authenticate the assertions made in the *Book of Mormon* that have not been verified from all of the other archeological sites examined in Mexico, Central, and South America. We should also find murals of the event found in 3 Nephi in the *BOM* of Jesus Christ coming down out of heaven to visit with the Nephites. A little bit of factual evidence would go a long way to not only help others believe in God, but show us that He may still care. This would make it easier to believe in a God that had continuous involvement with mankind, and not just interaction now and then—a God who does not change His involvement with mankind.

REASON 11
GOD IS NOT THE SAME YESTERDAY, TODAY, AND FOREVER

In Mormon 9:9–20 in the *BOM*, it states: "For do we not read that God is the same yesterday, today, and forever…" In *D&C*, 76:4, it states: "From eternity to eternity he [the Lord] is the same, and his years never fail." As Mormons, we were taught this concept our entire lives: that God does not change and His doctrine does not change. But is that really true?

In Genesis, Chapter 4 in the Old Testament, Cain, a son of Adam, slew his brother Abel, and was cursed by the Lord. This cursing upon Cain and the descendants of Cain was twofold: (1) they were given a black skin and (2) they were denied the Priesthood, which is the authority to act for God here upon Earth. In the *Pearl of Great Price*, Moses 7:8, it states:

> For behold, the Lord shall curse the land with much heat, and the barrenness thereof shall go forth forever; and there was a blackness came upon all the children of Canaan [Cain's descendants], that they were despised among all people.

Then in verse 22 we read:

> And Enoch also beheld the residue of the people which were the sons of Adam; and they were a mixture of all the seed of Adam save it was the seed of Cain, for the seed of Cain were black, and had not place among them.

However, the "curse" upon the descendants of Cain *changed* in 1978, when President Spencer W. Kimball, the prophet of the Mormon Church, made an Official Declaration of the Church that indicated that the black race of descendants of Cain could now hold the Priesthood, although the curse of the black skin was not removed. (See *D&C*, Official Declaration 2.) This does not support the proposition that God does not change.

Another example of God changing his doctrine is with the issue of polygamy and concubines. In Genesis in the Old Testament, we read about the early prophets taking more than one wife and having concubines, specifically Abraham, who was blessed by the Lord and given promises regarding his posterity. This continues with Kings David and Solomon, who had many wives and concubines. However, this practice was condemned by God in the *Book of Mormon*, Jacob 2:27, which states:

> Wherefore, my brethren, hear me, and hearken to the word of the Lord. For there shall not any man among you have save it by one wife; and concubines he shall have none;

Then in 1843, the Lord or God changes again, when He commands Joseph Smith to institute polygamy. This continued in the Mormon Church until 1890, when President Wilford Woodruff, the Prophet of the Mormon Church at the time, officially declared that the Mormons would no longer practice polygamy, thus changing back (*D&C*, Official Declaration 1).

One other example is found in Doctrine and Covenants where Joseph Smith and the early Saints were commanded by the Lord to purchase land in Independence, Missouri for the "New Jerusalem" (*D&C*, 42:35; 58:37). Then in *D&C*, 84:3–5, we read:

> Which city shall be built, beginning at the temple lot, which is appointed by the finger of the Lord, in the western boundaries of the State of Missouri, and dedicated by the hand of Joseph Smith, Jun., and others with whom the Lord is well pleased. Verily this is the word of the Lord, that the city New Jerusalem shall be built by the gathering of the saints, beginning at this place, even the place of the temple, which temple shall be reared in this generation. For verily this generation shall not all pass away until an house shall be built unto the Lord, and a cloud shall rest upon it, which cloud shall be even the glory of the Lord, which shall fill the house.

Nevertheless, the Lord changes his mind; and in *D&C*, 124:45–55, the "Saints are excused from building the temple" and New Jerusalem. (See Chapter Summary.)

What appears to have happened in each of these instances is that the circumstances changed; to wit, the U.S. government outlawed polygamy, civil unrest in the 1960's and 1970's over the black issue became intolerable to the Mormon Church, and the early Saints were driven out of Missouri by opposing forces. God knew all of this before it happened and He still gave the revelations! This does not make nor supports the proposition that God is the same yesterday, today, and forever.

REASON 12
GOD IS NOT FAIR

As a Mormon, I was taught that God was "no respecter of persons," (Acts 10:34–35 and *D&C*, 38:16). However, that just is not the reality of God's dealings with mankind. Where do we find the written accounts of God's dealings with the billions of people who have lived in Asia? There are none! Where do we find written accounts of God performing miracles or intervening on behalf of non-Israelites? Again, there are none! Where do we find God discriminating against Asians, non-Israelites, non-Mormons, women, and blacks? We find these discriminations in all of the standard scriptoria works of the Mormon Church, the Bible, *Book of Mormon*, *Doctrine and Covenants* and, the *Pearl of Great Price*. These discriminatory practices are discussed in many of the following "Reasons," but perhaps a short overview is appropriate here.

According to the Constitution of the United States, all men are created equal. The Mormon doctrine teaches that the Constitution was inspired by God. In *D&C*, 101:80 it states:

> And for this purpose have I [the Lord] established the Constitution of this land [America], by the hands of wise men whom I raised up unto this very purpose, and redeemed the land by the shedding of blood.

The U.S. Congress has passed numerous laws that have been upheld by the U.S. Supreme Court that prohibit discrimination based upon nationality, religion, race, or gender. However, the God that I was taught to believe in appears to discriminate in all four of these categories in His dealings with mankind which are discussed in other Reasons.

The Bible and the *Book of Mormon* are full of accounts where God only dealt with the Israelite people through their Prophets. His chosen people were the descendants of Abraham. Basically, all other nations were without prophets or intervention. According to Mormon philosophy, the ONLY religion recognized by God was the Israelite religion, then the teachings of Christ, and currently the Mormon religion. For over 4000 years, God looked upon the black- and yellow-skin races as not worthy of His presence, His contact, or His Priesthood. Women have always been subservient to man in all of the scriptures.

One example of this unfairness is the country of China and the Chinese people. China is currently the most populated country in the world and probably has been for centuries. Wikipedia, the free encyclopedia on the Internet, explains that what is now China was inhabited by **Homo erectus** more than a million years ago. There is evidence showing that between 12,000 and 10,000 B.C., the people living around the Yellow River in China were involved in agriculture.

> With agriculture came increased population, the ability to store and redistribute crops, and the potential to support specialty craftsmen and administrators.

By 7000 B.C., the Chinese were farming millet, giving

> rise to the Jiahu culture. …At Damaidi in Ningxia, 3,172 cliff carvings (dating from 6000 to 5000 B.C.) have been discovered, "featuring 8,453 individual characters such as the sun, moon, stars, gods, and scenes of hunting or grazing." These pictographs are reputed to be similar to the earliest characters confirmed to be written Chinese (*Wikipedia*, "History of China").

Another website states that the

> history of science and technology in China is both long and rich, with many contributions to science and technology. In antiquity, independently of other civilizations, ancient Chinese philosophers made significant advances in science, technology, mathematics, and astronomy. Traditional Chinese medicine, acupuncture, and herbal medicine were also practiced.
>
> Among the earliest inventions were the abacus, the "shadow clock," and the first flying machines such as kites and lanterns. The four Great Inventions of ancient China: the compass, gunpowder, papermaking, and printing were among the most important technological

advances, only known in Europe by the end of the Middle Ages ("Science and Technology in Ancient China").

These four discoveries had an enormous impact on the development of Chinese civilization and a far-ranging global impact. Gunpowder, for example, spread to the Arabs in the 13th Century and thence to Europe ("History of science and technology in China").

Therefore, the Chinese people were probably more educated, civilized, and advanced than the Israelite people of the Bible, the Nephites of the *Book of Mormon*, and the Christians from Christ onward, until the Industrial Revolution. Nevertheless, we have no known contact by the God or Gods believed in by the peoples of the Bible and *Book of Mormon* with the Chinese people. Even when the Gospel of Jesus Christ was allegedly restored by Joseph Smith, it was not shared with the Chinese people until the most recent few decades.

Some of that which has been said above about China could also be said about the countries of India and the former Soviet Union, which are the next most-populated countries in the world.

Why weren't the billions of people in China, India, the former Soviet Union, and other places in the world given prophets or the Gospel? Why did the black race have to wait until 1978 to have to right to receive the Mormon Priesthood? (See Reason 63.) Why do we have nothing written about the importance of and participation by women in the creation of the world? (See Reason 68.) Why has God been so unfair in His dealings with mankind? Wouldn't a God who was the spiritual Father of all mankind be "no respecter of persons" (*D&C*, 38:16), and reasonable and fair with *all* of mankind? The Mormon God or Gods do not seem to have this quality of fairness, which otherwise would enhance one's belief in them.

REASON 13
GOD IS A JEALOUS GOD

Throughout the Old Testament, God indicates that He is a jealous God and condemns his chosen people, the Israelites, continuously for worshipping other gods. As we all know, the first of the Ten Commandments given to Moses on Mount Sinai was, "Thou shall have no other gods before me," and the second was, "Thou shall not make unto thee any graven image" (Exodus 20:3–4). Then in verse 5, He states: "Thou shalt not bow down thyself to them, nor serve them: for I the Lord thy God am a jealous God."

Why would God be jealous when He knows that He is the only true God? Is this not a characteristic that is un-godlike? Wouldn't God, who is omnipresent, omniscient, and omnipotent care less about other graven images of concocted gods created by man? For some reason, a jealous God does not seem right. Bruce R. McConkie, in his book *Mormon Doctrine*, on page 391 states:

> Our Lord uses the word *Jealous* as one of his names. 'For thou shalt worship no other god: for the Lord, *whose name is Jealous*, is a jealous God. (Exodus 34:14)

This seems like it might be an appropriate explanation, but it is not, as explained hereafter. Elder McConkie goes on to say:

> Among other things, use of this name is a complete refutation of the sectarian heresy (found in the creeds) that Deity is devoid of passions.

(This ascribes to God the negative emotion or passion of jealousy).

We discuss in Reason 32 the enormous number of names attributed to God in the *Book of Mormon*. "Jealous" is not one of them. However, in Mosiah 11:22, it does state, "that I am the Lord their God, and am a jealous God" (also stated in Mosiah 13:13). The only other time the word "jealous" is used in the *Book of Mormon* is in Ether 9:7, describing an emotion or passion of Akish toward his son, causing the son to be placed in prison. Further, we find in Joseph Smith's alleged *Inspired Translation* of the Old Testament (*JST*), a change or modification made to Exodus 34:14. Joseph Smith's translation states: "for the Lord, whose name is Jehovah, is a jealous God," inserting "Jehovah" for "Jealous," therefore indicating that "jealous" is not an appropriate name for God.

Webster's Dictionary defines "jealous" as:

> intolerant of rivalry or unfaithfulness, disposed to suspect rivalry or unfaithfulness, or hostile toward a rival or one believed to enjoy an advantage.

Would God be intolerant, suspecting, or hostile when He would know that there are no other Gods? Alternatively, would He be an omniscient, loving, and merciful God who understands that the majority of mankind does not have the correct understanding or knowledge of God? A kind God and one in whom I could believe would not have the passion of jealousy.

REASON 14
GOD IS A GOD OF CONFUSION

The God we as members of the Mormon Church were taught to believe in sometimes appears to be confused or seems to have vacillated in regard to various laws. The first example is the story of Noah and the flood, where God knew the end from the beginning and what His children would do. However, God went ahead anyway, and allowed a majority of unrighteous spirit children to come to the earth around Noah's time, so that He could destroy them with the flood. Why not spread the unrighteous spirit children over generations of time and allow more righteous spirit children to inhabit the Earth during Noah's time, so that God didn't have to destroy all of the inhabitants on Earth?

Some members of the Mormon Church have put forth the idea that Earth needed to be baptized like the members of God's church, by immersion, so there needed to be a flood. However, this baptism of the Earth could have occurred prior to Adam being placed upon Earth. In fact, a baptism of the Earth most likely did occur prior to Adam, because, in the creation (as recorded in the *Pearl of Great Price*, Moses 2:6–10), the waters were created first and covered the Earth. Then God said, "Let the waters under the heaven be gathered together unto one place, and it was so, and I, God, said: Let there be dry land; and it was so" (verse 9).

Another example of confusion is when the Lord gave to Moses the Ten Commandments on Mt. Sinai, of which one was "Thou shalt not kill." However, shortly thereafter, when Moses came down from Mt. Sinai with the tablets of the Ten Commandments and saw his people worshipping a golden calf, he broke the tablets and said to the people:

> Who is on the Lord's side? Let him come unto me. And all the sons of Levi gathered themselves together unto him. And he said unto them. Thus saith the Lord God of Israel, Put every man his sword by his side, and go in and out from gate to gate throughout the camp, and slay every man his brother, and every man his companion, and every man his neighbor. And the children of Levi did according to the word of Moses:

and there fell of the people that day about three thousand men. (Exodus 32:26–28)

Apparently, the commandment not to kill is a qualified commandment. This is just like our court systems today, in which the "law" sometimes is only what the judges *say* the law is and not actually what the written law says. The Lord God of the Old Testament interpreted the law: *to not kill*, according to circumstances—and not in accordance to what was written. In the *Book of Mormon*, there is another example of the Lord commanding someone to kill even after the Ten Commandments were also given to the people of the *BOM*. God told Nephi to kill Laban, a keeper of records, and to steal the Plates of Brass from him, which Nephi did. This is again a confusing story as to God's violation of the Ten Commandments (1 Nephi 4:17–18).

Then there is the commandment not to steal. But the Lord commands Joshua and other prophets of the Israelites (as previously mentioned) to attack and war against many cities in the Promised Land and steal the people's treasures and gold, cattle and animals, and also to steal their land (see the books of Joshua and Judges). Is this not a little confusing?

Another example of confusion by the Mormon God has to do with the end of the Earth and the Second Coming of Christ. Jesus Christ and his Apostles, after Christ died, taught that the end of the earth was close at hand. In Matthew 16:28, Jesus said:

> Verily I say unto you, There be some standing here, which shall not taste of death, till they see the Son of man coming in his kingdom.

Some may believe that this scripture refers to John the Beloved, and the suggestion in the Bible that he did not die and apparently stayed upon Earth so he would be here for the Second Coming. However, the reference in this scripture is to "some" and not just "one." A similar verse in found Mark 9:1 states:

> And he said unto them, Verily I say unto you, That there be some of them that stand here, which shall not taste of death, till they have seen the kingdom of God come with power.

Again, the reference is to "some."

Jesus seemed to be teaching that the Son of Man was soon to arrive from heaven in judgment of mankind, with those who followed the laws being rewarded and those who did not being punished. Furthermore, it seems that this judgment would come in the lifetime of His disciples (Matthew 24:21–33). Specifically in Matthew 24:34, Jesus stated, "Verily I say unto you, this generation shall not pass, till all these things be fulfilled." The Apostle Paul also taught that those he was speaking to should be prepared for the coming of Christ (1 Thessalonians 5:1–6). Nevertheless, the Second Coming has never happened.

In his *History of the Church*, Joseph Smith talked about the timing of the Second Coming of Christ and a revelation that he received in regard to the same. In volume 5 at page 336, Joseph Smith states in April 1843 the following:

> Were I going to prophesy, I would say the end [of the world] would not come in 1844, 5, or 6, or in forty years. There are those of the rising generation who shall not taste death till Christ comes.

This is very similar to Jesus' statement in Mark 9:1 quoted above. However, just as in the time after Jesus made that statement, after Joseph Smith made this statement, Christ did not come and all of the rising generation passed away. So why did the Lord add to the confusion as to when the Second Coming was to occur by the revelations given to Joseph Smith?

Another point about "A God of Confusion," is found in the *Book of Mormon*. In 2 Nephi 27:23, it states:

> For behold, I am God; and I am a God of miracles; and I will show unto the world that I am the same yesterday, today, and forever.

This scripture indicates that the God we were taught to believe in as Mormons is a "God of Miracles." One simple miracle God could have performed would have eliminated much of the confusion as to what God or Jesus Christ wants us to believe and do. Jesus could have just written down what He said and what transpired while He was upon Earth.

Unfortunately, we do not have any original manuscripts of what Jesus actually said when he *was* on Earth. Why didn't Jesus write his own history and gospel and then preserve it? If we had the actual testament of Jesus written by him and authenticated, as the original, then we would know the entire story and the truth about His Gospel. Some might argue that being a carpenter he couldn't read or write. However, if he could walk on water and raise people from the dead, he certainly had the capability to learn to read and write. Indications are that He *did* read and write, as mentioned many times in the New Testament. (See Jesus reading in the synagogue in Nazareth, as recorded in Luke 4). The Gospel of Jesus or His Testament, written in his own hand, and preserved for today, would answer so many questions and eliminate so much confusion.

Further, because God is all-powerful, there would be numerous other ways that He could have protected and preserved the original manuscript written by Jesus until such time that it could be authenticated and reproduced. We know that He allegedly protected and preserved the "gold plates" from 400 A.D., when they were buried by Moroni, until 1829, when they were given to Joseph Smith. A preservation of the "Gospel of Jesus" would have eliminated a lot of confusion as to the actual Gospel of Jesus Christ. Why wouldn't God do this, to confront the confusion that leads so many of His children away from His Gospel?

There are numerous other examples of confusion throughout the history of the Bible, the *Book of Mormon,* and the LDS Church, where prophesies or the laws of God are changed or contradicted by God. This makes it extremely difficult to believe in a God of confusion, or one that vacillates according to the circumstances. Wouldn't God be a God that is constant and the same in His dealings with the people of old as well as the people of today? Shouldn't spiritual or moral laws be eternal and not changeable because of different times or circumstances?

REASON 15
GOD MAKES MISTAKES

Most religions, including the Mormon religion, view their God as one that is perfect, or in other words, would not make any mistakes in His dealings with the human race. However, the first example of a mistake by the God we were taught to believe in was the War in Heaven, discussed in Reason 69, where God lost one third of His spirit children. To allow the expulsion of one third of your spirit children from Your presence and deny them the opportunity to come to an earth seems to be a huge mistake to me. It is hard to imagine that God would not have been more persuasive to His spirit children, or more intuitive as to their spiritual needs, so that He might have prevented such a large loss of his spirit children to the "dark side."

The argument could be made that even in the War in Heaven all of His spirit children had free agency, or the freedom to choose what they felt was the right choice. However, it is difficult to believe that an all-knowing and all-powerful God would make the mistake of not teaching his spirit children the ability to choose the path that would bring them the most happiness and progression. If we as parents on Earth lose one third of our children to the "dark side," we believe we have failed and made many mistakes that caused said result. In fact, we are commanded to teach our children correct principles so that when they grow up they won't depart therefrom. The Prophet David O. McKay, of the Mormon Church, made a statement that seemed to indicate that no success in life could compensate for failure in the home by not teaching your children correctly (McCullough 116).

One might argue that there had to be sin or evil upon Earth so that mankind could be tested to see if they would follow God. Therefore, Satan needed to be cast out and given the power to tempt mankind and lead them astray. This doesn't quite make sense though, because one of the eternal laws is "opposition in all things" (2 Nephi 11-19). Therefore, good and evil have always been present, even in the pre-existence in the War in Heaven. Apparently, there was an opposition to the plan of Jesus Christ in the pre-existence: the one offered by Lucifer, which was apparently an "evil" plan, because it resulted in the expulsion of Lucifer or Satan and of one third of God's children from God's presence. Therefore, there must have been an evil influence present to influence Satan to rebel against God. So the conclusion that good and evil are eternal laws that co-exist with God seems to make the most sense.

Further, if God was perfect in the pre-existence and would have raised His spirit children perfectly, why didn't He raise all of His spirit children with the desire to do good and resist evil and therefore prevent losing one third of His spirit children? If God also knew everything, the beginning from the end, He would have known about the rebellion and the loss of his spirit children, just like He knew beforehand of the loss of millions to the flood at the time of Noah. Both of these seem to be mistakes. One cost the physical death of millions; the other cost the spiritual death of trillions, because the spirits that were cast out can never obtain a physical body or return to God's presence. Therefore, they have suffered a spiritual death (*D&C*, 29:36–45). Is it not a mistake to allow so many of your children to perish and be condemned to an eternal existence with Satan?

The flood at the time of Noah will be discussed in Reason 77 in regard to the confusion of God killing his own children upon Earth. It also appears to be a huge mistake when one considers the omniscient power of God. An argument could be made that God didn't know that all of his spirit children allowed to come to earth would become so wicked that they would have to be destroyed. But that would open up the possibility that, due to His not knowing everything, mistakes could be made.

According to the story of the *Book of Mormon*, God led a handful of his chosen people in 600 B.C. from Jerusalem to the American continent. The prophet, Lehi, was warned by the Lord that Jerusalem was going to be destroyed because the people would not repent. Many would be killed and many more carried off into captivity in Babylon (1 Nephi 1:4, 13). Unlike the flood, the wicked were allowed to live in captivity and eventually return to Jerusalem from Babylon so that Christ could be born there. On the other hand, Lehi and his family were saved by traveling in a ship across the ocean to the American continent. Did God learn from his earlier mistake of killing everyone with the flood? But that would mean that God could make mistakes. The God that we would want to believe in *would not* make mistakes.

As members of the Mormon Church, we have always been told (when we have proposed questions like the ones above) that God's thoughts are not man's thoughts and His plan and purposes are not known to us. Therefore, we need to accept everything that He does with faith. We can accept the fact that we don't have a clue what God thinks. But in searching for God, don't we need to feel in our hearts that the God we believe in is a rational, loving, and forgiving God and one whom would not make mistakes?

Other apparent mistakes that have been or will be discussed in other Reasons include 1) the fact that God sometimes allowed polygamy, and other times said it was a sin and an abomination (Reason 11); 2) the exclusion of women in His revelations with mankind (Reason 20); and 3) the lack of participation of His Goddess in the creation (Reason 68). The same could be said in regard to the Mormon Church denying blacks the Priesthood for so many years and then all of the sudden saying it was ok in 1978, as though a mistake had been made and needed to be corrected (Reason 19).

Both the *Doctrine & Covenants* and the *History of the Church* written by Joseph Smith contain accounts that appear to be mistakes in revelations given to Joseph Smith. Some of these are discussed in other Reasons, such as 1) buying the land in Independence, Missouri to build a temple for the New Jerusalem, and 2) the establishment of the United Order, or Law of Consecration by revelation from the Lord (see *D&C*, Section 104) in Kirtland, Ohio. In this revelation, all of the members would give all of their properties and income to the Church and allow the Church to manage them and give back to the members what the Church thought was fair and reasonable.

This didn't work and appears to have been a mistake, which was a fact that would have been known by an omniscient God. Joseph Smith also founded a bank called the Kirtland Safety Society and printed money in Kirtland, Ohio in accordance with revelations given to him (see *HC*, 2:472–73), but again, the same was a disaster.

Would the God that we would want to believe in make mistakes or command things to be done that He knows would fail or could not be accomplished? The argument could be made that we do not know God's purposes and that He commands some things for the single person or group of people's experience. But this seems unlikely, because we can see the results of the non-fulfillment of some commandments and the disasters of others.

REASON 16
GOD IS A GOD OF WAR AND VIOLENCE

As mentioned previously, the Mormon religion teaches that the God of the Old Testament is Jehovah or Jesus Christ. It also teaches that the God or Lord mentioned in the *Book of Mormon* is the same: Jehovah or Jesus Christ. The Old Testament is full of references to the fact that Jehovah was a God of war, vengeance, and violence. In many incidents in the Old Testament, God commands His people to go to war, seek vengeance, or to commit violence. I have mentioned a lot of these in other Reasons, like when Joshua became the Prophet of the Israelites upon Moses' death and God commanded him to lead the Israelite people into the Land of Promise. Joshua was told to attack the city of Jericho and "utterly destroyed all that was in the city, both man and woman, young and old, and ox and sheep, and ass, with the edge of the sword" (Joshua 6:21).

The Lord was a God of war and violence for Joshua and the Israelites. They did not rest from war until they had destroyed over thirty cities and dethroned over thirty-one Kings and took their lands (Joshua 12). The Lord continued to fight the battles of the Israelites from Joshua to Zechariah, and usually did so with violence.

The Old Testament has many other instances where the Lord either instituted the violence and war or supported the same. Some are as follows:

- Judges 1:4: "And Judah went up; and the Lord delivered the Canaanites and the Perizzites into their hand: and they slew of them in Bezek ten thousand men."
- Judges 14:19: "And the Spirit of the Lord came upon [Samson], and he went down to Ashkelon, and slew thirty men of them, and took their spoil."
- Judges 15:14, 16: "...the Spirit of the Lord came mightily upon [Samson]...and...with the jaw of an ass have I slain a thousand men."
- 1 Samuel 23:2, 5: "Therefore David inquired of the Lord, saying, Shall I go and smite these Philistines? And the Lord said unto David, Go, and smite the Philistines, and save Keilah. ...So David and his men...fought with the

Philistines, and brought away their cattle, and smote them with a great slaughter."
- 1 Kings 18:19–40: The Prophet Elijah kills the 450 prophets of Baal.
- 2 Kings 1:6–12: The Prophet Elijah brings down fire from heaven to consume two captains and their fifty men each.
- 2 Kings 6:18: "And when they came down to him, Elisha prayed unto the Lord, and said, Smite this people, I pray thee, with blindness. And he smote them with blindness according to the word of Elisha."
- Isaiah 34:2–3: "For the indignation of the Lord is upon all nations, and his fury upon all their armies: he hath utterly destroyed them, he hath delivered them to the slaughter. Their slain also shall be cast out, and their stink shall come up out of their carcasses, and the mountains shall be melted with their blood."
- Jeremiah 47–52: The Lord brings violence and death to many cities and people.

The eighth Article of the Faith of the LDS Church states, in part: "We believe the Bible to be the word of God as far as it is translated correctly." Many Mormon-faithful rely on this belief to excuse the stories of the God of the Old Testament—and His acts of war, vengeance, and violence—as not being translated correctly. However, we can find the same God of war, vengeance, and violence in the *Book of Mormon* which, according to the same Eighth Article of Faith, has been translated correctly.

Throughout the *Book of Mormon* there are many wars among the Nephites and the Lamanites, the two main groups of people discussed. In fact, probably at least one fifth of the entire *Book of Mormon* is a history of said wars. Again, the Lord or God in the *Book of Mormon* (Jehovah or Jesus Christ) fought the wars in behalf of the Nephites and brought vengeance, violence, and death to the Lamanites, as verified in the following passages:

> 2 Nephi 5:20–21: Wherefore, the word of the Lord was fulfilled which he spake unto me, saying that: Inasmuch as they will not hearken unto thy words they shall be cut off from the presence of the Lord. And behold, they were cut off from his presence. And he had caused the

> cursing to come upon them, yea, even a sore cursing, because of their iniquity. For behold, they had hardened their hearts against him…wherefore, as they were white, and exceedingly fair and delightsome, that they might not be enticing unto my people the Lord God did cause a skin of blackness to come upon them.
>
> Omni 1:3, 5, 7: And it came to pass that two hundred and seventy and six years had passed away, and we had many seasons of peace; and we had many seasons of serous war and bloodshed…and the more wicked part of the Nephites were destroyed. …Wherefore, the Lord did visit them in great judgment; nevertheless, he did spare the righteous.
>
> Words of Mormon 1:14: And in the strength of the Lord they did contend against their enemies, until they had slain many thousands of the Lamanites.
>
> Mosiah 9:18: And God did hear our cries and did answer our prayers; and we did go forth in his might; yea, we did go forth against the Lamanites, and in one day and a night we did slay three thousand and forty-three; we did slay them even until we had driven them out of our land.

In Alma 43, during another war between the Lamanites and the Nephites, a General named Moroni asked the prophet Alma to inquire of the Lord as to where the Nephites should go to gain an advantage over the Lamanites. In verse 24 it states:

> And it came to pass that the word of the Lord came unto Alma, and Alma informed the messengers of Moroni, that the armies of the Lamanites were marching…into the land of Manti.

Based upon said information provided by the Lord, the Nephites were victorious. Then in Alma 61:15, during the war between the Lamanites and the Nephites, the General Moroni is given instructions from the head of the government as follows:

> Therefore, come unto me speedily with a few of your men, and leave the remainder in the charge of Lehi and Teancum; give unto them power to conduct the war in that part of the land, according to the Spirit of God....

The death, vengeance, and violence attributed to the God in the *Book of Mormon* has been discussed in Reason 35 more specifically, when He destroys all of the cities and their inhabitants because of their wickedness, just prior to His visiting the people (3 Nephi 9). It is interesting to note that this same Lord of the Old Testament and of the *Book of Mormon*, who spoke to Joseph Smith so many times in the 1830's, failed to fight the battles of the early LDS Church members. Instead, He allowed them to be killed and expelled from their homes and lands numerous times, requiring them to move from state-to-state, until finally settling in Utah. This same God also failed to fight the battles of the Jewish people in the Holocaust in World War II, the innocent people of the massacres of Stalin, Genghis Kahn, and Mao, and many others. Wouldn't God be a God of peace and non-violence and protect righteous people by means other than causing death and destruction?

For example, in the *Book of Mormon*, Mosiah 24:16–23, where the Nephite people were in bondage to the Lamanites and suffering afflictions and burdens it states:

> And it came to pass that so great was their faith and their patience that the voice of the Lord came unto them again, saying: Be of good comfort, for on the morrow I will deliver you out of bondage. ...And in the morning the Lord caused a deep sleep to come upon the Lamanites, yea, and all their task-masters were in a profound sleep. And Alma and his people departed into the wilderness...and...poured out their thanks to God...for they were in bondage, and none could deliver them except it were the Lord their God. ...And now the Lord said unto Alma: Haste thee and get thou and this people out of this land, for the Lamanites have awakened and do pursue thee; therefore get thee out of this land, and I will stop the Lamanites in this valley that they come no further in pursuit of this people.

This is a God of non-violence.

Another example in the *Book of Mormon* is in Mosiah, Chapter 22, where the converted people of King Limhi escape from the bondage of the Lamanites by causing the guards to become drunk, and then leaving by night. Again, why is this not the God of the Old Testament and all of the *Book of Mormon*? Is it not appropriate to believe that the true God is not vengeful, violent, or a supporter of war when other solutions are available and possible?

REASON 17
THE MORMON GOD DISCRIMINATES BASED ON NATIONALITY

According to the Constitution of the United States of America, all men are created equal. The Mormon doctrine teaches that the Constitution was inspired by God. In *D&C*, 101:80, it states:

> And for this purpose have I [the Lord] established the Constitution of this land [America], by the hands of wise men whom I raised up unto this very purpose, and redeemed the land by the shedding of blood.

The U.S. Congress has passed numerous laws that have been upheld by the U.S. Supreme Court that prohibit discrimination based upon nationality, religion, race, or gender. However, the God that we were taught to believe in appears to discriminate in all four of these categories in His dealings with mankind.

In Acts 10:34–35, it states:

> Then Peter opened his mouth, and said, Of a truth I perceive that God is no respecter of persons: But in every nation he that feareth him, and worketh righteousness, is accepted with him.

If God is no "respecter of persons" then why would He have a chosen people?

According to the doctrine of the Mormon Church, God has a chosen people, the Israelites, or the descendents of the twelve tribes of Israel, although some of the twelve tribes eventually became lost. The term "Israelites" is the English name for the nation of Israel, which was divided into twelve tribes. Each tribe descended from one of the twelve sons of Jacob, the grandson of Abraham. Jacob was given the name "Israel" by the Lord (Genesis 32:28). The Israelites were the dominant cultural and ethnic group living in the area located near and around modern-day Israel and Palestine between 1273 B.C. and 423 B.C. Apparently, Jehovah (Jesus Christ) made a covenant with Abraham and his descendants (the Israelites) that they would be his chosen people upon Earth. Therefore, Jehovah did not appear to give revelations to, nor have prophets among, all of the other people living upon Earth at that time, which included the millions living in Europe, Scandinavia, India, Russia, China, and basically the rest of the world.

The Mormon religion teaches that through baptism and receiving the Gift of the Holy Ghost, a member of the Church becomes an Israelite. This is because those not directly descended from Israel are therefore Gentiles, and can be adopted and grafted into Israel through baptism, thus become part of the "chosen people" of God. (*See PGP*, Abraham 2:9–11 and McConkie 389–90).

The *Book of Mormon* is full of references to this "chosen people of God." Many patriarchal blessings (given to church members by patriarchs in the church) indicate that members of the Mormon Church have been adopted into the tribe of Ephraim of the House of Israel through their baptism into the Mormon Church. In fact, that is what mine said. Some members of the Mormon Church believe that only certain sons and daughters of God are members of the "chosen people" due to their pre-earth life existence, when as spirits, they lived with God. Apparently, some spirit children were more valiant in the pre-existence than others and therefore had the right to be part of the chosen people when they came to earth. This seems to be supported by the fact that the God who Mormons are taught to believe in only had contact with a few of His children upon Earth; and those were born into the House of Israel.

The Old Testament is also full of passages discussing the "chosen people," the Israelites. They are described as descendents of both Abraham (with whom God made a promise) and Abraham's grandson, Jacob, whose name was changed to "Israel." The *D&C*, 107:40 also states:

> The order of this priesthood was confirmed to be handed down from father to son, and rightly belongs to the literal descendants of the chosen seed, to whom the promises were made.

The Old Testament does not explain why some people are born descendents of Abraham and Israel, but it is explained in the teachings of the Mormon Church. In the *PGP*, Abraham 3:22–23, it states:

> Now the Lord had shown unto me, Abraham, the intelligences that were organized before the world was; and among all these there were many of the noble and great ones; And God saw these souls that they were good, and he stood in the midst of them, and he said: These I will make my rulers; for he stood among those that were spirits, and he saw that they were good; and he said unto me: Abraham, thou art one of them; thou wast chosen before thou wast born.

Then in *D&C*, 138:55–56, which is a vision of the spirit world, it states:

> I observed that they [referring to Joseph Smith, Hyrum Smith, Brigham Young, John Taylor and Wilford Woodruff, all Presidents and Prophets of the Mormon Church] were also among the noble and great ones who were chosen in the beginning to be rulers of the Church of God. Even before they were born, they, with many others, received their first lessons in the world of spirits and were prepared to come forth in the due time of the Lord to labor in his vineyard for the salvation of the souls of men.

This belief of the Mormon religion—that some people were chosen before they were born to be rulers in the Church of God and that others were chosen before they were born to be members of God's chosen people—seems to be contrary to the God-inspired Constitution that states: "All men are created equal." Of more importance is the fact that God has discriminated against more than 90 percent of his children here upon Earth, based upon whether they belong to the nation of Israel or not. If they did not and were born into another nation, then they were not visited by God, did not have prophets who spoke with God, and did not have His Gospel or teachings. Isn't it hard to believe in a discriminatory God?

REASON 18
THE MORMON GOD DISCRIMINATES BASED ON RELIGION

When Joseph Smith went into the woods to pray in 1820, he wanted to find out which of the churches he should join. When he saw God the Father and Jesus Christ in his first vision, Joseph Smith stated in his History (1:18–19):

> My object in going to inquire of the Lord was to know which of all the sects was right, that I might know which to join. No sooner, therefore, did I get possession of myself, so as to be able to speak, than I asked the Personages who stood above me in the light, which of all the sects was right (for at this time it had never entered into my heart that all were wrong)—and which I should join. I was answered that I must join none of them, for they were all wrong; and the Personage [Jesus Christ] who addressed me said that all their creeds were an abomination in his sight; that those professors were all corrupt; that: "they draw near to me with their lips, but their hearts are far from me, they teach for doctrines the commandments of men, having a form of godliness, but they deny the power thereof."

What were some of the religious creeds in 1820 that the Lord told Joseph Smith "were an abomination in his sight?" The Methodists, which was the sect that Joseph Smith was going to join, believed in Jesus Christ as the Savior and Redeemer of the world. Part of their creed was their desire to be more Christlike, as suggested in the following twenty-two questions that members of the Methodist church were invited to ask themselves every day in their private devotions:

1. Am I consciously or unconsciously creating the impression than I am better than I really am? In other words, am I a hypocrite?
2. Am I honest in all my acts and words, or do I exaggerate?

3. Do I confidentially pass on to another what I was told to me in confidence?
4. Can I be trusted?
5. Am I a slave to dress, friends, work, or habits?
6. Am I self-conscious, self-pitying, or self-justifying?
7. Did the Bible live in me today?
8. Do I give it time to speak to me every day?
9. Am I enjoying prayer?
10. When did I last speak to someone else about my faith?
11. Do I pray about the money I spend?
12. Do I get to bed on time and get up on time?
13. Do I disobey God in anything?
14. Do I insist upon doing something about which my conscience is uneasy?
15. Am I defeated in any part of my life?
16. Am I jealous, impure, critical, irritable, touchy or distrusting?
17. How do I spend my spare time?
18. Am I proud?
19. Do I thank God that I am not as other people, especially as the Pharisees who despised the publican?
20. Is there anyone whom I fear, dislike, disown, criticize, hold a resentment toward or disregard? If so, what am I doing about it?
21. Do I grumble or complain constantly?
22. Is Christ real to me?

(*See* "Everyday Disciples.")

This doesn't appear to be a creed that would be an abomination in the sight of God.

Quakers were members of another religion in 1820. They believed in an almighty, all-wise, and everlasting God, His only Son, the Lord, and in one Holy Spirit. They also believed in the Bible, the resurrection of Christ and mankind, a final judgment, prayer, marriage, peace instead of war, the Sabbath day, and obeying enactments of civil government. Their creed also included abolishing slavery, improving women's rights, and prison reform ("Declaration of Faith"). Again, this does not appear to be a creed that would be an abomination in the sight of God. Why wouldn't God acknowledge the good in all religions and creeds? Why wouldn't God state to Joseph Smith in 1820 that most Christians, Muslims, and many other religious people had their hearts close to God, but that some of their teachings were in error?

It seems evident from reading *D&C*, Section 76 on the Three Degrees of Glory (discussed in Reason 43) that some people had the misfortune of being born at the wrong time and in the wrong place upon Earth. Those people, who lived when the Gospel of Jesus Christ was not on Earth, or who were raised in and believed in another religion other than the alleged *true* Mormon religion, were discriminated against. This would be the majority of the people who have lived on Earth in last two thousand years and all of the people who lived in places like Russia, China, and India for the last six thousand years. According to Mormon theology, because those people did not have the chance to have the Gospel of Christ and receive the testimony of Jesus in the flesh, they had to wait until they died to receive said testimony of Jesus in the Spirit World. Therefore, as described in *D&C*, 76:71–79, those people were denied the opportunity to obtain the Celestial Kingdom due to being born at the wrong place and time, when they could not belong to the true religion of Jesus Christ.

This appears to be discrimination against nearly 90 percent of the spirit children of God the Father, who have been born upon Earth. Wouldn't we like to believe in a God who gave every one of His spirit children the opportunity to return to live with Him in the Celestial Kingdom (if there is such a place), regardless of whether they had the chance upon Earth to obtain a testimony of Jesus Christ or not, and regardless of what religion they belonged to or were baptized into?

More specifically, God seems to discriminate against the Catholic religion "carte blanche." In the *BOM*, 1 Nephi 12, the Prophet Nephi (in 592 B.C.) sees in a vision the "land of promise" (America) and the visitation of Jesus Christ to the people there after His resurrection. Nephi then sees the next four hundred years after the visit of Christ and the destruction of Nephi's descendants around 400 A.D., which is recorded in Mormon 6:1–15. Then in 1 Nephi 13, the Prophet Nephi sees the formation of the church of the devil set up among the Gentiles, who were separated by many waters from his descendants living in the "promised land" (America). 1 Nephi 13:2–6 states:

> And the angel said unto me: What beholdest thou? And I said: I behold many nations and kingdoms. And he said unto me: These are the nations and kingdoms of the Gentiles. And it came to pass that I saw among the nations

of the Gentiles the formation of a great church. And the angel said unto me: Behold the formation of a church which is most abominable above all other churches... And it came to pass that I beheld this great and abominable church; and I saw the devil that he was the founder of it.

The Prophet Nephi goes on in 1 Nephi 13 to see in his vision a man (Columbus) who went upon the many waters to the descendants of Nephi in the "promised land" (America), and other Gentiles (Europeans) going across the many waters to the "promised land" (America). These Gentiles were leaving religious intolerance to go to America. They humbled themselves and the power of the Lord was with them and helped them win the Revolutionary War.

Nephi then sees in his vision, in verses 20–29, that the Gentiles in America, apparently in the 1700's, had a religious book (the Bible) with them and that "the great and abominable church...[had] taken away from the gospel of the Lamb many parts...and many covenants of the Lord." There was only one church that had the book (Bible) during the time period from Christ to the colonization of America, who would have taken "parts" out of the Bible through the many translations and revisions. That church was the Catholic Church. Although there are many instances in the history of the Catholic Church where it did not act in a Christian way (such as during the Inquisition), it is hard to believe that God would condemn said Church and refer to it as the "church of the devil," when it teaches about Christ and living a Christian life.

In 1 Nephi 14:9–10, which is a continuation of Nephi's vision, we read:

> And it came to pass that [the angel] said unto me: Look, and behold that great and abominable church, which is the mother of abominations, whose founder is the devil. And he said unto me: Behold there are save two churches only; the one is the church of the Lamb of God, and the other is the church of the devil; wherefore, whoso belongeth not to the church of the Lamb of God belongeth to that great church, which is the mother of abominations; and she is the whore of all the earth.

It is difficult to believe in a God that discriminates against all other churches or religions other than the Mormon religion, which is characterized as the *only* "true church" of Jesus Christ, and refers to all of the other churches as the church of the devil.

Why should someone of a different faith or religion, or someone who has been excommunicated from the LDS Church, be discriminated against just because they are not of the same religion? It is hard to believe in a God that would require that a person could only live with Him in the Celestial Kingdom in heaven, if he or she belonged to the "correct religion," instead of basing entrance into the Celestial Kingdom just on living a good, righteous life.

REASON 19
THE MORMON GOD DISCRIMINATES BASED ON RACE

In Reason 63, we discuss the black race and the topic of Priesthood and the reasons given in scripture as to why the black race was cursed and could not have the Priesthood until 1978. Although the Prophet Joseph Smith did not give any revelations relating to the black race and their denial of the Priesthood and temple blessings in the Mormon Church, he did translate the *Book of Mormon*, which specifically equates a person with black skin as an unrighteous person. In 2 Nephi 5:21, we read:

> And [the Lord] had caused the cursing to come upon them, yea, even a sore cursing, because of their iniquity. For behold, they had hardened their hearts against him that they had become like unto a flint; wherefore, as they were white, and exceedingly fair and delightsome, that they might not be enticing unto my people the Lord God did cause a skin of blackness to come upon them.

This cursing was upon the "Lamanites," the larger of the two groups of people that descended from Lehi, who came to the Americas from Jerusalem in 600 B.C. The Lamanites did not have prophets like the Nephites and did not have the same beliefs as the Nephites. So apparently, the Lord God cursed people in the *Book of Mormon* with a black skin. Then when they became righteous, "their curse was taken from them, and their skin became white like unto the Nephites" (3 Nephi 2:15).

Apparently, the Mormon God, as told in the *Book of Mormon*, equates a black skin with unrighteousness. Once the different color of skin was given to the Lamanites, all of their descendants were then discriminated against, based solely upon their race. It is also interesting to note that we have no records showing that God dealt at any time or in any way with the non-Caucasian races that lived in India, China, Japan, etc. The only people who God spoke to or was concerned about directly were the white races.

The discrimination against the alleged "descendants of Cain," or the black race, which descendants today would seem almost impossible to determine, does not seem to be a position that God would take in relationship to His spirit children here upon Earth. It is a discrimination that had no basis in regard to how a person lived here on Earth and how that person treated others. It was solely based upon being a member of a certain race, and is contrary to my beliefs and those of others members of the Mormon Church. It is also contrary to the doctrine established by the Constitution of the United States, which was supposedly inspired by God.

Wouldn't God grant similar opportunities to all of His spirit children that came upon Earth? Would He discriminate against one race just because their alleged ancient ancestor (Cain) killed his brother? The Second Article of Faith of the LDS Church states: "We believe that men will be punished for their own sins, and not for Adam's transgression" (*HC*, 4:540). However, Brigham Young stated, "Why are so many inhabitants of the earth cursed with a [skin] of blackness? It comes in consequence of their fathers rejecting the power of the Holy Priesthood, and the law of God" (Watt 272).

Shouldn't all of God's children be treated the same regardless of race and regardless of what their ancestors did? Should we believe in and worship a God that discriminates between races of His children and only appears to and reveals His word to the white races?

REASON 20
THE MORMON GOD DISCRIMINATES BASED ON GENDER

We have mentioned in Reasons 12 and 15 some problems with God and the female gender; but further discussion is appropriate in regard to this issue. There is very little dispute over the position of women in the Gospel of Jesus Christ, as taught by the Mormon Church. Like the black race, they are not allowed to hold the Priesthood because that is entirely a male function in the Church. Further, women are not allowed to hold any significant position of authority in the Church such as Prophet, Apostle, General Authority, Regional Representative, Patriarch, Stake President, Bishop, or numerous other positions.

There is also discrimination against women that came from the doctrine of polygamy instituted by the Prophet Joseph Smith and which was prevalent in the Old Testament. Polygamy is further discussed in Reason 46, but it is interesting to note here that in the *D&C*, 132:51–54, the Lord gave a revelation to Joseph Smith, commanding his wife, Emma Smith, to submit to the doctrine of polygamy or be destroyed. Furthermore, nowhere in any of the scriptures do we find an instance where God gave a woman more than one husband or concubines.

Why aren't women equal in the sight of God? The Mormon religion teaches that a man cannot obtain godhood without being married in the temple under the Law of the New and Everlasting Covenant of Celestial Marriage for time and all eternity, performed by someone who has been anointed and appointed by God (*D&C*, 132:15–22). Therefore, in this instance, the LDS religion teaches that women are equal in the sight of God, because a man cannot be exalted without a woman. Nevertheless, there are inconsistencies in regard to equality for women in the Mormon Church, as stated above in regard to holding the Priesthood, authoritative positions, and polygamy. Some members of the Mormon Church believe that women have a different role to play here upon Earth, and therefore are not discriminated against. Obviously though, that role upon Earth is subservient to the man's role and not equal in comparison.

In the temple endowment ceremony performed by the LDS Church, the woman does in fact play a subservient role. Because the entire temple ceremony is no longer secret and has been placed on different Internet sites in its entirety, anyone can verify the subservient role of the woman. Although there have been many changes to the temple endowment ceremony since Joseph Smith first initiated the same, it still represents the same hierarchy of importance and authority. In the temple ceremony, the woman is placed in a subservient role when there is no mention of Elohim's wife, our Heavenly Mother, in the creation of Earth or the creations of Adam and Eve.

In the creation of this earth, as taught in the Mormon religion in the temple ceremony, there were only three participants: God the Father (Elohim), Jesus Christ (Jehovah), and Adam (Michael). The process and description of the creation of Earth and of Adam and Eve by said participants is part of the temple ceremony. Conspicuously absent from the creation of Earth and the creation of Adam and Eve is the Heavenly Mother or Mothers of our spirit bodies, and the eternal Goddess or Goddesses of God the Father. Some of the General Authorities of the LDS Church have indicated that the reason for the absence of any mention of God the Father's eternal companion or companions in the scriptures, the Bible, *Book of Mormon*, *Doctrine and Covenants*, and *Pearl of Great Price* is because God the Father would not want to expose Her to any ridicule or negativity from Her children who dwell upon the earth. However, this would not explain Her absence as a participant in the creation, as discussed in the temple, because that ceremony has been secret for over 150 years and participants are under an oath of secrecy.

If the woman is as important as the man in the eternal nature of our existence, then shouldn't God's Goddess be part of the holiest of ceremonies in the Mormon religion and known to her spirit children who dwell upon Earth in physical bodies? But she is not known or discussed anywhere in the scriptures or Mormon doctrine. In fact, the only place where our Heavenly Mother is mentioned is in one LDS hymn titled "O My Father."

Further, in the original temple ceremony, it is the man that covenants to obey God. The woman, in her subservient role, covenants to obey the man. This hierarchy is prevalent in the Mormon Church because the man holds the Priesthood and the wife is supposed to follow the husband's directions as long as they are given in righteousness as a worthy Priesthood holder. It is the man who presides, whether it is at a church function or in the home for family prayer. It isn't hard to accept the fact that a man and a woman are different physically and do in fact have different roles in the reproduction of the species. Shouldn't they both be equal in the sight of God as to His religion or church?

All of the books of scripture are dominated by man. In fact, in the *Book of Mormon*, we are never given the names of the wives of the Prophets Nephi, Jacob, Mosiah, Alma, Mormon, Moroni, and others; and they are not even mentioned except as a *wife*. There are very few women in the *Book of Mormon* that are even mentioned by name; and very few that play any significant role in the dealings between the God of the *Book of Mormon* and the people therein. The Bible is similar, although there are more instances where women do play a role in God's dealings with His children upon Earth. Again, they are few and far between.

Would the God in whom one wants to believe discriminate based upon gender and not allow both sexes the same rights, privileges, and opportunities? Wouldn't a woman be as important in the history of God's dealings with mankind as the man and have more than a subservient role? Shouldn't her role be equal to that of man's in most instances?

REASON 21
THE MORMON GOD CHANGES HIS REVEALED WORD

The four books of scripture for the Mormon Church are the Bible, the *Book of Mormon*, the *Doctrine and Covenants*, and the *Pearl of Great Price*. These are considered the "revealed Word of God" to His "chosen people." However, according to Mormon theology, God is supposed to continue to speak to his Prophet on Earth, which also constitutes His "revealed word." These alleged communications between God and his Prophet on earth, from 1845 (after the death of Joseph Smith) to the present, are believed by Mormons to be recorded in the semi-annual general conferences of the Mormon Church, where the Prophet speaks to the members of the Church as the spokesman for what God wants them to hear at that time.

We discuss in Reason 59 the fact that we do not have any written revelations since Joseph Smith that are claimed by the Mormon Church to be directly from God. On numerous occasions in the revelations in the *Doctrine and Covenants*, Joseph Smith used the phrase, "Behold I am God, give heed to my word," and then recorded exactly what God had said to him. The speeches given by the Prophets at the semi-annual general conferences, although recorded, do not contain similar phrases. However, our comparisons for any changes in God's revealed word take into consideration the above-mentioned four books of scripture and past conference talks given by the Prophets and Apostles of the Mormon Church.

In Reason 82, we discuss the changes made by Joseph Smith to the Bible in his *"Inspired Translation."* We also discuss the inconsistencies between certain scriptures from the Bible found in the *Book of Mormon* and the *Inspired Translation* of the Bible, so those changes in the "revealed word of God" will not be discussed in this Reason.

As to other changes in God's revealed word, there is one significant change concerning the Word of Wisdom found in *D&C*, Section 89, that is also discussed in Reason 45. *D&C*, 89:1–2 states:

> A Word of Wisdom, for the benefit of the council of high priests, assembled in Kirtland, and the church, and also

the saints in Zion – To be sent greeting; ***not by commandment or constraint,*** but by revelation and the word of wisdom, showing forth the order and will of God in the temporal salvation of all saints in the last days (emphasis added).

The Word of Wisdom was not originally given by God as a commandment to mankind; but was later made a commandment through the word of Brigham Young, the Prophet of the Mormon Church after the death of Joseph Smith. Therefore, this was a change in the revealed word of God. Today, a member of the Mormon Church must strictly adhere to the Word of Wisdom: no alcohol, tobacco, tea, or coffee, in order to obtain a recommend to attend the temple and be considered a devout Mormon.

Another significant change relates to the black race and the Priesthood of God, discussed in Reason 63. Brigham Young, as the Prophet, declared that the black race (or descendants of Cain) could not hold the Priesthood. This was accepted by the Church as the "revealed word of God" until it was changed in 1978 by a Declaration given by the Prophet at that time, Spencer W. Kimball, allowing the blacks to hold the Priesthood.

The revelation from God on polygamy found in *D&C*, Section 132, further discussed in Reason 46, commanding the Mormon people to practice polygamy, was also changed by a Declaration from the Prophet Wilford Woodruff in 1890, which abandoned said practice of polygamy. Further, the practice of polygamy was prohibited and judged as "evil" in the *Book of Mormon* when the Prophet Jacob said,

> Wherefore, my brethren, hear me, and hearken to the word of the Lord: For there shall not any man among you have save it be one wife; and concubines he shall have none; (Jacob 2:27)

In Reason 34, we discuss the story of Nephi and Laban found in the *Book of Mormon*. In both the Old Testament and the *Book of Mormon* in numerous places, God reveals his commandment not to kill; but then changes this revelation in God's discussion with Nephi and commands Nephi to kill Laban. Reason 78 (concerning Moses and the Passover), Reason 80 (concerning Joshua and the invasion of the Promised Land), and Reason 35 describing the destruction of cities and their inhabitants by God in the *Book of Mormon*, are additional examples of God changing his "revealed word" concerning killing.

There are other Reasons discussed in this book that could also be cited as examples of the changing revelations of God; but the conclusion would still be the same: "Why should I believe in a God that changes his revelations?"

REASON 22
GOD, THE FATHER ONCE BEING A MAN

The Prophet Joseph Smith taught, and the Mormon Church accepts as true, that God the Father was once a man like us, with a physical body living on an earth maybe similar to ours. In Joseph Smith's "King Follett Discourse" of 1844 (as printed in *HC*, 6:302–17), Joseph Smith declared:

> God himself was once as we are now, and is an exalted man, and sits enthroned in yonder heavens! That is the great secret. If the veil were rent today, and the great God who holds this world in its orbit, and who upholds all worlds and all things by His power, was to make himself visible,—I say, if you were to see him today, you would see him like a man in form like yourselves in all the person, image, and very form as a man; for Adam was created in the very fashion, image and likeness of God, and received instruction from, and walked, talked and conversed with Him, as one man talks and communes with another (305).

Joseph Smith went on to state:

> In order to understand the subject of the dead, for consolation of those who mourn for the loss of their friends, it is necessary we should understand the character and being of God and how He came to be so; for I am going to tell you how God came to be God. We have imagined and supposed that God was God from all eternity. I will refute that idea, and take away the veil, so that you may see. These are incomprehensible ideas to some, but they are simple. It is the first principle of the gospel to know for a certainty the character of God, and to know that we may converse with Him as one man converses with another, and that He was once a man like us; yea, that God himself, the Father of us all, dwelt on

an earth, the same as Jesus Christ Himself did; and I will show it from the Bible (305).

Therefore, according to Joseph Smith, God went through an existence similar to ours and to that of Jesus Christ. God would have had a Father in heaven who would have begot his spiritual body. He would have been born with earthly parents also. (Perhaps like Jesus Christ, he would have been born of a virgin, being conceived by the Holy Spirit.) He would have been tempted by evil during His life and prevailed, been obedient to the laws of His God and Father given to Him, including perhaps being married in a temple ceremony for all eternity. (The LDS Church teaches that neither a man or a woman can be an heir to the highest kingdom of the Celestial Kingdom, and thus become a God, without being married in the temple and entering into the "new and everlasting covenant of marriage." (*See D&C*, 131:2–4; Section 132; and Smith, *Doctrines*, vol. 2)

Then, Lorenzo Snow, the fifth President and Prophet of the Mormon Church, explained the same concept in one of his discourses using a couplet, which is often repeated within the LDS Church:

As man now is, God once was;
As God now is, man may be (Snow Smith 46).

God may have had physical children during His earthly existence; but that would only be speculation, because we don't know if Jesus Christ had children. Apparently, as stated by Joseph Smith, God also "laid down his [life] and [took] it up again," as Jesus Christ did ("King Follett Discourse," found in the *HC*, 6:305). Therefore, God must have lived upon an earth that also needed a Savior to atone for the sins of the people living on *that* earth. Then God would have died and been the first to receive a resurrected, perfect body (consisting of His spirit body and His resurrected physical body together) and become an heir of the Celestial Kingdom.

God would have progressed in His Celestial Kingdom to become a God (which apparently takes over millions of years) and be entitled to eternal increase of begetting spirit children with His eternal wife or wives. He then would have created worlds where His begotten sons and daughters could dwell and also begin *their* eternal progression of trying to become a God.

The Prophet Joseph Smith also explained these concepts in a sermon that he gave in the grove just east of the Temple in Nauvoo, Illinois on June 16, 1844, just eleven days before he was murdered in Carthage, Illinois (*HC,* 6:473–79). In this sermon on the Godhead and the plurality of Gods he said:

> I will preach on the plurality of Gods. ...I wish to declare I have always and in all congregations when I have preached on the subject of the Deity, it has been the plurality of Gods. It has been preached by the Elders for fifteen years. I have always declared God to be a distinct personage, Jesus Christ a separate and distinct personage from God the Father, and that the Holy Ghost was a distinct personage and a Spirit: and these three constitute three distinct personages and three Gods. ..."In the beginning the head of the Gods...called the Gods together." ...In the beginning the heads of the Gods organized the heavens and the earth. ...The heads of the Gods appointed one God for us; ...I learned a testimony concerning Abraham, and he reasoned concerning the God of heaven. "In order to do that," said he, "suppose we have two facts: that supposes another fact may exist–two men on the earth, one wiser than the other, would logically show that another who is wiser than the wisest may exist. Intelligences exist one above another, so that there is no end to them." If Abraham reasoned thus—If Jesus Christ was the Son of God, and John discovered that God the Father of Jesus Christ had a Father, you may suppose that He had a Father also. Where was there ever a son without a father? And where was there ever a father without first being a son? Whenever did a tree or anything spring into existence without a progenitor? ...Hence if Jesus had a Father, can we not believe that *He* had a Father also (474–76)?

A logical conclusion from all of the above would be that there is no end to Gods and to Sons and to earths where they could dwell. The Mormon God had a Father and a Son and he had a Father and a Son, and on and on with no end. Further, under Mormon doctrine, we can become a God and have a Son, who can become a God and have a Son, and on and on with no end. This would mean there has and will be an infinite number of Gods, Sons, and earths!

Perhaps it is because of my limited intellect, but I have a hard time accepting the above-alleged facts, including that a man can become a God, have spiritual offspring, create an earth for them to dwell on, and then have one of his spiritual sons be a Savior and Redeemer for the rest of his spiritual children. Likewise hard to believe is that one of his spiritual sons would rebel against him and become a Devil (discussed in Reason 71). What would determine if a man like me or like you, the reader, becomes a God? Is it dependent upon what kind of intelligence we are and what we accomplished in the pre-existence? Alternately, perhaps it is just an unattainable goal given to us to keep us believing in the Mormon Gods and Mormon theology.

No other religious theology that I know of asserts that God was a man like us and that we can become a God like Him. That fact doesn't make it untrue. What causes me problems with this theological assertion is that we do not have enough information from God to support it. If God wants us to believe that we can become a God like Him, then there should be more evidence or revealed information about what we have to do to accomplish the same. Another problem for me, as explained in other Reasons, is the extreme limitation most human beings have of even getting a chance to be a God, due to the obvious discriminations against them.

REASON 23
DOCTRINE OF MAN BECOMING A GOD

In Reason 22, we discussed the Mormon concept that God was once a man like us and that there is a potential in us to also become a god. This concept is probably only believed in by the Mormon Church, because most other religions place God on such a higher level of existence than man that it would be impossible for any man to become a god. However, the statements of Prophets of the Mormon Church who allegedly speak for God, plus some Mormon scriptures, represent that this is possible. Perhaps the best of these scriptures is the one found in *D&C*, 132:19–21:

> And again, verily I say unto you, if a man marry a wife by my word, which is my law, and by the new and everlasting covenant, and it is sealed unto them by the Holy Spirit of promise, by him who is anointed, unto whom I have appointed this power and the keys of this priesthood; and it shall be said unto them—Ye shall come forth in the first resurrection; ...which glory shall be a fulness [*sic*] and a continuation of the seeds forever and ever. Then shall they be gods, because they have no end; ...Then shall they be gods, because they have all power, and the angels are subject unto them. Verily, verily, I say unto you, except ye abide my law ye cannot attain to this glory.

So, what does it take for a man here upon Earth to become a god in the hereafter, according to the Mormon doctrine? Although the following list is not exhaustive, it does state most of the things we would have to do to have a chance to become a god:

1. Be one of the "noble and great" intelligences that were organized before the world was (Abraham 3:22–23).
2. Be born upon the Earth at a time and place when and where the Gospel of Jesus Christ was upon the Earth (*D&C*, 76:51–59).
3. Be baptized by immersion by one having the authority (*D&C*, 76:51).

4. Receive the Holy Ghost "by the laying on of...hands [by] him who is ordained" (*D&C*, 76:52).

5. Believe in God and keep His commandments while upon Earth and "endure to the end" (2 Nephi 31:17–21 and *Lectures on Faith* 70–71).

6. Always repent of any violations of God's commandments (*D&C*, 58:42–43).

7. For men, become a Melchizedek "Priest of the Most High" (*D&C*, 76:57).

8. Be married in a Celestial marriage in a Mormon temple under the "new and everlasting covenant" and sealed to your spouse "by the Holy Spirit of promise" by one "who is anointed" (*D&C*, 132:19–20).

9. Be righteous and live by every word that comes from God (2 Peter 1:3–11).

10. In the hereafter, learn how to be a God (J. Fielding Smith, *Teachings* 345–47).

One of my problems with becoming a god is that it seems to have already been determined in the pre-existence, based upon what kind of intelligence or spirit being you were there. Were you, in fact, a "noble and great intelligence" that existed before God created a spiritual body for you? The time and location that you were born on Earth (also apparently based on your choices in the pre-existence) would also determine if you had the teachings of God. If you did, that would help you to accomplish the above-listed criteria to become a God. The main problem I have with the concept of a "man becoming a god" is that it just seems to be an incentive to keep us believing in Mormon theology. It *is* a positive incentive to have us live a certain way on Earth (which I believe is good). Nevertheless, God knows that you and I will never be a god, so why would God tease us with this concept when He knows that we will fail?

REASON 24
ONLY SOME OF US CAN BECOME GODS

In addition to what was stated in Reason 23, according to Mormon theology, only certain ones of the human race can become Gods. In the *Pearl of Great Price*, Abraham 3:22 states:

> Now the Lord had shown unto me, Abraham, the intelligences that were organized before the world was; and among all these there were many of the noble and great ones.

Then in verse 26 we read:

> And they who keep their first estate shall be added upon; and they who keep not their first estate shall not have glory in the same kingdom with those who keep their first estate; and they who keep their second estate shall have glory added upon their heads for ever and ever.

The first estate is the pre-existence, where we were first intelligences and then literal spirit children of God the Eternal Father. The second estate is our earth life, where mankind is tested "to see if they will do all things whatsoever the Lord their God shall command them" (*PGP*, Abraham 3:22).

In *D&C*, 138:53–56, we read:

> The Prophet Joseph Smith, and my father, Hyrum Smith, Brigham Young, John Taylor, Wilford Woodruff, and other choice spirits who were reserved to come forth in the fulness [sic] of times to take part in laying the foundations of the great latter-day work. Including the building of temples and the performance of ordinances therein for the redemption of the dead, were also in the spirit world. I observed that they were also among the noble and great ones who were chosen in the beginning to be rulers in the Church of God. Even before they were born, they, with many others, received their first

lessons in the world of spirits and were prepared to come forth in the due time of the Lord to labor in his vineyard for the salvation of the souls of men.

Therefore, there were "choice spirits" in the pre-existence who were chosen there to be exceptional people upon Earth, with an apparent advantage to become a God.

The ultimate goal of a member of the Mormon Church is to reach the highest degree of the Celestial Kingdom after they die, so that they can: 1) become a God; 2) have spiritual children there; and 3) create an earth for *their* spirit children to dwell on. This is one of the purposes of being married in the Mormon Temple and entering into "the New and Everlasting Covenant of Marriage." Joseph Smith explained this in *D&C*, Section 76 and in his teachings. In the book *Teachings of the Prophet Joseph Smith*, compiled by Joseph Fielding Smith, we read on pages 300–01:

> Except a man and his wife enter into an everlasting covenant and be married for eternity, while in this probation, by the power and authority of the Holy Priesthood, they will cease to increase when they die; that is, they will not have any children after the resurrection. But those who are married by the power and authority of the priesthood in this life, and continue without committing the sin against the Holy Ghost, will continue to increase and have children in the celestial glory. ...In the celestial glory there are three heavens or degrees; and in order to obtain the highest, a man must enter into this order of the priesthood [meaning the new and everlasting covenant of marriage]; and if he does not, he cannot obtain it. He may enter into the other, but that is the end of his kingdom: he cannot have an increase.

Then on page 374, we read:

> Go and read the vision in the Book of Covenants [*D&C*, Section 76]. There is clearly illustrated glory upon glory—one glory of the sun, another glory of the moon, and a glory of the stars; and as one star differeth from another star in glory, even so do they of the telestial

world differ in glory, and every man who reigns in celestial glory is a God to his dominions.

Who becomes an heir of, or qualifies for, the Celestial Kingdom? The answer is found in the Section 76 of the *D&C*, verses 50–53 and 58, where we read the following:

> And again we bear record—for we saw and heard, and this is the testimony of the gospel of Christ concerning them who shall come forth in the resurrection of the just—They are they who received the testimony of Jesus, and believed on his name and were baptized after the manner of his burial, being buried in the water in his name, ...That by keeping the commandments they might...receive the Holy Spirit by the laying on of the hands... And who overcome by faith, and are sealed by the Holy Spirit of promise, which the Father sheds forth upon all those who are just and true. ...Wherefore, as it is written, they are gods, even the sons of God.

Further, in verses 71–79, we learn that those people on Earth who do not have a chance to receive the Gospel of Christ while living, because of the time and place they are born, and those who are "honorable men of the earth," will only receive the Terrestrial Kingdom and cannot become Gods. Therefore, this predestination is the determining factor in becoming a god. Very few actually qualify—even the billions who were born upon Earth when the Gospel of Jesus Christ was not available during their lifetime. Perhaps this concept creates as many problems for you, the reader, as it does for me.

REASON 25
CHRIST AS A SPIRIT SON BEING A GOD

The LDS Church teaches that Jesus Christ was the firstborn of God the Father, after God the Father became a God. All the rest of mankind upon Earth were born of God the Father as spirit children after the spiritual birth of Jesus Christ (*D&C*, Section 93). Lucifer, or Satan, was also a begotten son of God. There was a War in Heaven between the spirit children of God to see whether they would follow Jesus Christ or Lucifer. Apparently, one third of the spirit children of God the Father followed Lucifer and were cast out of heaven and were denied the opportunity of coming to this earth to obtain a physical body (Revelation 12:7–9). This is further discussed in Reasons 66–70.

The sexual or other process by which spirit children are begotten by a Heavenly Mother and Father has not been revealed. However, there is no question that by some process, God the Father procreated with His eternal wife or wives an astronomical number of spirit children, who have and do inhabit this earth or other earths, and that Jesus Christ was His first spirit child.

It is interesting to note, according to Mormon doctrine, that because Jesus Christ was the firstborn spirit child of God the Eternal Father, that he (Christ) has not always been a God. Sometime after His spiritual birth though, He became a God. We know that Christ participated in the creation of the earth and of mankind as a God with His Eternal Father (as told in the Mormon Temple Ceremony). Therefore, his becoming a God had to occur before that. Further, prior to the War in Heaven, we were told that both Jesus Christ and Satan presented plans to God the Eternal Father as to how they would save the spirit children who were allowed to come to Earth, so that those spirit children could return to live with their spiritual Father. (See *PGP*, Moses 4:1–3 and Abraham 3:24–28.) Then, in Abraham 3:24, it states: "And there stood one among them [the great and noble intelligences in the pre-existence] that was like unto God." So perhaps Jesus Christ was only "like unto God" *before* his plan for mankind was accepted by God the Eternal Father; and thereafter, he became a God. According to the fourth chapter in Abraham, it was the Gods, plural, who then went down and created the earth and mankind. Again, Jesus Christ had not followed all of the steps required of God the Father to become a God. There is no dispute in Mormon doctrine that Jesus Christ, as a spiritual being, *did* act as the God to the Israelites in the Old Testament and to the Nephites in the *Book of Mormon* (See *D&C*, 136:21–22; *PGP*, Abraham 2:6–11; and *BOM*, Ether 3:6–16).

The question arises though as to *how* a spirit (Jesus) can become a God without similar requirements that God the Father had to accomplish. As discussed in Reason 22, God the Father had to 1) go to an earth and gain a physical body; 2) qualify by the way he lived his life; 3) be married to a woman in a temple of God and sealed eternally; 4) be resurrected; and 5) progress for millions of years, after His physical death, before He became a God. Was Jesus Christ pre-destined to become a God, and therefore God the Eternal Father allowed him to act as a God, even though he hadn't gone to an earth yet, been tested, or been resurrected? Further, we have no scriptural support that Jesus Christ was married and sealed to a woman eternally, which is also a prerequisite to becoming a God. Why is there this confusion or contradiction about how Christ became a God? It would have been easy to explain through a revelation to Joseph Smith or some other Prophet, just as Joseph Smith explained how God the Father became a God (Reason 23).

REASON 26
QUESTIONS ABOUT THE HOLY GHOST

We don't have enough information about how the Holy Ghost became a God and a member of the Godhead, so we do not have clear information regarding the origin of the Holy Ghost. As mentioned in *D&C*, 130:22, the Holy Ghost

> has not a body of flesh and bones, but is a personage of Spirit. Were it not so, the Holy Ghost could not dwell in us.

Was the Holy Ghost also a spirit child of God the Eternal Father, like Jesus Christ and Satan, and then became a member of the Godhead? Because the Holy Ghost does not have a resurrected body of flesh and bone, it is apparent that the Holy Ghost did not live upon an earth like God the Eternal Father and Jesus Christ. They were both physical beings who died and were resurrected, and thus acquired their resurrected bodies of flesh and bone, as revealed to Joseph Smith in the above scripture reference.

Bruce R. McConkie in *Mormon Doctrine* (359) states:

> Because he is a Spirit Personage, he has power—according to the eternal laws ordained by the Father—to perform essential and unique functions for men. In this dispensation, at least, nothing has been revealed as to his origin or destiny; expressions on these matters are both speculative and fruitless.

Apparently, it would be "fruitless" to try and determine where the Holy Ghost came from, because God the Eternal Father has not revealed anything to his Prophets in the last 6,000 years regarding the origin of the Holy Ghost. The Holy Ghost is the third distinct and separate member of the Godhead. So why hasn't God revealed anything about his origin? It is through the Holy Ghost that a person obtains spiritual knowledge, or "the truth of all things" (Moroni 10:4–5). The Lord speaks to the mind and heart of mankind through the Holy Ghost (*D&C*, 8:2). It is the Holy Ghost who bears record of the Father and the Son (3 Nephi 11:32). Further, according to Mormon doctrine, a person must receive the "gift of the Holy Ghost" by the "Laying on of hands" by one who has the authority, before they can become an heir of the Celestial Kingdom (*PGP*, Fourth Article of Faith and *D&C*, 76:52). Because it is through the Holy Ghost that God and Jesus Christ work with mankind, it would be beneficial to know more about him and his origin.

Throughout the scriptures and the doctrine of the Mormon Church, it is assumed that the Holy Ghost is of the male gender, although I don't believe this has been directly revealed. That would be an essential fact also worth knowing. It is probably safe to assume that because God the Eternal Father was once a man (discussed in Reason 22), and had to progress to become a God, that the Holy Ghost also had to progress to become a member of the Godhead. How that progression took place we don't know. We also don't know how a spirit personage like the Holy Ghost can progress as far as a resurrected being like Jesus Christ.

Presumably, the Holy Ghost is the only member of the Godhead that can enter into our physical bodies and dwell there (*D&C*, 130:22). The Holy Ghost is only one spirit personage and

> can be in only one place at one time, and he does not and cannot transform himself into any other form or image than that of the Man who he is (McConkie 359).

Therefore, it is difficult to comprehend how the Holy Ghost gets around so fast to dwell in so many people on Earth at the same time! Members of the Mormon Church consistently testify (especially during "fast and testimony meetings" on the first Sunday of each month) that they are filled with the Holy Ghost when they state that they know the Mormon Church is true. This occurs simultaneously at numerous LDS sacrament meetings.

There are so many unanswered questions about the Holy Ghost; but members of the Mormon Church are asked to just accept what they have been told. One would think that it would be important to know more about the third member of the Godhead, which would increase one's susceptibility to believe in the Mormon God(s).

REASON 27
BECOMING A GOD WITHOUT GAINING A PHYSICAL BODY

As mentioned previously, Mormons believe that the pre-mortal Jesus Christ became a God prior to coming to Earth. As the firstborn spiritually to God the Eternal Father, and the one chosen to come to Earth as the Son of God, Jesus Christ (or Jehovah) participated as a God in the creation of the Earth and of man (*PGP*, Abraham, Chapters 3–5). He was also the Lord, Jehovah, and the God of the Old Testament. But how does a spirit being become a God without first obtaining a physical body?

God, the Eternal Father apparently only became a God after going through a physical existence as a man on an earth, and thereafter being resurrected and progressing to Godhood as explained by Joseph Smith in his teachings, and discussed in Reasons 22 and 23. Therefore, Mormons believe that God was once a man like us, and that Jesus Christ was also a man that dwelled on this earth.

However, as also previously discussed, both Jesus Christ and the Holy Ghost apparently became Gods without first going through a physical existence. Jesus Christ was a God before being physically born upon Earth. The Holy Ghost has never obtained a physical body, nor does he currently have one, as stated *in D&C*, 130:22.

Mormons believe that a man who comes to earth and obtains a physical body may become a God, have spiritual children, and create an earth for those spiritual children to dwell. This is their ultimate goal after death: to reach the highest degree of the Celestial Kingdom. This was discussed in Reason 24 and is what God, the Eternal Father, did as well. To reiterate, in *Teachings of the Prophet Joseph Smith*, compiled by Joseph Fielding Smith, we read on page 374:

> Go and read the vision in the Book of Covenants [*D&C*, Section 76]. There is clearly illustrated glory upon glory—one glory of the sun, another glory of the moon, and a glory of the stars; and as one star differeth from another star in glory, even so do they of the telestial world differ in glory, and every man who reigns in celestial glory is a God to his dominions.

For some reason though, Jesus Christ became a God before coming to Earth to obtain a physical body and the Holy Ghost became a God without even coming to an earth *or* obtaining a physical body. An argument could be made for Jesus Christ that His role as a God, with only a spiritual body, was based upon the fact that He was destined to come to Earth and receive his physical body. However, this argument can't be made for the Holy Ghost.

Why is the revealed plan of becoming a God, and the revealed description of the Godhead, so contradicting? If we are commanded to follow in God, the Eternal Father's footsteps to become a god, why wasn't the Holy Ghost required to as well? Of course Mormons can state that we don't need to know how the Holy Ghost became a God. But why did it occur that way and why hasn't the truth of it been made known in plainness?

On numerous occasions, Joseph Smith (as stated in Reasons 22–24), discussed the path to follow to become a God. The path included receiving a physical body and being resurrected. The Holy Ghost was an exception and Jesus Christ's path was different though. Nevertheless, they both became Gods. Confusion and lack of revealed simplicity only add to the dilemma of whether to believe in the Mormon God(s) or not.

REASON 28
PROBLEMS WITH JOSEPH SMITH'S FIRST VISION

In Reason 18, the First Vision of Joseph Smith was mentioned. However, there are some problems with the history of the First Vision that diminish its authenticity and it being a benefit to those seeking to find out if God exists. The official account of the First Vision is found in the *History of the Church*, 1:4–6. It indicates that 1) there was a religious revival in the spring of 1820 that caused Joseph Smith to wonder which religion was right; 2) he prayed in a grove of trees and was immediately overcome by an evil power; 3) he saw a pillar of light and was delivered from his enemy; 4) he saw two personages with one saying, "This is My Beloved Son, Hear Him;" and 5) he was told that all the sects were wrong and an abomination to God.

One problem is the timing of the First Vision. The historical evidence from newspapers and the records of the Baptist, Methodist, and Presbyterian churches indicate that there was no religious revival in 1820—that did not occur until spring of 1824. This is supported by Joseph Smith's mother in her first draft of Lucy Mack Smith's *History*, 1845, p. 93–94, where she states that the revival did not occur until after her son, Alvin's death, in November 1823.

Other problems come with the different written records of the First Vision. There are at least nine (9) different recorded versions and most of them differ significantly! A summary of nine of the versions are given below, as given in greater detail in *What Every Mormon (and Non-Mormon) Should Know* by Edmond C. Gruss and Lane A. Thuet.

Version 1: The earliest version of the First Vision was written by Joseph Smith in 1831–1832 in his own handwriting and was made public in 1965 by Paul Cheesman in his master thesis, An *Analysis of the Accounts Relating Joseph Smith's Early Visions*. In this account, Joseph stated that he was 16 years old, already knew the Churches were wrong from reading the Bible, sought forgiveness, and was only visited by one personage, Jesus Christ.

Version 2: In February 1835, an account of the First Vision given by Joseph Smith to Oliver Cowdery was published in the *LDS Messenger and Advocate*, a Mormon publication (42, 78–79; vol. 1). In this account, Joseph was age 17, the revival was in 1823, Joseph claimed he prayed to find out if God existed and if his sins could be forgiven, and he was only visited by one messenger from God, who forgave his sins.

Version 3: Later in 1835, Joseph Smith dictated to a scribe (either Warren Parish or Warren Cowdery) his own account of the First Vision for his (Joseph's) personal diary. This account was published in *Dialogue: A Journal of Mormon Thought* (Jessee 85–87; vol. 6) and is the first mention of the evil power. Additionally, Joseph does not claim that God and Jesus visited him, but only many angels.

Version 4: In 1837, Orson Pratt related the story of the First Vision that was recorded by William Appleby in his (William's) diary. The revival was in 1822, Joseph was 17, and the visitors were not God and Jesus, but rather other beings who stated they were angels and who claimed to have forgiven Joseph's sins.

Version 5: In 1841, William Smith, Joseph's brother, related the story of the First Vision to James Murdock, which was published in *A New Witness for Christ in America* (Kirkham 414–15; vol. 2). In this account, Joseph was 17 and it was a glorious angel that appeared to him, rather than God and Jesus.

Version 6: On March 1, 1842, the *Times and Seasons*, a Mormon publication, published a letter written by Joseph Smith to John Wentworth. In this account of the First Vision, Joseph did not give his age, mentioned no evil power, and said two personages visited him, but did not identify them (706–10).

Version 7: This is the official Mormon version of the First Vision that was published in the *Times and Seasons* on April 1, 1842 (748–49) and is presently found just after the *Pearl of Great Price* in the Triple Combination of the Mormon scriptures and in the *History of the Church*, vol. 1, no. 1.

Version 8: In 1843, Joseph Smith did an interview for the *Pittsburgh Gazette* that was printed on September 15, 1843. In this account, Joseph was 14, but there was no mention of the evil power.

Version 9: Joseph Smith told Alexander Neibaur the story of the First Vision and on May 24, 1844, Neibaur wrote it in his journal. This account is similar to the official account except there was no mention that all the sects were wrong, but only that the Methodists were.

There is no dispute that by 1844 Joseph Smith had clarified the Godhead so that there was no misunderstanding that God, Jesus Christ, and the Holy Ghost were three distinct and separate personages. This concept was stated in *D&C*, 130:22 and in two sermons given by

Joseph Smith in 1844, known as the "King Follett Discourse" and the "Sermon in The Grove" (J. Smith, *History* 302–17; 473–79; vol. 6). The question here is not whether God and Jesus Christ are two separate beings in Mormon doctrine, but *who* actually appeared to Joseph Smith in the First Vision. This problem could have been resolved fairly easily by Joseph writing down the First Vision at the time that it happened. It is extremely curious and unbelievable that he did not, even though he was only 14 years old. What is more unbelievable is that God did not require Joseph to write it down at that time.

In *D&C*, Section 76, Joseph Smith and Sidney Rigdon (in 1832) have a vision of the three degrees of glory of kingdoms in heaven. In verse 113 we read, "This is the end of the vision which we saw, which we were commanded to write while we were yet in the Spirit." Apparently, that vision was written down right then, pursuant to a commandment of God. The First Vision seems to be of greater importance than the vision of the three degrees of glory; and although it took place twelve years previous, Joseph Smith could write at that time as well. Why wouldn't God command Joseph Smith to write down the First Vision right after the time that it happened so that everyone would know that he had verified seeing God and Jesus Christ at that time? The confusion of the First Vision would have been eliminated and such an important event would have been memorialized in writing at the time that it happened.

REASON 29
ABSENCE OF PLAIN AND PRECIOUS TRUTHS RESTORED

There is so much confusion in the LDS Church as to whom and what God is compared to what is written in the Holy Bible. Mormons believe that the following scripture in 1 Nephi 13:24–26 in the *Book of Mormon* explains why. It also justifies in their minds why there are so many Christian religions with different interpretations of the Bible and questions about whether God and Jesus Christ are the same being or two distinct separate beings:

> And the angel of the Lord said unto me: Thou hast beheld that the book proceeded forth from the mouth of a Jew; and when it proceeded forth from the mouth of a Jew it contained the fulness [*sic*] of the gospel of the Lord, of whom the twelve apostles bear record; and they bear record according to the truth which is in the Lamb of God. Wherefore, these things go forth from the Jews in purity unto the Gentiles, according to the truth which is in God. And after they go forth by the hand of the twelve apostles of the Lamb, from the Jews unto the Gentiles; thou seest the formation of that great and abominable church, which is most abominable above all other churches; for behold, they have taken away from the gospel of the Lamb many parts which are plain and precious; and also many covenants of the Lord have they taken away.

Then the following scripture, 1 Nephi 13:40, explains why the *Book of Mormon* is so important in making known the plain and precious things that were taken out of the Bible:

> And the angel spake unto me, saying: These last records, which thou hast seen among the Gentiles, shall establish the truth of the first, which are of the twelve apostles of the Lamb, and shall make known the plain and precious things which have been taken away from them; and shall

make known to all kindreds, tongues, and people, that the Lamb of God is the Son of the Eternal Father, and the Savior of the world; and that all men must come unto him, or they cannot be saved.

However, the *Book of Mormon* didn't restore the plain truth about whom or what God is, or resolve the confusion as to the Godhead, as discussed in Reason 31.

Some of the other alleged plain and precious truths that currently are major doctrines of the Mormon Church that do not appear in the *Book of Mormon* are:

1. Temple work and its purpose and relevancy.
2. Celestial marriage and its necessity.
3. Reasons for doing baptisms and endowments for the dead.
4. Explanation of the Three Degrees of Glory in heaven.
5. Word of Wisdom.
6. Paying tithing of ten percent.

We could have listed numerous other tenets of the Mormon religion that are not found in the *Book of Mormon*; but the point is that if the entire and full Gospel of Jesus Christ was upon Earth at the time of Jesus, then that same Gospel would have been available to the people of the *Book of Mormon.* This is based upon the assertion that the *BOM* contains all of the "plain and precious truths" that were taken from the Bible. Why would God's alleged word to mankind contradict itself, as stated above? In addition, why wouldn't the *Book of Mormon* contain all of the Gospel of Jesus Christ?

REASON 30
PROBLEMS WITH THE BOOK OF MORMON GOD

The God of the *Book of Mormon* is also Jesus Christ, according to the Mormon religion. However, there is a lot of confusion and ambiguity in the *BOM* as to whether God, the Father, is in fact separate from the Son, Jesus Christ, as discussed in Reason 25 and other Reasons. What causes some concern in regard to the God of the *Book of Mormon* are the similarities with the God of the Old Testament—when it comes to killing the unrighteous, being inconsistent in dealing with all of His children on Earth, and killing innocent children.

The *Book of Mormon* people are divided between the righteous and unrighteous, to wit, the Nephites and the Lamanites, similar to the division in the OT between the Israelites and the non-Israelites. For over 1000 years, God is involved with the Nephites and fights their battles, similar to the God of the OT. However, God mostly ignores the Lamanites, just as the OT God ignored the non-Israelites.

In those 1000 years, the *Book of Mormon* has accounts of the Lord (Jehovah) destroying cities, killing people, and discriminating between the righteous and unrighteous, similar to the OT. The Mormon religion teaches that the *Book of Mormon* is the most perfect book upon the face of the earth and does not have any mistranslations. Therefore, the following examples of the *Book of Mormon* God's vengeance are true and accurate, according the LDS doctrine.

The first incident is where Nephi is commanded by the Lord to cut off the head of a drunken Laban, as recorded in 1 Nephi 4:6–18 and discussed further in Reason 34. Next is the curse of a "skin of blackness," given by the Mormon God to those who would not "hearken unto the words" given to them by the prophet Nephi, as recorded in 2 Nephi 5:20–25. Then there is the account in Alma 14:26–28, where Alma and Amulek are in prison and the Lord answers their prayer and destroys the prison, killing "the chief judge, the lawyers, priests, teachers…and every soul within the walls." A later prophet named Nephi, as recorded in Helaman 11:1–7, persuades the Lord to cause a famine and kill thousands of Lamanites and Nephites. This is the same Lord or God of the OT who was responsible for so many atrocities mentioned in other Reasons, and the Lord or God that the LDS Church teaches was in fact Jesus Christ.

The greatest atrocities in the *Book of Mormon* take place when numerous cities and all the inhabitants therein—including men, women and innocent children, probably totaling in the hundreds of thousands—are destroyed and killed by the Lord Jesus Christ, as recorded in 3 Nephi 9:1–15 and discussed further in Reason 35.

According to Mormon theology, prior to the book of 3 Nephi, the *Book of Mormon* God is the same God as the God of the Old Testament. That God was Jesus Christ as a "Spirit Being" before He came to earth to live, to die, and to be resurrected. Then, in 3 Nephi, He appears to the Nephites as a resurrected Being and continues thereafter to be the *Book of Mormon* God. However, there is very little written about that particular God's dealings with the people of the *Book of Mormon* for the succeeding 300 years, after His appearance to them. Thereafter, He allows the total destruction of the Nephite people in approximately 380 A.D., wherein hundreds of thousands of them are slain because of their unbelief in the *BOM* God (Mormon, Chapters 1–8). It is hard to believe in the *Book of Mormon* God that behaves this way to the people here upon Earth.

REASON 31
THE CONFUSING GODHEAD IN THE BOOK OF MORMON

The God or Gods that I was taught to believe in as a member of the Mormon Church are mentioned in the first of thirteen "Articles of Faith" of the Mormon Church. They were written by Joseph Smith in March 1842 (*HC*, 4:535–41). In the first Article of Faith, it states; "We believe in God the Eternal Father and in His Son, Jesus Christ and in the Holy Ghost" (*PGP*, The Articles of Faith 1:1). According to the doctrine of the Mormon Church, God the Eternal Father has a resurrected body of flesh and bones just like ours, as does Jesus Christ; and they are two separate Beings. The Holy Ghost is a third separate being with only a spiritual body, but in the same form as our physical bodies. This is verified in *D&C*, Section 130:22, written in April 1843. It states:

> The Father has a body of flesh and bones as tangible as man's; the Son also; but the Holy Ghost has not a body of flesh and bones, but is a personage of Spirit.

These three separate beings make up the Godhead in the Mormon religion and are each considered a god.

Even though the Godhead was explained in simple terms in 1842 in the First Article of Faith and in 1843 in *D&C*, 130:22, there was some confusion prior to 1838 in regard to these Gods. The confusion as to the First Vision of Joseph Smith in 1820 as to whether he saw one or two personages is discussed in detail in Reason 28. What doesn't make sense is that there seems to be a lot of confusion in the *Book of Mormon* (written in 1829) as to whom God, the Eternal Father and Jesus Christ are, and who is actually speaking to the ancient prophets and dealing with mankind. Are they the same entity but dealing with mankind in different capacities? Alternatively, are they two different and distinct beings, both dealing with mankind?

Mormons have always taught that the *BOM* should make known who God and Jesus Christ are, because one of its main purposes is to restore the plain and precious truths about God and the Gospel that have been lost over time. Further, as Joseph Smith said in the *HC*, 4:461:

> I spent the day in the council with the Twelve Apostles at the house of President Young, conversing with them upon a variety of subjects. ...I told the brethren that the Book of Mormon was the most correct of any book on earth, and the keystone of our religion, and a man would get nearer to God by abiding by its precepts, than by any other book.

Therefore, we should be able to examine the *BOM* to see if it does help us understand God and the Godhead. In 1 Nephi 13:40, it states: "the Lamb of God is the Son of the Eternal Father." It does not indicate for sure if they are two distinct personages. However, the concept of two separate beings appears to be contradicted by the Prophet Abinadi in Mosiah 15:1–5, which states:

> And now Abinadi said unto them: I would that ye should understand that God himself shall come down among the children of men, and shall redeem his people. And because he dwelleth in flesh he shall be called the Son of God, and having subjected the flesh to the will of the Father, being the Father and the Son—The Father, because he was conceived by the power of God; and the Son, because of the flesh; thus becoming the Father and Son—And they are one God, yea, the very Eternal Father of heaven and earth. And thus the flesh becoming subject to the Spirit, or the Son to the Father, being one God, suffereth temptation, and yieldeth not to the temptation, but suffereth himself to be mocked, and scourged, and cast out, and disowned by his people.

However, in Mosiah, chapter 13, Abinadi refers to "God," "the Lord thy God," and "the Lord" as the same person who made the heaven and earth, gave Moses the Ten Commandments, and who would become the Messiah.

This seems to indicate that the Eternal Father or God is also Christ. Furthermore, in Alma 11:38–39 and 44, the Prophet Amulek says that the Son of God "is the very Eternal Father" and that God the Father, Christ the Son and the Holy Spirit "is one Eternal God."

The Prophet Mormon states in Mormon 7:7 that the Father, the Son, and the Holy Ghost "are one God." The Prophet Mormon also says:

> For do we not read that God is the same yesterday, today, and forever, and in him there is no variableness neither shadow of changing? ...But behold, I will show unto you a God of miracles, even the God of Abraham, and the God of Isaac, and the God of Jacob; and it is that same God who created the heavens and the earth, and all things that in them are. Behold, he created Adam, and by Adam came the fall of man, And because of the fall of man came Jesus Christ, even the Father and the Son; and because of Jesus Christ came the redemption of man." (Mormon 9:9, 11–12.)

How confusing is this? We are taught in the Mormon Church that Jesus Christ was the Jehovah in the Old Testament and the One who made covenants with the house of Israel, but the *BOM* states it was God the Father who made said covenants, again seeming to indicate that God the Father and Jesus Christ are one and the same.

Then, when Jesus Christ appears to the Nephites, as recorded in 3 Nephi 11:7, He is introduced by a voice that says, "Behold my Beloved Son, in whom I am well pleased, in whom I have glorified my name—hear ye him." Jesus goes on to state in 3 Nephi 11:27 and 36 the following:

> And after this manner shall ye baptize in my name; for behold, verily I say unto you, that the Father, and the Son, and the Holy Ghost are one; and I am in the Father, and the Father in me, and the Father and I are one. ...And thus will the Father bear record of me, and the Holy Ghost will Bear record unto him of the Father and me; for the Father, and I, and the Holy Ghost are one.

Following the above, Jesus goes on to state in 3 Nephi 20:35 that

> The Father hath made bare his holy arm in the eyes of all the nations; and all the ends of the earth shall see the salvation of the Father; and the Father and I are one.

The *BOM* does not specifically explain, in simple and plain language, how the Father and the Son are one; or how the Father, the

Son, and the Holy Ghost are one; or that in reality, God the Eternal Father, Jesus Christ the Son, and the Holy Ghost are three separate and distinct personages. It also does not explain *D&C*, 130:22: "The Father has a body of flesh and bones as tangible as man's; the Son also, but the Holy Ghost is a personage of Spirit," as believed by the Mormon Church.

The *BOM* also fails to plainly explain how God the Father and Jesus Christ are "one" or are "two," as taught by the Mormon Church. Although in 3 Nephi 19:23 and 29 it states:

> And now Father, I pray unto thee for them, and also for all those who shall believe on their words, that they may believe in me, that I may be in them as thou, Father, art in me, that we may be one. ...Father, I pray not for the world, but for those whom thou hast given me out of the world, because of their faith, that they may be purified in me, that I may be in them as thou, Father, art in me, that we may be one, that I may be glorified in them.

There are a few other passages in the *Book of Mormon* that allude to a oneness other than being the exact same personage; but again, these passages are not very plain and instead are quite ambiguous.

Further, like the Bible, the words "God," "the Lord," and "Christ" are used in the *BOM* to apparently describe the same entity and are sometimes interchangeable; but there is no explanation as to why. In addition, why should the description of God and His separateness from Jesus Christ be so ambiguous in the *BOM* when the *BOM* was supposed to have restored the plain things of the Bible that had been removed? Why is the *BOM* so confusing when describing "God the Eternal Father," void of any description of the "Holy Ghost," yet specific when describing "Christ" (see Ether 3)?

Perhaps a person reading the *BOM*, independent of the beliefs and doctrines of the Mormon religion, could interpret the *BOM* as supporting the idea that God the Eternal Father and Jesus Christ are indeed one and the same person and entity. A person could also interpret it this way: that when it describes Jesus Christ, it is also describing God the Eternal Father. Again, this seems to be contradicted in 3 Nephi, Chapters 11 through 28, where Jesus Christ appears to the people of the *BOM* after His resurrection. While talking to them over a few days, he uses the term "Father" approximately 158 times in referring to "thy Father," my Father," "the Father in heaven," "your

Father," "our Father," and "the Father and I are one." Further, Jesus prays **to** the Father, talks **to** the Father, and many times states that He is going to the Father, all of which support a conclusion that Jesus Christ and "the Father" are two separate beings, even though the *BOM* passages quoted above keep stating that they are one. It appears that the *BOM* is just as confusing as the Holy Bible, or perhaps more confusing in attempting to explain who and what God is and whether God the Eternal Father and Jesus Christ are indeed the same person and entity and not two.

It has been and is still difficult for me to believe in a God or Godhead that is so confusing. Why wouldn't God explain to His children upon Earth in simple, plain language who and what He is, who was speaking to all of the prophets, and how He (as God the Father) and Jesus Christ function, in relationship to humankind and this world? Wouldn't it have been easier and less confusing for God the Eternal Father to say every time He was speaking to mankind that this is "God the Eternal Father of your spirits" and for Jesus Christ to say that he is "Jesus Christ, the Son of God the Father?" In addition, whenever the Holy Ghost was involved, he could have identified himself as well.

Throughout the *Book of Mormon*, God and Jesus Christ could have simply indentified themselves (when speaking to mankind or the prophets) as suggested above. If it was only Jesus Christ speaking to the ancient prophets as a spiritual being, like recorded in book of Ether mentioned above, then why didn't He always identify himself as such? How simple it would have been, and then we would have known each time who was speaking! If Jesus Christ was speaking on behalf of His Father, then He could have said, "I am speaking for and in behalf of God, the Eternal Father."

This confusion in the Godhead and lack of a simple and plain explanation of who and which God is speaking or dealing with mankind is also present in the *Doctrine and Covenants*, the revelations given to Joseph Smith in the 1830's and 40's. This is discussed in Reason 41. But if there are three distinct Gods, as believed in the Mormon Church, then simplicity should prevail in their dealings with mankind. We should always know from the scriptures referred to as the "word of God," which One we are listening to, or with whom we are involved. There doesn't seem to be an adequate explanation as to why there is so much confusion on this subject if the Mormon Church is the "one and only true church of Jesus Christ" and the only one upon Earth that teaches the correct Gospel of Jesus Christ!

REASON 32
GODS WITH TOO MANY NAMES

A review of the entire *Book of Mormon* reveals that there are over ninety (90) different names or terms used to define or identify deity, which only adds to the confusion and ambiguity. We still don't know whether God the Father and His Son, Jesus Christ are the same entity or separate personages, as presently taught by the Mormon Church; nor do we know which God is speaking to or dealing with mankind.

The following are the numerous names or terms used in the *BOM* to refer to or identify the Gods in the *BOM* and how many times they are used:

ALMIGHTY	1
ALMIGHTY GOD	3
ALPHA AND OMEGA	1
BELOVED	1
BELOVED SON	3
CHRIST	282
CHRIST THE LORD	4
CHRIST THE SON	1
CHRIST WAS GOD THE FATHER	1
COMFORTER	1
COUNSELLOR [*sic*]	1
CREATOR	9
ETERNAL FATHER	6
ETERNAL GOD	6
ETERNAL HEAD	1
ETERNAL JUDGE	1
EVERLASTING FATHER	1
FATHER	177
FATHER OF HEAVEN	4
FATHER IN HEAVEN	4
FATHER AND THE SON	5
FATHER (thy, my, your, our)	36
FATHER AND I ARE ONE	1
GOD	1189
GOD OF ABRAHAM, ISAAC AND JACOB	9

GOD THE FATHER	7
GOD THE ETERNAL FATHER	5
GOD OF ISRAEL	12
GREAT SPIRIT	18
GREAT SPIRIT IS GOD	2
HEAVENLY FATHER	4
HOLY CHILD JESUS	2
HOLY GHOST	101
HOLY GOD	2
HOLY MESSIAH	2
HOLY ONE	13
HOLY ONE OF ISRAEL	36
HOLY SPIRIT	13
HOLY SPIRIT OF GOD	2
I AM	4
I AM GOD	2
I AM LIGHT, LIFE AND TRUTH	1
I AM THE FATHER	1
I AM THE LORD	1
JESUS	98
JESUS CHRIST	51
JEHOVAH	1
KING	2
LAMB or LAMB OF GOD	68
LORD	1105
LORD GOD ALMIGHTY	1
LORD IS GOD	1
LORD THE ALMIGHTY GOD	2
LORD (their, your) GOD	75
LORD OUR GOD	13
LORD THY GOD	124
LORD GOD OF HOSTS	3
LORD GOD OMNIPOTENT	2
LORD JEHOVAH	1
LORD JESUS CHRIST	15
LORD OF HOSTS	55
LORD OMNIPOTENT	3
LORD AND SAVIOR JESUS CHRIST	2
LORD (their, thy) REDEEMER	4
MAKER	4

MESSIAH	25
MIGHTY GOD	1
MIGHTY ONE	4
MOST HIGH GOD	6
ONE GOD	6
ONLY BEGOTTEN OF FATHER	4
ONLY BEGOTTEN SON	4
ONE ETERNAL GOD	1
PRINCE OF PEACE	1
REDEEMER	29
SAVIOR	8
SAVIOR JESUS CHRIST	1
SHEPHERD	6
SON	34
SON OF GOD	50
SON OF ETERNAL GOD	1
SON OF ETERNAL FATHER	1
SON OF LIVING GOD	2
SON JESUS CHRIST	3
SON OF RIGHTEOUSNESS	3
SPIRIT	66
SPIRIT OF CHRIST	2
SPIRIT OF GOD	20
SPIRIT OF LORD	37
SPIRIT OF THE LORD OMNIPOTENT	1
SUPREME CREATOR	1
WONDERFUL	1

It is not unusual to have different ways of describing the Gods of the Mormon religion. However, it would seem more logical for God in His communications with mankind to simplify the "Godhead" and refer to the three Gods in terms that all of us could understand. Why add to the confusion that was created in the Bible by using over 92 terms in the *Book of Mormon* just to describe three (3) Gods? This confusion and lack of simplicity discussed here and in other Reasons is another reason for questioning one's belief in the Mormon God(s).

REASON 33
LACK OF EVIDENCE SUPPORTING THE BOOK OF MORMON

Since 1829, the main argument by the Mormon Church supporting its alleged "divine origin" has been the *Book of Mormon*. While preaching as a missionary for the Mormon Church from 1966–68 in New Zealand, I used the *Book of Mormon* as the main focus and selling point for interested investigators. It was the most relied-upon book to help them obtain a testimony of the divinity of the Church and that Joseph Smith was a prophet called of God. We constantly challenged investigators to read the *BOM* and to pray about it. We testified to them that, pursuant to Moroni 10:4 in the *BOM*, they would know that the book was true and from God.

As missionaries, we were continuously asked to provide physical evidence supporting the authenticity of the *Book of Mormon* other than the book itself. We presented them with the small amount of physical evidence that we had at that time: an archeological finding showing both dark- and white-skinned people (as stated in the *BOM*) and a small figurine that looked like a horse. (The *BOM* claims the existence of horses in the Americas around 600 B.C.) We further assured our investigators that a lot more physical evidence would eventually be found to support the *BOM*, because there were such extensive archeological digs going on in the Americas at the time, and enormous still-uncovered ruins.

However, almost fifty years later, not only has additional physical evidence *not* been found, but the evidence we had at that time now appears less credible. *Wikipedia*, the free encyclopedia, under "Archeology and the Book of Mormon," reveals many problems about the lack of physical evidence including the following:

1. The National Geographic Society, in a 1996 letter written to the Institute for Religious Research, stated that archaeologists and other scholars have long probed the hemisphere's past and the Society does not know of anything found so far that has substantiated the *Book of Mormon*.

2. From the mid-1950's onwards, the Church-owned Brigham Young University has sponsored (under the banner of the New World Archaeological Foundation, or NWAF) a large number of

archaeological excavations in Mesoamerica, with a focus on the Mesoamerican time period known as the Preclassic (earlier than *c.* A.D. 200). The results of these and other investigations, while producing valuable archaeological data, have not led to any widespread acceptance by non-LDS archaeologists of the *Book of Mormon* account. Citing the lack of specific New World geographic locations to search, Michael D. Coe, a prominent Mesoamerican archaeologist and Professor Emeritus of Anthropology at Yale University, wrote:

"As far as I know there is not one professionally trained archaeologist, who is not a Mormon, who sees any scientific justification for believing the historicity of The Book of Mormon, and I would like to state that there are quite a few Mormon archaeologists who join this group."

3. Some Mormon archaeologists and researchers claim

various archaeological findings such as place names, and ruins of the Inca, Maya, Olmec, and other ancient American and Old World civilizations as giving credence to the Book of Mormon record. [Critics and non-Mormon archaeologists] disagree with these conclusions, arguing that the Book of Mormon mentions several animals, plants, and technologies that are not substantiated by the archaeological record between 3100 B.C. to 400 A.D. in America

including the ass, cattle, horses, oxen, domesticated sheep, swine, goats, elephants, wheat, barley, silk, steel, metal swords, cimitars, chariots, and other elements.

4. In 1955, Thomas Ferguson, an LDS member and founder of the NWAF, with five years of funding from The Church of Jesus Christ of Latter-day Saints,

began to dig throughout Mesoamerica for evidence of the veracity of the *Book of Mormon* claims. In a 1961 newsletter, Ferguson predicted that although nothing had been found, the *Book of Mormon* cities *would* be found within 10 years. In 1972, Christian scholar Hal Hougey wrote Ferguson[,] questioning the progress[,] given the stated timetable in which the cities would be found (Larson 55–93). Replying to Hougey, as well as secular and non-secular requests, Ferguson wrote in a letter dated 5 June 1972:

"Ten years have passed. ...I had sincerely hoped that Book-of-Mormon [*sic*] cities would be positively identified within 10 years—and time has proved me wrong in my anticipation (Larson 76)."

During the period of 1959 to 1961, NWAF colleague Dee Green was editor of the *BYU Archaeological Society Newsletter* and had an article from it published in the summer of 1969 edition of *Dialogue: A Journal of Mormon Thought*, [pp 76–78] in which he acknowledged that the NWAF findings did not back up the veracity of the Book of Mormon claims. After this article and another six years of fruitless search, Ferguson published a 29-page paper in 1975 where he concluded, "I'm afraid that up to this point, I must agree with Dee Green, who has told us that to date there is no Book-of-Mormon [*sic*] geography.

In 1976, referring to his own paper, Ferguson wrote a letter in which he stated

"The real implication of the paper is that you can't set the Book-of-Mormon [*sic*] geography down anywhere—because it is fictional and will never meet the requirements of the dirt-archeology. I should say—what is in the ground will never conform to what is in the book (Larson 79)."

...Though the NWAF failed to establish *Book of Mormon* archaeology, the archaeological investigations of NWAF-sponsored projects were a success for ancient

American archaeology in general[,] which has been recognized and appreciated by non-Mormon archaeologists. Currently[,] BYU maintains 86 documents on the work of the NWAF at the BYU NWAF website; these documents are used outside both BYU and the LDS Church by [other] researchers.

5. LDS scholars

have estimated that at various periods in Book of Mormon history, the populations of civilizations discussed in the book ranged between 300,000 and 1.5 million people. The size of the late Jaredite civilization was even larger. According to the Book of Mormon, the final war that destroyed the Jaredites resulted in the deaths of at least two million men.

The *Book of Mormon* describes peoples who were literate, had knowledge of Old World languages, and possessed Old World-derived writing systems.

From Book of Mormon population estimates, it is evident that the civilizations described are comparable in size to the civilizations of Ancient Egypt, ancient Greece, ancient Rome, and the Maya. Such civilizations left numerous artifacts in the form of hewn stone ruins, tombs, temples, pyramids, roads, arches, walls, frescos, statues, vases, and coins. [We have none of these from the *BOM* civilizations] ("Archeology," *Wikipedia.org*).

From the onset of the *Book of Mormon* in 1829 up to the present, slightly less than 200 years, the amount of physical evidence supporting the *Book of Mormon* is almost non-existent. In *D&C*, 19:26, Jesus Christ states to Joseph Smith that the *Book of Mormon* "contains the truth and the word of God." Why would God give to mankind His word, and then fail to provide any physical evidence to support the fact that it was true?

REASON 34
THE BOOK OF MORMON'S MURDER OF LABAN

The first part of the first book of Nephi in the *Book of Mormon* tells the story of Lehi and his family (including his righteous son, Nephi) leaving Jerusalem in approximately 600 B.C., due to the wickedness there. However, after they leave Jerusalem and go into the wilderness, Nephi and his brothers are sent back to Jerusalem by their father, Lehi, to obtain the "plates of brass." These plates contained the history of the Jews up to that time, the genealogy of Lehi's forefathers, and the first five books of the Old Testament, alleged to have been written by Moses.

The keeper of the plates of brass was a man named Laban. Nephi and his brothers "cast lots" to see who had to go to Laban and request the plates of brass from him. Nephi's older brother Laman lost and had to go, but when he asked Laban for the records, Laban refused to give them to him, became angry, and kicked Laman out of his house. Nephi's brothers wanted to go back to the wilderness and tell their father that they could not get the plates, but Nephi convinced them to try again. So Nephi and his brothers went back to their home in Jerusalem and obtained all of their gold, silver, and precious things (I don't know why they didn't take them in the first place) and took these assets to Laban to buy the plates of brass.

Laban again refused and also sent his servants to kill Nephi and his brothers and to steal the assets. Nephi and his brothers escaped from the servants of Laban, but left their property behind, which Laban acquired. Nephi's brothers were really angry with Nephi and began beating him up; but an angel of the Lord interceded and told them that the Lord would deliver Laban to them. Then in Chapter 4 of 1 Nephi, Nephi convinces his brothers to go back with him to Jerusalem again. He leaves the brothers outside the wall and goes in to Laban's house himself. On the way there, he finds Laban drunk and passed out. Nephi didn't know what to do, but was "constrained" by the "Spirit" to kill Laban. Therefore, Nephi took Laban's sword and cut off Laban's head. After Nephi cut off Laban's head, he took all of Laban's clothes and armor and put it on to deceive the servants of Laban and obtain the plates of brass, which he accomplished.

The rationale for the "Spirit" directing Nephi to kill Laban is stated in 1 Nephi 4:12–17. Verse 13 states:

> Behold the Lord slayeth the wicked to bring forth his righteous purposes. It is better that one man should perish than that a nation should dwindle and perish in unbelief.

Nephi further rationalizes that they needed the "law of Moses" (the brass plates) to keep the commandments, so that they would prosper in the "promised land," where they were going. However, what does not make sense is the fact that God or the Lord could still give Nephi and his family the commandments when they reached the "promised land" by just revealing them to the prophets there. Therefore, Nephi's rationale does not appear to be credible or a justifiable reason to kill someone.

Further, God being all-powerful, He could have accomplished the task of Nephi obtaining the plates of brass in many other ways that would not have required Nephi killing Laban. One way could have been using additional wine or drugs to keep Laban passed out while the plates were obtained, and then causing Laban to forget who took the plates. One of God's *BOM*-chosen actually directed this approach of getting the enemy drunk, as recorded in Alma 55:8–24, where hundreds of Nephite prisoners were rescued without the shedding of blood. It would not take much of an imagination to think of additional ways as well, in order to obtain the plates from Laban without a prophet of God murdering him.

This story has bothered me since the first time I read it in my teenage years. In my mind, there is no way that God would kill someone just to obtain plates or records, when so many other ways exist to accomplish the goal. Nevertheless, the Mormon God did in fact order Laban's head to be cut off. Although this is only one story in the *Book of Mormon*, it represents a religious philosophy that condones murder to accomplish a goal, which, in my mind, is contrary to an acceptable view of God. Mormons believe this story to be true, but it goes against my inner compass and registers as "wrong."

REASON 35
GOD'S DESTRUCTION OF CITIES IN THE BOOK OF MORMON

Another story in the *Book of Mormon* that has always bothered me is found in 3 Nephi Chapters 8 and 9. This story takes place at the same time that Jesus Christ was crucified in Jerusalem, but involves the people and cities in the Americas, who descended from Lehi and Nephi who landed there 600 years previous.

In 3 Nephi 8, we read about earthquakes, fires, whirlwinds (tornadoes), and other physical upheavals happening to many of the cities where the Nephites lived. Verse 14 states:

> And many great and notable cities were sunk, and many were burned, and many were shaken till the buildings therefore had fallen to the earth, and the inhabitants thereof were slain, and the places were left desolate.

Other cities were damaged and apparently millions of people were destroyed. Why were all of these people (men, women, and children) destroyed, and by whom? The answer is found in 3 Nephi 9:1–15, where the voice of Jesus Christ explains that He destroyed the cities and killed the inhabitants thereof because "of their iniquity and abominations" (verse 2). The story goes on in the following verses:

> Behold, that great city Zarahemla have I burned with fire, and the inhabitants thereof. And behold, that great city Moroni have I caused to be sunk in the depths of the sea, and the inhabitants thereof to be drowned. And behold, that great city Moronihah have I covered with earth, and the inhabitants thereof, ...And behold, the city of Gilgal have I caused to be sunk, And the inhabitants thereof to be buried up in the depths of the earth. Yea and the city of Onihah and the inhabitants thereof, and the city of Mocum and the inhabitants thereof, and the city of Jerusalem and the inhabitants thereof; and waters have I caused to come up in the stead thereof, ...And behold, the city of Gadiandi, and the city of Gadiomnah,

and the city of Jacob, and the city of Gimgimno, all these have I caused to be sunk, and made hills and valleys in the places thereof; and the inhabitants thereof have I buried up in the depths of the earth, ...And behold, the great city of Jacobugath, which was inhabited by the people of King Jacob, have I caused to be burned with fire ... And behold, the city of Laman, and the city of Josh, and the city of Gad, and the city of Kishkumen, have I caused to be burned with fire, and the inhabitants thereof, ...And many great destructions have I caused to come upon this land, and upon this people, because of their wickedness and their abominations. Behold, I am Jesus Christ the Son of God.

This is the time when Jesus Christ, after His crucifixion and resurrection in Jerusalem, appeared to the surviving people of the *Book of Mormon*, who were "spared because ye were more righteous than they" (verse 13). This is the resurrected Jesus Christ, who taught in Jerusalem and to the surviving people in the *BOM*, that,

it is written, an eye for an eye, and a tooth for a tooth; But I say unto you, that ye shall not resist evil, but whosoever shall smite thee on thy right check, turn to him the other also," and "love your enemies, bless them that curse you, do good to them that hate you, and pray for them who despitefully use you and persecute you." (See Matthew 5:38–44 and 3 Nephi 12:38–44.)

Apparently, Jesus Christ spared the more righteous people in the Americas at that time. Thereafter, with an introduction from his father, God the Eternal Father, Jesus Christ appeared to the remaining people gathered in the land of Bountiful, which was located in either Central of South America (3 Nephi 11).

This story sounds a lot like the events described in the Old Testament, when God destroyed mankind with the flood and rained fire and brimstone upon Sodom and Gomorrah, killing all of the inhabitants thereof. But why kill innocent children just because the men and women are wicked? Moreover, why even kill all of the inhabitants in so many cities when God with all of His knowledge and wisdom knew what was going to happen to all of them? Further, are we to conclude that there were not even just a few of the inhabitants of these cities that were not so wicked that they needed to be killed?

Then there is the question posed in Reason 16 herein as to why God has failed to destroy the wicked people and cities that have existed since the time of his crucifixion, when He destroyed the wicked people and cities in the Old Testament and *Book of Mormon*. It all seems so arbitrary and unnecessary when there are so many other ways of solving an alleged problem. Why didn't God destroy other cities in Asia, Europe, or other parts of the world that were not worshipping the correct God or living their lives in accordance with the way that God wants us to live? This useless killing of people, including innocent children, is not an attribute of a God in whom I should believe.

REASON 36
LACK OF DNA IN AUTHENTICATING THE BOOK OF MORMON

The understanding of Joseph Smith and traditionally of Mormons in general, is that the *Book of Mormon* indicates that the Indians found in the Americas are Lamanites. These Lamanites descended from Lehi and his family after they left Jerusalem, traveled by land and sea, and settled in the Americas in 600 B.C. They are known as a "remnant of the House of Israel" (see original title page of the *BOM*). This traditional understanding was indeed found in the wording of the Preface to the *BOM*, although it was not part of the actual text. The Preface was updated in 2007, removing that wording. The Lamanites were the largest group of people that descended from Lehi and his family and allegedly destroyed almost all of the Nephites, the other main group of people in the *BOM*, in approximately 400 A.D. The "House of Israel" refers to the people that lived in the ancient Middle East.

Scientists note that genetic studies show that the Indians or Amerindian peoples are most likely of Asiatic origin, which appears to conflict with the *Book of Mormon* account of their ancestry. Mormon archaeologists deal with the genetics problem in a variety of ways. The following are some excerpts from the article, "Genetics and the Book of Mormon," found on *Religion Wiki*:

> In 1929 President Anthony W. Ivins of the LDS church's First Presidency cautioned church members: "We must be careful in the conclusions that we reach. The Book of Mormon teaches the history of three distinct peoples ... who came from the old world to this continent. It does not tell us that there was no one here before them. It does not tell us that people did not come after. And so if discoveries are made which suggest differences in race origins, it can very easily be accounted for, and reasonably, for we do believe that other people came to this continent [(Moore)].

Mormon researchers such as anthropologist Thomas W. Murphy (who is a member of the Church of Jesus Christ Latter-day Saints, henceforth LDS) and former-LDS and molecular biologist Simon Southerton state that the substantial collection of Native American genetic markers now available are not consistent with any detectable presence of ancestors from the ancient Middle East, and argued that this poses substantial evidence to contradict the account in the Book of Mormon. Both Murphy and Southerton have published their views on this subject (Southerton 2004).

Southerton's work was later used as a source for a 2006 article written by William Lobdell and published in the *Los Angeles Times*, which stated: "For Mormons, the lack of discernible Hebrew blood in Native Americans is no minor collision between faith and science. It burrows into the historical foundations of the Book of Mormon, a 175-year-old transcription that the church regards as literal and without error" [(Lobdell)].

…LDS scholars also say that the DNA taken from modern day Israelis has been intermixed with DNA from many other nations, thus they do not contain the same traits that Israelites had when Lehi left Israel (Stubbs 2003). Also, modern Native Americans have intermixed, which has changed their DNA from that of their ancestors' as well. It is also noted by LDS researchers that another factor affecting genetic diversity of New World inhabitants is the fact that 90% of the population died as the result of disease introduced by the Spaniards after their arrival (Coe 2002, p. 231).

Michael F. Whiting, director of Brigham Young University's DNA Sequencing Center and an associate professor in BYU's Department of Integrative Biology, concluded in his article "DNA and the Book of Mormon: A Phylogenetic Perspective" that Book of Mormon critics attempting to use DNA "have not given us anything that would pass the muster of peer review by scientists in this field, because they have ignored the real complexity of the issues involved. Further, they have overlooked the entire concept of hypothesis testing in science and believe that just because they label their results as "based on DNA," they have somehow proved that the results are accurate or that they have designed the experiment correctly. At best, they have demonstrated that the global colonization hypothesis is an oversimplified interpretation of the Book of Mormon. At worst, they have misrepresented themselves and the evidence in the pursuit of other agendas." Additionally, although he admits the usefulness of population genetics and of DNA in inferring historical events, he contests that, "given the complexities of genetic drift, founder effect, and introgression, the observation that Native Americans have a preponderance of Asian genes does not conclusively demonstrate that they are therefore not descendants of the Lamanite lineage, because we do not know what genetic signature that Lamanite lineage possessed at the conclusion of the Book of Mormon record." Lastly, he concludes, "[There is] a strong possibility that there was substantial introgression of genes from other human populations into the genetic heritage of the Nephites and Lamanites, such that a unique genetic marker to identify someone unambiguously as a Lamanite, if it ever existed, was quickly lost." and that, "There are some very good scientific reasons for why the Book of Mormon is neither easily corroborated nor refuted by DNA evidence, and current attempts to do so are based on dubious science" (Whiting 24–35).

Continuing from *Wikipedia* under the same topic heading ("Genetics and the Book of Mormon"):

Murphy has responded to Whiting's comments as follows: "While Whiting, in his presentation for FARMS at BYU, exclaimed delight at the prospect of evolutionary biology coming to the defense of the Book of Mormon, he offered no scientific data to substantiate an Israelite origin of indigenous peoples anywhere in the Americas. In fact, he conceded, 'current genetic evidence suggests that Native Americans have a genetic history representative of Asia and not the Middle East.'" Murphy further states: "One of the most surprising critiques to emerge was the false allegation that I am evading peer review or that the research I reviewed would not stand up to peer review. ...[T]he article ["Lamanite Genesis, Genealogy, and Genetics"] was a summary of genetic research on Native American origins, nearly all of which had been subjected to peer review prior to publication in leading scientific journals such as *American Journal of Human Genetics, Proceedings of the National Academy of Sciences,* and *American Journal of Physical Anthropology.* ...Whiting's and Lambert's claims are little more than an inaccurate projection of the inadequacies of LDS apologetics onto my publications." (Murphy 113)

In my mind, the arguments made by the LDS apologetics are extremely weak and of little substance. There just is not any evidence to support the allegation in the *BOM* and Joseph Smith's position (stated numerous times in various writings) that the Indians are descendants of the Israelite people. Further, the Mormon God specifically states in the *BOM* in numerous places that they were. In Mormon Chapter 7, the great General of the Nephite people in 400 A.D., whose name was Mormon, invites the Lamanites of the latter days to believe in Christ. In verses 1 and 2 he states:

> I speak unto you, ye remnant of the house of Israel; and these are the words which I speak; Know ye that ye are of the house of Israel.

Who else was Mormon talking about except the people who lived in the Americas today? Why prophesy about a people if they would not exist at the time?

This lack of any DNA evidence to support the contention of the *BOM* and the Mormon God or Gods that the Indians have Israelite blood in them is a powerful reason to question the *Book of Mormon* and its God.

REASON 37
THE BOOK OF MORMON'S LANGUAGE IS LOST

The peoples of the *Book of Mormon*, both the Nephites and the Lamanites, were extremely civilized with both verbal and written languages. When Lehi, Nephi, and their families arrived in the Americas, they had the written plates of brass with them and continuously wrote down their history. In 1 Nephi 1:2, recorded in 600 B.C. we read, "Yea, I make a record in the language of my father, which consists of the learning of the Jews and the language of the Egyptians." Then 1000 years later, in approximately 400 A.D., the prophet Moroni records in the book called Mormon 9:32–34:

> And now, behold, we have written this record according to our knowledge, in the characters which are called among us the reformed Egyptian, being handed down and altered by us, according to our manner of speech. And if our plates had been sufficiently large we should have written in Hebrew; but the Hebrew hath been altered by us also, and if we could have written in Hebrew, behold, we would have had no imperfection in our record. But the Lord knoweth the things which we have written, and also that none other people knoweth our language; and because that none other people knoweth our language, therefore he hath prepared means for the interpretation thereof.

It would appear that the plates of brass, obtained by Nephi in 600 B.C. from Laban in Jerusalem, were written in Hebrew and still existed 600 years later, when Jesus Christ appeared to the Nephites (3 Nephi 1:2). So for that period of time, they had the Hebrew language. Then in 400 A.D., Mormon had all of the plates that had been written upon for 1000 years from which he did the abridgement and then gave the records to his son, Moroni (see Words of Mormon 1:1–9).

We know that the Lamanites also had a written language that most likely would have lasted the 1000 years as well. During the last great war between the Nephites and Lamanites that occurred from 360–

420 A.D., the king of the Lamanites sent an epistle to Mormon, the General of the Nephites (Mormon 3:4). Then a few years later, when Mormon again became the General of the Nephites, he sent an epistle to the Lamanite king, as recorded in Mormon 6:2-3, which states:

> And I, Mormon, wrote an epistle unto the king of the Lamanites, and desired of him that he would grant unto us that we might gather together our people unto the land of Cumorah, by a hill which was called Cumorah, and there we could give them battle. And it came to pass that the king of the Lamanites did grant unto me of the thing which I desired.

It appears then that both the Nephites and the Lamanites understood each other and used the same written language. The question then is, "What happened to the language that existed in 400 A.D. that was derived from Hebrew and/or Egyptian (because it cannot be found anywhere in any of the languages of the American Indians)?" This question was given to the Mormon Church in 1921 by a Mr. Couch from Washington, D.C., who was investigating the *Book of Mormon*. An Apostle of the LDS Church at that time, James E. Talmage, asked B. H. Roberts, a General Authority of the Mormon Church, to provide an answer. Mr. Couch's exact question was, "How could the great diversity in primitive Indian languages have occurred in such a short period of time after about A.D. 400, when the Nephites, whose Hebrew language was so highly developed, disappeared?"

B. H. Roberts examined this question in his book, *Studies of the Book of Mormon*, published in 1985. He acknowledged the following (91):

> 1. That there are a large number of separate language stocks in America that show very little relationship to each other. ...

> 2. That it would take a long time—much longer than that recognized as "historic times,"—to develop these dialects and stocks where the development is conceived of as arising from a common source or origin—some primitive language.

3. That there is no connection between the American languages and the language of any people of the Old World. New World languages appear to be indigenous to the New World.

After his careful analysis and research, B. H. Roberts came up with four possible ways of attempting to answer the question, but each of them had "formidable difficulties" (92). He then concluded that he hoped that someone could come up with a better answer that was "free from the serious difficulties" that were contained in his attempts (94).

Another interesting issue relating to the written language of the *Book of Mormon* people, either Hebrew or Reformed Egyptian, is that no one has ever found any evidence of those written languages existing in the "New World." However, there *are* existing ancient records of the New World that verify other languages. In *Wikipedia*, there is an analysis of this issue in the article titled "Archeology and the Book of Mormon." The following quotes are taken from that article:

> The National Geographic Society has noted, "Reports of findings of ancient Egyptian Hebrew, and other Old World writings in the New World and pre-Columbian contexts have frequently appeared in newspapers, magazines, and sensational books. None of these claims has stood up to examination by reputable scholars. No inscriptions using Old World forms of writing have been shown to have occurred in any part of the Americas before 1492 except for a few Norse rune stones which have been found in Greenland.

> Losses of ancient writings occurred in the Old World, in deliberate or accidental fires, in wars, earthquakes, and floods. Similar losses occurred in the New World. Much of the literature of the pre-Columbian Maya was destroyed during the Spanish conquest in the 16th century. On this point, Michael Coe noted: "Nonetheless, our knowledge of ancient Maya thought must represent only a tiny fraction of the whole picture, for of the thousands of books in which the full extent of their learning and ritual was recorded, only four have survived to modern times (as though all that posterity

knew of ourselves were to be based upon three prayer books and *Pilgrim's Progress*)."

The Maya civilization also left behind a vast corpus of inscriptions (upwards of ten thousand are known) written in the Maya script, the earliest of which date from around the 3rd century BC with the majority written in the Classic Period (c. 250–900 AD). Mayanist scholarship is now able to decipher a large number of these inscriptions. These inscriptions are mainly concerned with the activities of Mayan rulers and the commemoration of significant events, with the oldest known Long Count date corresponding to December 7, 36 BC, being recorded on Chiapa de Corzo *Stela 2* in central Chiapas. None of these inscriptions make contact with events, places, rulers, or timeline of Book of Mormon.

From a layman's viewpoint, it seems apparent that the American Indians did not descend from the Lamanites. If they did, there would be some remnant of the Hebrew language in the languages spoken by the American Indians and the archeological findings of the written language. We have absolutely no physical evidence of the Hebrew or Egyptian language ever being spoken or written on the American continents. Why would God have his prophets in the Americas keep such extensive written records for over 1000 years in the Hebrew and Egyptian languages and then fail to preserve any of it, except for the gold plates?

In 1947, near the Dead Sea in the Middle East, hundreds of scrolls were found in a cave and were verified to have been written between approximately 200 B.C. and 100 A.D. These scrolls contained portions of many of the books of the Old Testament and had been preserved for almost 2000 years. Joseph Smith claimed to have had the "gold plates," written by Mormon and Moroni around 400 A.D., that survived for over 1400 years. Therefore, if the written word of God was important for us to have, God would have found some way to reserve those writings, so that they could be verified today. But again, we have no originals, and no writings, inscriptions, or other carvings found in the Americas, to substantiate the existence of the people of the *Book of Mormon*.

REASON 38
JOSEPH SMITH, THE REAL AUTHOR OF THE BOOK OF MORMON

Throughout the first sixty years of my existence, I defended the position that Joseph Smith could not have personally written the *Book of Mormon* by himself and been the author of the same. I used the common arguments of other Mormons that Joseph Smith was too young and under-educated to have accomplished such a task. The *BOM* seems to be such a complicated and profound book of history and religious belief that it would almost be impossible for a man in his early twenties in the late 1820's to have fabricated the entire book by himself.

But this question of whether Joseph Smith could have personally written the *Book of Mormon* was examined extensively by B. H. Roberts (a General Authority for the Mormon Church in 1922). His research and report was presented in "A Book of Mormon Study," found in *Studies of the Book of Mormon*, published in 1985, referred to in the previous Reason 37. Roberts looked at the early literature that would have been available to Joseph Smith in the 1820's, Joseph Smith's intelligence and imagination, and the religious attitude and conversions of the time.

After Roberts had written his treatise on the difficulties of the *Book of Mormon*, referred to above, he wrote to the President of the Mormon Church, Heber J. Grant. He was granted an appointment with the First Presidency, the Twelve Apostles, and the Council of Seventy to discuss the "discrepancies between that record [*BOM*] and the results of archeological and other scientific investigations." He had more than one session with the leaders of the Church, but was so disappointed with the sessions that he decided to continue on his own in his research, looking for possible explanations as to the origin of the *Book of Mormon*.

Roberts main study was a book written by the Reverend Ethan Smith of Vermont, titled *View of the Hebrews*, which was published in two editions in 1823 and 1825. These books, therefore, could have been available to Joseph Smith prior to the publication of the *BOM* in 1829. After carefully reviewing the *View of the Hebrews*, and the similarities between it and the *Book of Mormon*, Roberts surprisingly concludes that it could have been the "ground plan" for Joseph Smith's authorship of the *Book of Mormon* (Roberts 149).

Further, on the same page, in a portion written by Brigham D. Madsen (editor for Robert's *Studies*), the following:

> Robert's "A Book of Mormon Study" considers this approach in some detail [Joseph Smith using the *View of the Hebrews* in authoring the *Book of Mormon*] and he bolsters it by extensive reference to the latest scientific investigations available to him during the years 1922–27. Not content with this examination, Roberts also spends the last part of his "Study" examining the "Imaginative Mind" of Joseph Smith, certain internal inconsistencies in the Book of Mormon, and, finally, the similarity of conversions in the book to Christian conversions of the period in the times and vicinity when and where the Book of Mormon was "translated."

I would suggest reading *Studies of the Book of Mormon* in its entirety. Roberts does a thorough job of analyzing all of the evidence available at that time and a superb job of comparing the *View of the Hebrews* to the *Book of Mormon*. He also reviews internal evidence that the *Book of Mormon* is of human origin. However, it is Robert's conclusion about Joseph Smith's ability to personally write the *BOM* that is important to me. It is found on page 250 and states:

> In the light of this evidence, there can be no doubt as to the possession of a vividly strong, creative imagination by Joseph Smith, the Prophet, an imagination, it could with reason be urged, which, given the suggestions that are to be found in the "common knowledge" of accepted American antiquities of the times, supplemented by such a work as Ethan Smith's *View of the Hebrews*, would make it possible for him (Joseph Smith) to create a book such as the Book of Mormon is.

In *D&C*, 1:24; 6:25; 9:8–10 and numerous other scriptures, the Lord indicates that Joseph Smith was given the gift and the power to translate, and by this gift, the gold plates were translated into the *Book of Mormon*. However, as discussed above, it is my impression that Joseph Smith had the capability to imagine and write the *Book of Mormon* without any gift of God.

REASON 39
GOD WOULDN'T HAVE AUTHORED THE BOOK OF MORMON

According to the theology of the Mormon Church, the *Book of Mormon* is the literal word of God. The Eighth Article of Faith of the Mormon Church states: "We believe the Bible to be the word of God as far as it is translated correctly; we also believe the Book of Mormon to be the word of God." (*HC*, 4:541). Furthermore, *Mormon Doctrine*, by Bruce McConkie, at page 845 states:

> By the *word of God* is also meant the scriptures, the revelations, the message of salvation which God sends by the mouths of holy men called to his ministry.

Therefore, it is the words that God would speak to us if He conversed with us face to face.

However, an analysis of the exact words and messages found in the *BOM* indicate that they may have not come from God. When discussing God's revealed word, our first assumption would be that God would speak in simple, concise, and understandable words and phrases. His messages would be worthy of something coming from God. They would not be confusing or contradicting, but majestic and universally understood.

In Reason 31, we discussed the confusing Godhead as described in the *BOM*. The Godhead is perhaps the most important and significant issue addressed in religion. It is an issue that needs to be revealed by God in simple and majestic terms and not in confusing or contradicting terms. This does not happen in the *BOM*. If God were the author of the *BOM*, wouldn't He make sure that the description and discussion of the Godhead would be worthy of its author?

Another factor to analyze in regard to the authorship of the *BOM* is whether the content is concise, spiritually important, and godlike in its form. There are 531 pages in the *BOM*, 6604 verses, and approximately 268,163 words. God would have chosen the correct words to express His meaning and message and would have done this in a godly manner. He would not have used the phrase, "And it came to pass," some 1,476 times, which comprises about 2% of the *BOM*.

He would not have used over 92 different terms, 400 times, to identify the three Gods of the Mormon Godhood.

Another apparent non-godlike part of the *BOM* is the recitation of the wars and contentions between the Nephites and Lamanites found throughout the *BOM*. Furthermore, there are chapters that only give historical information. None of those portions of the *BOM* contain any religious or spiritual information of any significance. I don't believe God would have wasted so many chapters and verses telling about the history, wars, and contentions between the Nephites and Lamanites that have no religious or spiritual relevance.

For example, Mosiah, Chapters 19–23 (approximately 9 pages) only discusses King Noah (an unrighteous man), the invasion by the Lamanites, wars and battles between Nephites and Lamanites, and the escape by the Nephites from Lamanite bondage. Other apparent non-godlike parts of the *BOM* are found in the book of Alma, where there is a lot of non-spiritual information. Chapters 2 and 3 of Alma recite history and wars; Chapters 28–29 describe battles; Chapters 43–63 (comprising 55 pages and some 706 verses) only tell about the wars and dissensions between the Nephites and Lamanites from approximately 73 B.C. until 53 B.C., or about 20 years. In these 55 pages, we do not find any significant religious or spiritual messages that would be beneficial to us in learning about God and what He wants us to do while we are upon the Earth.

The above-mentioned chapters in Mosiah and Alma comprise approximately 72 pages, or almost 13.5 % of the *BOM*. Would God waste over one-eighth of His words to us to tell us about a time in history that does not impact our lives whatsoever? If God is giving us His word or message that is intended to be a guide in how we live our lives, He would not waste space telling a short part of the history of the wars and contentions between only two groups of people. This information has already been repeated and recorded thousands of times in the history of mankind.

There is also the book of Ether, which contains 31 chapters and 433 verses, or about 6.5 % of the *BOM*. Chapters 7–11 and 14–15 contain 207 verses, or almost one half of the book of Ether. These chapters are also void of any spiritual significance and only describe the wars, contentions, and extermination of the people.

There are a total of approximately five hundred and twenty-nine (529) verses from the Old and New Testament, as stated in the King James Version of the Bible, that are also found in the *Book of*

Mormon. Most of these verses were allegedly taken from the Plates of Laban that were obtained by Nephi in 620 B.C. (see Reason 34). There are some differences between the verses found in the *BOM* and the same verses found in the Bible, but there was an attempt to resolve these by Joseph Smith when he published his *Inspired Translation* of the Old and New Testaments (see Reason 82). Most of these verses in the *BOM* are from the book of Isaiah. Those verses from Isaiah are also contained in the *Dead Sea Scrolls* that were discovered in 1947, after being preserved for almost 2000 years. So there is approximately 8% of the *BOM* that is repetitive and that can be found in the Bible, the *Dead Sea Scrolls*, or Joseph Smith's *Inspired Translation*.

The approximations of the percentages of the *BOM* that are not spiritual or of significant religious value, as indicated above, may not be exactly correct, but they are fairly close. Therefore, we have just under **one third** of the *Book of Mormon* that does not appear to be what God would reveal to mankind as His word. Why would a book or record, claiming to be the "Word of God," be so voluminous and still somewhat void of what an all-knowing and all-loving God would want us to know, as His spiritual children?

It is interesting to note that we probably have only "one" writing that is believed by Christians (including Mormons), Jews, and Muslims to be the actual word of God written by God: the "Ten Commandments" given to Moses. This is according to the Qur'an (The Prophets) 21:48; Exodus 34:1 and 20:1–17 in the Old Testament; and Mosiah 12:33 in the *Book of Mormon*. The Ten Commandments are simple, concise, direct, and not confusing. If we add to the Ten Commandments, the Golden Rule of "doing unto others what we want done to us," given by Jesus Christ in Matthew 7:12, we have God's direct words of how we should live our lives, given to us in less than one page of scripture.

Wouldn't the *Book of Mormon* be more concise, simple, and non-confusing if God had been the author? Wouldn't it have been condensed into a lot fewer pages of scriptures than it was? Moreover, wouldn't the *Book of Mormon* have been less confusing, as to whom God the Father and Jesus Christ were, had it been authored by God?

REASON 40
LACK OF GOLD PLATES

Joseph Smith received the gold plates from the Angel Moroni on September 22, 1827 and had them in his possession (except for a short time in July 1828) until approximately June or July 1829, although we don't know the exact date for sure when he gave the gold plates back to the Angel Moroni. At the conclusion of the *Pearl of Great Price*, the Mormon Church has included excerpts from Joseph Smith's *History of the Church*. In verse 60 of that excerpt, we read the following in regard to Joseph receiving and returning the gold plates:

> I soon found out the reason why I had received such strict charges to keep them safe, and why it was that the messenger [Moroni] had said that when I had done what was required at my hand, he would call for them. For no sooner was it known that I had them, than the most strenuous exertions were used to get them from me. Every stratagem that could be invented was resorted to for that purpose. The persecution became more bitter and severe than before, and multitudes were on the alert continually to get them from me if possible. But by the wisdom of God, they remained safe in my hands, until I had accomplished by them what was required at my hand. When, according to arrangements, the messenger called for them, I delivered them up to him; and he has them in his charge until this day, being the second day of May, one thousand eight hundred and thirty-eight.

A description of the gold plates is made by Joseph Smith in his *HC*, 4:537. It states as follows:

> These records were engraven on plates which had the appearance of gold, each plate was six inches wide and eight inches long, and not quite so thick as common tin. They were filled with engravings, in Egyptian

characters, and bound together in a volume as the leaves of a book, with three rings running through the whole. The volume was something near six inches in thickness, a part of which was sealed. The characters on the unsealed part were small, and beautifully engraved. The whole book exhibited many marks of antiquity in its construction, and much skill in the art of engraving.

So my question in regard to the gold plates is simple: why hasn't God returned them to one of the Prophets of the Mormon Church during my lifetime? The gold plates could be verified as ancient records and the translation of the "Egyptian characters" could authenticate the translation contained in the *Book of Mormon*. One answer given to my query is based upon the fact that part of the gold plates were sealed and that according to 2 Nephi 27:7–8:

> ...the book shall be sealed; and in the book shall be a revelation from God, from the beginning of the world to the ending thereof. Wherefore, because of the things which are sealed up, the things which are sealed shall not be delivered in the day of the wickedness and abominations of the people. Wherefore, the book shall be kept from them.

However, this too does not make sense as an argument for not allowing the unsealed portion of the gold plates to either remain upon the earth, or be returned to the earth in today's time for verification and authentication.

As described by Joseph Smith, the gold plates were single leaves held together by three rings. How hard would it be to unhook the plates from the three rings and separate the unsealed from the sealed portion of the plates? Obviously, it would not be hard at all, especially for an "Angel of God."

It is my understanding that, according to the Mormon religion, one of the main purposes of the restoration of the Gospel through Joseph Smith and the translation of the *BOM* was to give to everyone that was interested an opportunity to hear the Gospel and accept it. In this way, their lives would be happier and they could enjoy the blessings of the Gospel. So wouldn't the presence of the unsealed portion of the gold plates from which came the translation of the *Book of Mormon* be an even greater incentive for people to listen to the Gospel and accept it? What a great conversion tool the Gold Plates would be today with the verification of the same by modern-day scholars and experts on ancient records and translations! There would be no downside to God having the Angel Moroni return the Gold Plates to the Prophet of the Mormon Church today, but a tremendous upside.

An argument has been made by some in the Mormon Church that we should be required to accept the *Book of Mormon* on faith. Then why have the written and signed statement of eleven (11) witnesses, found at the beginning of the *BOM*, claiming that they saw the Gold Plates, if we are required to accept them today by faith? There would be no need of any witnesses. Apparently though, God decided that there was a need in 1829 for the same.

We should have the Gold Plates available today to examine and use to verify the authenticity of the *Book of Mormon* and the validity of the Mormon Church. Why wouldn't God agree with my proposal, since it would be a conduit for millions of people to be given the Gospel of Jesus Christ and thereby live happier lives?

REASON 41
QUESTIONS ABOUT THE D&C GOD

The God of the *Doctrine and Covenants* (*D&C*) is also Jesus Christ, according to Mormon theology. In Section 10, verse 1 in the *Doctrine and Covenants* we read, "I am Alpha and Omega, Christ the Lord; yea, even I am he, the beginning and the end, the Redeemer of the World." Then in verse 4, it states: "for I, God, am endless."

One of the problems with the God of the *D&C* seems to be a lack of foreknowledge of some of the statements made about future events. The *D&C* and the *History of the Church* (written by Joseph Smith) contain accounts that appear to be mistakes in revelations given to Joseph Smith. In *D&C*, 84:2–5, it states:

> Yea, the word of the Lord concerning his church, established in the last days for the restoration of his people, as he has spoken by the mouth of his prophets, and for the gathering of his saints to stand upon Mount Zion, which shall be the city of New Jerusalem. Which city shall be built, beginning at the temple lot, which is appointed by the finger of the Lord, in the western boundaries of the State of Missouri, and dedicated by the hand of Joseph Smith, Jun., and others with whom the Lord was well pleased. Verily this is the word of the Lord that the city New Jerusalem shall be built by the gathering of the saints, beginning at this place [Missouri], even the place of the temple, which temple shall be reared in this generation. For verily this generation shall not all pass away until an house shall be built unto the Lord."

Nonetheless, that generation passed away and the "house [was not] built unto the Lord."

Further, in *D&C*, 42:35, the Lord commanded Joseph Smith to buy land in Missouri for New Jerusalem and stated,

> And for the purpose of purchasing lands for the public benefit of the church, and building houses of worship,

and building up of the New Jerusalem which is hereafter to be revealed.

Again, apparently this was a mistake to buy the land in Missouri for the reason that the Saints were driven from Missouri and lost all of the lands that they had purchased to build the New Jerusalem. However, the Lord told Joseph Smith in *D&C*, 124:51:

> Therefore, for this cause have I accepted the offerings of those whom I commanded to build up a city and a house unto my name, in Jackson county, Missouri, and were hindered by their enemies, saith the Lord your God.

Another example in the history of the LDS Church is the establishment of the United Order or Law of Consecration, given by revelation from the Lord (see *D&C*, Section 104). This occurred in Kirtland, Ohio, where the members of the Mormon Church would give all of their properties and income to the Church and allow the Church to manage them. Then the Church would give back to the members what the Church thought was fair and reasonable. This didn't work and appears to have been a mistake, which was a fact that would have been known by an omniscient God. Joseph Smith also founded a bank known as the "Kirtland Safety Society" and printed money in Kirtland, Ohio in accordance with revelations given to him (see *HC*, 2:472–73); but again, the same was a disaster.

There is also the issue of polygamy, which instruction was given to Joseph Smith as a revelation from the God in *D&C*, Section 132 in 1843, but then repealed by the Prophet Wilford Woodruff in 1890. This is discussed extensively in Reason 46. Also of interest is the issue of the blacks not being allowed to hold the Priesthood, discussed in Reason 63, which was reversed by the Prophet Spencer W. Kimball in 1978.

The argument could be made that we do not know God's purposes and that He commands some things for the person or people's experience, but this seems unlikely, because we can see that the results of the non-fulfillment of the above commandments. The disasters of the failed Kirtland bank and the printed notes/money only brought additional persecution upon the early members of the Mormon Church (see *HC*, 2:487–88). Further, the issues of polygamy and blacks not holding the priesthood caused tremendous problems for many years in the Mormon Church.

The God of the *D&C* also gave revelations to Joseph Smith about almost everything, including somewhat minor issues. Some examples are:

1. The story of James Covill, a Baptist minister, accepting and then rejecting Mormonism (Sections 39–40)
2. Building Joseph Smith a house (Section 41)
3. calling John Whitmer to be a scribe (Section 47)
4. Stating that some beliefs of the Shakers religion were wrong (Section 49)
5. Calling W. W. Phelps to write books for children in church schools (Section 55)
6. Telling various people where they should go in the country to proclaim the Gospel (Section 75)
7. Advising who should spend the tithing (Section 120)

Apparently, the God of the *Doctrine and Covenants* was involved in the daily affairs of the Mormon Church and many of its members for only about 10–14 years, and then quit being involved through revelations given to the Prophet of the Church. Why would God be involved in such minor issues and only for such a short period of time?

REASON 42
A CONFUSING EXCEPTION TO THE GOSPEL PLAN

In *Doctrine and Covenants*, Section 137, there is a vision given to Joseph Smith of the Celestial Kingdom. It reads as follows:

> The heavens were opened upon us, and I beheld the celestial kingdom of God, and the glory thereof, whether in the body or out I cannot tell. I saw the transcendent beauty of the gate through which the heirs of that kingdom will enter, which was like unto circling flames of fire; Also the blazing throne of God, whereon was seated the Father and the Son. I saw the beautiful streets of that kingdom, which had the appearance of being paved with gold. I saw Father Adam and Abraham; and my father and my mother; my brother Alvin, that has long since slept; And marveled how it was that he had obtained an inheritance in that kingdom, seeing that he had departed this life before the Lord had set his hand to gather Israel the second time, and had not been baptized for the remission of sins. Thus came the voice of the Lord unto me, saying: All who have died without a knowledge of this gospel, who would have received it if they had been permitted to tarry, shall be heirs of the celestial kingdom of God; Also all that shall die henceforth without a knowledge of it, who would have received it with all their hearts, shall be heirs of that kingdom; For I, the Lord, will judge all men according to their works, according to the desire of their hearts. And I also beheld that all children who die before they arrive at the years of accountability are saved in the celestial kingdom of heaven.

The above scripture creates some confusion as to the relationship of earth life to where we end up for eternity. If someone like the brother of Joseph Smith and everyone since this vision or revelation can be an heir of the Celestial Kingdom without hearing the Gospel or accepting it here upon Earth—based upon God's knowledge that they would have accepted the Gospel with all their hearts—then what is the purpose of even having the Gospel on Earth? God could just look at what we did upon the Earth with the knowledge that we had and judge us according to the desire of our hearts. Because he already knows the desires of our hearts, then it is possible to obtain the Celestial Kingdom without the Gospel. Does this make sense? Or is it just a confusing exception to the Plan of Salvation in which the Gospel is a crucial part?

This concept also appears to be contradictory to the 76th Section of the *D&C* discussed in Reason 43. In that Section, the Lord tells Joseph Smith concerning the second degree of heaven, or Terrestrial Kingdom:

> Behold, these are they who died without law; And also they who are the spirits of men kept in prison, whom the Son visited, and preached the gospel unto them, that they might be judged according to men in the flesh: Who received not the testimony of Jesus in the flesh, but afterwards received it. These are they who are honorable men of the earth, who were blinded by the craftiness of men. (*D&C*, 76:72–75)

I had a good friend who died without knowing the Gospel of Jesus Christ as taught by the Mormons; but he lived a very good life upon Earth and was an "honorable man." He sincerely believed that the Catholic religion was true and had extreme faith in the same. He lived a very Christian life, doing good to others and living the commandments found in the Bible. Apparently, according to the above scripture, he was "blinded by the craftiness of men," and did not have the correct desire in his heart to become an heir of the Celestial Kingdom. I admit that I am not a great intellect or scholar, but this kind of confusion creates doubts in my mind about believing in the Mormon God(s).

REASON 43
THE THREE DEGREES OF GLORY CONTROVERSY

The issue of the relationship between this earth life and eternity becomes even more confusing when we look closer at another vision given to Joseph Smith and Sidney Rigdon. It is found in the 76th Section of the *Doctrine and Covenants*. This Section is known in the Mormon Church as the "vision of the three degrees of glory," which are the Celestial, or glory of the sun; the Terrestrial, or glory of the moon; and the Telestial, or glory of the stars.

The individuals who become heirs of the first kingdom discussed (or the lower one, named the Telestial Kingdom), are those who do not receive the gospel of Christ or the testimony of Jesus, either upon Earth or thereafter:

> These are they who are liars, and sorcerers, and adulterers, and whoremongers, and whosoever loves and makes a lie. ...But behold, and lo, we saw the glory and the inhabitants of the telestial world, and they were as innumerable as the stars in the firmament of heaven or as the sand upon the seashore (See *D&C*, 76:103, 109.)

The individuals who become heirs of the second kingdom listed, named the Terrestrial Kingdom, are described in verses 72–75:

> Behold, these are they who died without law; And also they who are the spirits of men kept in prison, whom the Son visited, and preached the gospel unto them, that they might be judged according to men in the flesh; Who received not the testimony of Jesus in the flesh, but afterwards received it. These are they who are honorable men of the earth, who were blinded by the craftiness of men.

One wonders why the Gospel needed to be preached to them, because (as stated in the previous Reason) God already knows whether they would have received it in the hearts or not. Further confusion occurs because of *D&C*, Section 137 (quoted in the previous Reason). In this Section, Alvin (brother of Joseph Smith) and all others who God knows would have accepted the Gospel on Earth—if presented to them while they were alive—become heirs of the Celestial Kingdom. This is contrary to what is specified in Section 76 above (outlining those who will inherit the Terrestrial Kingdom).

Bruce R. McConkie, in *Mormon Doctrine* at page 784, further states that those assigned to the Terrestrial Kingdom are

> Those who reject the gospel in this life and who reverse their course and accept it in the spirit world; [and] Honorable men of the earth who are blinded by craftiness of men.

This does not explain why God would not know what is in a person's heart that would enable them to accept the Gospel after they die. The Celestial Kingdom inhabitants are

> they who received the testimony of Jesus, and believed on his name and were baptized [upon the earth] ...That by keeping the commandments they might be washed and cleansed from their sins, ...And who overcome by faith, and are sealed by the Holy Spirit of promise, which the Father sheds forth upon all those who are just and true. ...Wherefore, as it is written, they are gods, even the sons of God" (verses 51–58).

Therefore, heirs of this kingdom can become "gods" as is discussed in other Reasons. Again, it is confusing.

Why can't God communicate to us through His prophets in plain and simple language, so we can understand and not be confused as to such important principles as to where we may end up for the rest of our eternal lives? If God knows what is in our hearts, then the scriptures could just state that we will inherit that kingdom after we die based upon what is in our hearts, regardless of when we were born on Earth and whether the Gospel was even available for us during our lives.

REASON 44
ISSUES WITH THE DOCTRINE AND COVENANTS' REVELATIONS

In restoring the Gospel of Jesus Christ through Joseph Smith in the early 1800s, apparently it was necessary for God to give Joseph Smith numerous revelations and commandments as to what he and others should do. Some of these revelations are found in *D&C*, Section 1:17–18, 30:

> Wherefore, I the Lord, knowing the calamity which should come upon the inhabitants of the earth, called upon my servant Joseph Smith, Jun., and spake unto him from heaven, and gave him commandments; And also gave commandments to others, that they should proclaim these things unto the world; and all this that it might be fulfilled, which was written by the prophets. ...And also those to whom these commandments were given, might have power to lay the foundation of this church, and to bring it forth out of obscurity and out of darkness, the only true and living church upon the face of the whole earth.

However, some of the revelations, commandments, or directions of God given to Joseph Smith turned out to be wrong or at least inadvisable. One such revelation is found *D&C*, Section 9, given in April 1829 through Joseph Smith to Oliver Cowdery. Oliver Cowdery was given the gift or power to translate ancient records just like Joseph Smith, which is stated in *D&C*, Section 8. But the gift or power was taken away from him in Section 9:5, which states:

> And, behold, it is because that you did not continue as you commenced, when you began to translate, that I have taken away this privilege from you.

(One wonders why God would give Oliver Cowdery the gift and power to translate the Gold Plates when God knew that Oliver would fail and the gift would have to be taken away).

Then, *D&C*, 9:1–3 states:

> Behold, I say unto you, my son, that because you did not translate according to that which you desired of me, and did commence again to write for my servant, Joseph Smith, Jun., even so I would that ye should continue until you have finished this record [Book of Mormon], which I have entrusted unto him. And then, behold, other records have I, that I will give unto you power that you may assist to translate. Be patient, my son, for it is wisdom in me, and it is not expedient that you should translate at this present time.

(So then Oliver was only a scribe for Joseph Smith and did not assist in the translation of the Gold Plates).

The above scripture suggests that Oliver Cowdery would eventually again be given the gift and power to translate ancient records; but he never did translate any other ancient records and eventually apostatized from the Mormon Church. He did help Joseph Smith (along with W. W. Phelps) as a scribe when Joseph allegedly translated some papyrus purchased by some of the Saints at Kirkland (Ohio) in 1835. However, Oliver did not translate any of the ancient papyrus himself.

Another example of a wrong or inadvisable revelation is found in *D&C*, 42:30; 51:3; and 58:35, where the Lord commanded the Saints to observe the Law of Consecration or the United Order. In these verses, it is explained that the Saints would give everything they owned to the Church and the Church would decide how to divide it among the Saints. This plan failed and was eventually discontinued in the Church.

Other examples of revelations in the *Doctrine and Covenants* that seem to have been wrong and that are discussed in other Reasons are:

1. Buying land in Independence, Missouri for the New Jerusalem and for a temple, but then the New Jerusalem was not established and a temple was never built.

2. Establishing polygamy and then outlawing it later.

3. Warnings of the Second Coming given to the Saints, but the Second Coming did not occur.

Lastly, there are numerous revelations in the *Doctrine and Covenants* given to Joseph Smith where specific directions are given to specific individuals. Some examples are Section 30, directed specifically to David Whitmer, Peter Whitmer, Jr., and John Whitmer (although this revelation was originally three different revelations, it was combined into just one revelation by Joseph Smith in 1835); Section 32 directed to Parley P. Pratt and Ziba Peterson; Section 33 directed to Ezra Thayre and Northrop Sweet; and Section 34, directed specifically to Orson Pratt. There are other *D&C* Sections as well, but this all stopped with the death of Joseph Smith. Why do we not have continual revelations given to the prophets after Joseph Smith and directed to specific individuals in the Mormon Church? The incongruence of these revelations, the failure of some of them, and the lack of additional revelations add to my dilemma in believing in the Mormon God(s).

REASON 45
THE WORD OF WISDOM PROBLEMS

One belief that has identified Mormon people is the prohibition by the Mormon religion against the use of tobacco and drinking wine or strong drink, and coffee and tea. This doctrine was first given by a revelation to Joseph Smith in 1833 to the early Saints and is found in *D&C*, Section 89. It became a commandment by the word of Brigham Young, as stated in *Gospel Doctrine* by Joseph F. Smith, 11th ed., at page 365. It states: "It was given unto us 'not by commandment'; but by the word of President Brigham Young, it was made a commandment unto the Saints." Although the revelation only refers to "hot drinks," the Mormon Church has clarified that term to mean tea and coffee (McConkie 369).

Before a member of the Mormon Church can obtain a Temple recommend, the member must be interviewed by his/her Bishop and then by a member of the Stake Presidency. One of the questions asked the member is whether he or she observes the Word of Wisdom and refrains from using tobacco, alcohol, tea, and coffee. If the answer is "No," even though the member may be worthy in all other aspects of the Gospel, the temple recommend is denied. The Word of Wisdom is touted by the Church as its health law given for the benefit of mankind. If a member is using any of these substances, they cannot attend the Temple. This seems somewhat harsh for someone who only has a glass of wine occasionally with dinner, or a cup of coffee in the morning. One might ask "What is wrong with a cup of coffee?" The answer given by Mormons is that it contains caffeine, because other hot drinks like hot chocolate or Postum are *not* prohibited. However, there is no prohibition against soda drinks that contain caffeine, or against energy drinks that contain a lot more caffeine than coffee. Why the distinction? No one seems to know, except to say that is the Mormon Church's stand.

The Mormon Church has not discredited the studies of today that have shown that drinking wine in moderation may help prevent heart attacks and that some teas are also beneficial to the human body. But what is more amazing is that a member of the Mormon Church can weigh over 350 pounds, which is clearly detrimental to that person's health, drink more caffeine daily through soda drinks and energy booster drinks than what would be in ten cups of coffee per day, but they can still obtain a temple recommend. However, if they drink a cup of coffee or a glass of wine, they cannot.

It is acceptable that God would be concerned about our health and well-being. However, His law of health would be defensible under scrutiny by all of the studies about what is and what isn't good for our health. I never smoked or drank alcohol, coffee, or tea for the first 60 years of my life; but many of my brothers and friends did. However, they lived most of the rest of the Mormon philosophy and were great Christian people. This revelation about the Word of Wisdom seems to me to be outdated and in need of revision.

What needs even more revision is the emphasis placed upon the Word of Wisdom by the Mormon Church. Joseph Smith did not put that must emphasis on it when he was incarcerated in the Carthage Jail just prior to his martyrdom in 1844. In fact, according to John Taylor, the third Prophet and President of the Mormon Church, the Prophet Joseph Smith and other Church leaders needed some wine during the evening of his death on June 27th, 1844. In *HC*, 7:101, we read:

> Sometime after dinner we sent for some wine. It has been reported by some that this was taken as a sacrament. It was no such thing; our spirits were generally dull and heavy, and it was sent for to revive us. ...I believe we all drank of the wine, and gave some to one or two of the prison guards.

Obviously the wine was not "pure wine of the grape of the vine, of your own make," as required by *D&C*, 89:6, because pure grape juice would not have had a "reviving" quality to it.

Further, Brigham Young and the early Mormon settlers of Utah did not put as much emphasis on the Word of Wisdom and many chewed tobacco and drank alcohol. Brigham Young quit chewing tobacco in 1848, but then started again in 1857, when his teeth hurt and the tobacco relieved the pain. Many of the brethren of the Church chewed tobacco and President Young advised them to be modest about it (Arrington 312–13).

Del Vance's book, *Beer in the Beehive*: *A History of Brewing in Utah* looks at one of the world's oldest industries and its place in Utah History. Some trivia gleaned from browsing that book are as follows:

1. By 1850, several breweries were established in the Salt Lake Valley, presumably by Mormon pioneers. Vance has documentation that one of these early settlers, John Reese, was even granted a license to brew beer from beets.

2. Orrin Porter Rockwell, the notorious gunslinger and enforcer, built a roadhouse brewery in Bluffdale, Utah called the "Hot Springs Brewery Hotel." He had gained some practical experience years before in Nauvoo, when he set up a bar in Joseph Smith's Nauvoo House.

3. The first major Utah brewery was built in 1864 by a German immigrant, Henry Wagener, and called the California Brewery. It was located at the mouth of Emigration Canyon within a stone's throw of the "This Is the Place" monument.

4. In the 1800s, ZCMI sold beer, wine, and liquor in its downtown location.

5. Mark Twain was familiar with a distilled spirit called Valley Tan. He said it was "a kind of whiskey, or first cousin to it; it is of Mormon invention and manufactured only in Utah. Tradition says it is made of imported fire and brimstone."

6. The strict adherence to the Word of Wisdom was not required by the Mormon Church until the early 1900s.

Why hasn't God thought it appropriate to revise the Word of Wisdom? Moreover, why does God allow the Mormon Church to place unbelievable and disproportionate emphasis on the same?

REASON 46
DOCTRINE AND COVENANTS SECTION 132 (POLYGAMY)

Of all of the doctrines of the Mormon Church, polygamy is probably the one that has received the most publicity, been written about the most, and caused the most problems for the Church, since the time that it was instituted by Joseph Smith in the 1830s. It has been estimated that even today (2018), somewhere between thirty and forty percent of non-Mormons believe that Mormons still practice polygamy, even though polygamy was terminated and discontinued by the mainstream LDS Church in 1890. Not only have there been numerous books and articles written about polygamy, there have even been recent popular television series about it, to wit, *Sister Wives* and *Big Love*. Most recently, there have been criminal prosecutions for polygamy in both Utah and Texas that have been in the national spotlight.

As an attorney specializing in family law for the past 40 years, I have been involved in over 1,200 divorces, many of which have involved polygamy or polygamous clients. Those polygamous clients that I represented were hard-working citizens who sincerely and deeply believed that they were called by God to continue the practice of polygamy here upon Earth until the Second Coming of Christ. They relied upon an alleged revelation given by the Lord to John Taylor in 1886, the third prophet and president of the Mormon Church. They believed polygamy, being a commandment from God, was required by God to remain upon Earth at all times, and therefore a few chosen servants of God were set apart for them and their descendants to continue the practice of polygamy. (See "Question.")

The basis for the practice of polygamy by the Mormon Church is found in *Doctrine and Covenants*, Section 132, where, by revelation, the Lord discusses "Celestial marriage and a continuation of the family unit [which] enable[s] men to become gods," and gives the "laws governing the plural marriage." (*D&C*, Chapter 132 header) First, the Lord explains to Joseph Smith that the Old Testament Prophets did not sin in having more than one wife and concubines. In verses 34–37 the Lord says:

God commanded Abraham, and Sarah gave Hagar to Abraham to wife. And why did she do it? Because this was the law; and from Hagar sprang many people. ...Was Abraham, therefore, under condemnation? Verily I say unto you, Nay; for I, the Lord, commanded it. ...Abraham received concubines, and they bore him children; and it was accounted unto him for righteousness, because they were given unto him, and he abode in my law; as Isaac also and Jacob did none other things than that which they were commanded; and because they did none other things than that which they were commanded, they have entered into their exaltation, according to the promises, and sit upon thrones, and are not angels but are gods.

There is no dispute by the mainstream Mormon Church that polygamy is a divine law of the Priesthood of God, instituted and justified by God, and a practice that occurred in the Church from 1831 to 1890. Further, as discussed in Section 132, the doctrine of polygamy was given by God to Abraham, Isaac, Jacob, David, Solomon, and Moses; and they have become gods, as stated above. However, God forbade the practice of polygamy by the Nephites in the *Book of Mormon* as recorded in Jacob 2:22–35.

Notwithstanding the changes by God as to who can practice polygamy and when it can be practiced, what seems to be the major problem with polygamy is that it allows men, in the name of God, to marry under-aged girls, based upon the premise found in Section 132 that plural wives need to be virgins. This practice prevents young girls from enjoying their teenage years and enjoying that part of their life without the requirement of conceiving and bearing children.

One of my clients was a prime example of this. He and his wife, when in their early twenties, obtained a Celestial Marriage in the Mormon Temple for time and all eternity. However, after twenty years of marriage, and his wife no longer being able to bare children, my client received his revelation that he was required to take additional wives (who were virgins) so he could further "multiply and replenish the earth according to my [God's] commandment" (*D&C*, 132:63). His wife did not want to participate in polygamy, so I handled their divorce, which allowed my client to then marry three 14-year-old girls and "multiply and replenish," which he did. He had an additional fifteen

(15) children with his three teenage brides before they each reached the age of twenty-one (21).

This same scenario occurred with the early members of the Mormon Church from 1831 to 1890, and even thereafter. Joseph Smith is alleged to have married at least 33 wives, eleven of them between the ages of 14 to 20 (Compton 11). Brigham Young is alleged to have married more wives than Joseph Smith and had over 57 children (Arrington, Appendix C).

This doctrine and practice of polygamy, according to Mormon doctrine, is all part of God's plan and something that He instituted, condoned, and then repealed. Why would God establish polygamy in the Mormon Church, when God knew full well the problems that it would create and that God would later repeal His own commandment?

REASON 47
DOCTRINE OF MULTIPLE WIVES IN HEAVEN

I married my first wife in the Salt Lake City, Utah Temple, being married and sealed for time and all eternity. After 13 years, we divorced civilly, but were still married according to our God for eternity. Then I married my second wife, also in the Salt Lake Temple, and we were also married and sealed for time and all eternity. I now had two eternal wives. We divorced after 5 years, but only civilly, so under our God's plan, we were still eternal companions. My third wife and I were then married in the Salt Lake Temple for time and all eternity; therefore I was then blessed with three eternal wives.

According to LDS doctrine, had I died while being married to my third wife, neither she nor my first two wives would have been able to cancel the temple sealing, and they would have been my wives forever. I would have been re-united with all three (3) wives in heaven and they would be my eternal companions and no one else's. Further, I could have continued divorcing my wives under the laws of the State of Utah and then marrying additional women in the Temple, thus adding to my Celestial wives in Heaven. It did not matter that all my wives were alive at the same time and that we had been divorced under the applicable civil laws, we would still be married under God's law and I would be a polygamist.

Although the Mormon Church outlawed polygamy in 1890, it has never changed its belief as to a man having multiple wives sealed to him while living. According to their doctrine, those wives would only be that man's wives in heaven even if their civil marriage was terminated by divorce (See *D&C*, Section 132). On the other hand, the woman is stuck with whomever she is married to in the Mormon Temple, unless the man agrees to have the temple sealing cancelled. Of course, if the man dies before that takes place, then the woman cannot marry for time and all eternity in the temple again.

There is an example of this injustice in my own family. One of my older brothers was married in the temple to a woman when they were in their early twenties. However, my brother died at age 23 and his wife was left with two young children. She remarried a great guy, but they were not allowed to get married in the Temple for time and all eternity. In their belief, their marriage will terminate at death. They have now been married for over forty-five (45) years; raised my brother's two children and four additional children of their own, have numerous grandchildren, and have become soul mates. Nevertheless, according to Mormon doctrine, they will not be together in the eternities because she was first sealed eternally to my brother, even though they were only married a few short years. This does not make sense to me. Another solution must be possible.

A man having multiple wives in the hereafter and a woman being limited to one husband seems to be discriminatory. I am hopeful that the problem discussed above concerning my brother and his wife will be solved by a merciful and wise God, and not according to the concepts of the Mormon Church.

REASON 48
THE NEW JERUSALEM AND INDEPENDENCE, MISSOURI

After Joseph Smith was murdered in June 1847, his wife Emma, and her children, including one who was not yet born, stayed in Nauvoo, Illinois rather than travel west to Utah with Brigham Young. Emma Smith married Lewis Bidamon in 1847 and they raised all of Joseph's Smith's children in Nauvoo. Later, an older son, Joseph Smith III, received his own revelation and helped found the Reorganized Church of Jesus Christ of Latter-day Saints, which continued to believe in the *Book of Mormon* and in Joseph Smith as the prophet who restored the Gospel of Jesus Christ. Today, the Reorganized Church is known as the *Community of Christ Church*, with its headquarters in Independence, Missouri and worldwide membership of approximately 250,000.

It is interesting that the *Community of Christ* church has chosen Independence, Missouri as its headquarters, because this is where Joseph Smith prophesized that the New Jerusalem would be built, a holy city during the millennium after Jesus Christ's Second Coming (see *D&C*, 42:8–9; 45:66–67; 57:1–5; and 84:2–5).

In 1831, the saints, through a revelation given to Joseph Smith, were commanded to purchase tracts of land in Independence, Missouri. Joseph Smith prayed to God to know "When will Zion be built up in her glory, and where will Thy temple stand, unto which all nations shall come in the last days?" (*HC*, 1:189–90) He was answered by the Lord as recorded in *D&C*, 57:1–5:

> Hearken, O ye elders of my church, saith the Lord your God, who have assembled yourselves together, according to my commandments, in this land, which is the land of Missouri, which is the land which I have appointed and consecrated for the gathering of the saints. Wherefore, this is the land of promise, and the place for the city of Zion. And thus saith the Lord your God, if you will receive wisdom here is wisdom. Behold, the place which is now called Independence is the center place; and a spot for the temple is lying

westward, upon a lot which is not far from the courthouse. Wherefore, it is wisdom that the land should be purchased by the saints, and also every tract lying westward, even unto the line running directly between Jew and Gentile. And also every tract bordering by the prairies, inasmuch as my disciples are enabled to buy lands. Behold, this is wisdom, that they may obtain it for an everlasting inheritance.

Later in 1832, Joseph Smith received another revelation concerning Independence, Missouri and the New Jerusalem, as recorded in *D&C*, 84:2–5:

Yea, the word of the Lord concerning his church, established in the last days for the restoration of his people, as he has spoken by the mouth of his prophets, and for the gathering of his saints to stand upon Mount Zion, which shall be the city of New Jerusalem. Which city shall be built, beginning at the temple lot, which is appointed by the finger of the Lord, in the western boundaries of the State of Missouri, and dedicated by the hand of Joseph Smith, Jun., and others with whom the Lord was well pleased. Verily, this is the word of the Lord, that the city New Jerusalem shall be built by the gathering of the saints, beginning at this place, even the place of the temple, which temple shall be reared in this generation. For verily this generation shall not all pass away until an house shall be built unto the Lord, and a cloud shall rest upon it, which cloud shall be even the glory of the Lord, which shall fill the house.

Pursuant to these revelations, the early Saints bought properties in Independence, Missouri to build a temple and a New Jerusalem. They and Joseph Smith believed, as stated in the above scripture, that Joseph Smith's generation would not pass away before a temple was built there and the city of the New Jerusalem was established. Well, this did not happen and the Saints lost their money and property when they were driven out of Missouri, while the Lord God did nothing. Apparently though, the Reorganized Church (*Community of Christ Church*) *does* own some of the properties in Independence, Missouri.

What God would command his Saints to purchase land with a promise that they would be building a temple and new city there, when in fact an all-knowing God would know that it would not happen? Further, the land would not have had to have been purchased then, if the temple was going to be built after the Second Coming of Christ!

REASON 49
NECESSITY OF TEMPLES AND TEMPLE WORK

One of the many issues that separate the Mormon Church and the Mormon God(s) from other Christian faiths and their God is the building of temples by the Mormons for the purpose of doing temple ordinances. There are certain ordinances pertaining to the Gospel of Jesus Christ, which, according to Mormon doctrine, need to be performed only within temples that have been dedicated for that purpose. These ordinances are as follows:

1. Baptisms for the Dead
2. Washings and Anointings
3. Endowments
4. Sealings
5. Celestial Marriages

Doing baptisms for the dead is a temple ordinance performed by living members of the Church for the names of those persons who died without having the opportunity here upon Earth to be baptized. Baptisms for the dead will be discussed in Reason 53.

Washings, Anointings, and Endowments are completed by the members of the Church for themselves one single time, and then in behalf of a dead individual all subsequent times thereafter. A member of the Church can go to the temple as many times as they like, if they are worthy and have a temple recommend (after they have performed their own washings, anointings, and endowment) and do the same temple work for different persons who have died. Endowments for the dead will be discussed in Reason 54.

The sealings performed in the temple are to seal husbands and wives together for time and all eternity, which is part of the Celestial Marriage and also to seal children to their parents for eternity. Celestial marriages are performed only in the temple. The husband and wife are married civilly and further sealed to each other for time and all eternity. These ordinances are also performed for both the living and for the dead, and will be discussed in Reason 55.

Joseph Smith and the early saints were commanded to build temples so that they could perform these temple ordinances. In *D&C*, 124:39–40, it states:

> Therefore, verily I say unto you, that your anointings, and your washings, and your baptisms for the dead, and your solemn assemblies, and your memorials for your sacrifices by the sons of Levi, and for your oracles in your most holy places wherein you receive conversations, and your statutes and judgments, for the beginning of the revelations and foundation of Zion, and for the glory, honor, and endowment of all her municipals, are ordained by the ordinance of my holy house, which my people are always commanded to build unto my holy name. And verily I say unto you, let this house be built unto my name, that I may reveal mine ordinances therein unto my people.

The early Mormons built a temple in Kirtland, Ohio, planned to build a temple in Independence, Missouri, and built a temple in Nauvoo, Illinois. When the Mormons arrived in Salt Lake City, Utah in 1847, they immediately dedicated a plot of land upon which to build a temple, which was finished many years later. The Mormons continued to build temples in Utah. As the Church expanded, so did the building of temples. Today, the Mormon Church has more than 150 temples built or planned to be built throughout the world, where temple work can be performed.

Anyone who has seen a Mormon temple and toured the inside before it has been dedicated knows that no expense is spared to give each temple an outstanding view and presentation. Millions of dollars are spent to build each temple since the temples are the "Houses of God" and should be built with only the best results possible.

I have never had a testimony of temples or temple work. In fact, to try and obtain a testimony, I became a temple worker in the Jordan River Temple in Salt Lake County, Utah for almost a year and faithfully served every week at the veil in the temple. To my disappointment, I still never obtained a testimony of temples or temple work. It has always seemed to me to be a fantastic waste of money to build such a building and to build so many temples, when the ordinances performed therein could be performed in the other church structures and meeting chapels constructed by the Mormon Church. Further, it seems that all of the temple ordinances performed for the dead could be done in one day by just performing one baptism for all those that have died upon Earth or that will die and not have a chance to be baptized. Likewise, we could perform just one washing, anointing, endowment, sealing, and celestial marriage for all those that have died or will die that haven't or won't have the opportunity to do the ordinances themselves.

Would God require all of this enormous effort, time, and money in building temples and doing temple work, rather than using the same to alleviate the hunger and suffering of the living in the world?

REASON 50
THE TEMPLE CREATION CEREMONY INCONSISTENCIES

When a member of the Mormon Church goes to the temple to perform their own endowment or do an endowment for a person who has died, they participate in the endowment session. At the beginning of the session, it tells the story of the creation of the Earth and of the fall of Adam and Eve. The entire temple ceremony has been recorded on the Internet and is available to anyone who wants to look it up, although members of the Mormon Church take a vow of secrecy during the temple ceremony to not divulge what goes inside. The penalties for divulging various aspects of the temple ceremony are discussed in Reason 52.

The following is taken from the first part of the Endowment Ceremony that discusses the creation of the earth as indicated in the article, "Comparison between the pre and post 1990 [Mormon Temple Endowment] versions."

> Brethren and sisters, as you sit here, you will hear the voices of three persons who represent Elohim, Jehovah, and Michael. Elohim will command Jehovah and Michael to go down and organize a world. The work of the six creative periods will be represented. They will also organize man in their own likeness and image, male and female. [Elohim is God, the Eternal Father, Jehovah is Jesus Christ, and Michael is Adam.]
>
> **THE CREATION – FIRST DAY**
>
> **ELOHIM**: Jehovah, Michael, see: yonder is matter unorganized, go ye down and organize it into a world like unto the worlds that we have hereunto formed. Call your labors the First Day, and bring me word.
>
> **JEHOVAH**: It shall be done Elohim. Come Michael, let us go down.

MICHAEL: We will go down, Jehovah.

JEHOVAH: Michael, see: here is matter unorganized. We will organize it into a world like unto worlds that we have heretofore formed. We will call our labors the First Day, and return and report.

...

SECOND DAY

ELOHIM: Jehovah, Michael, go down again. Gather the waters together and cause the dry land to appear. The great waters call ye seas, and the dry land call ye earth. Form mountains and hills, great rivers and small streams, to beautify and give variety to the face of the earth. When you have done this, call your labors the Second Day, [and] bring me word.

JEHOVAH: It shall be done, Elohim. Come Michael, let us go down.

MICHAEL: We will go down, Jehovah.

JEHOVAH: Michael, we will gather the waters together and cause the dry land to appear. The great waters we will call seas, and the dry land we will call earth. We will form mountains and hills, great rivers and small streams to beautify and give variety to the face of the earth. We will call our labors the Second Day, and return and report.

...

THIRD DAY

ELOHIM: Jehovah, Michael, return again to the earth that you have organized. Divide the light from the darkness. Call the light "day", and the darkness "night." Cause the lights [i]n the firmament to appear; the greater light to rule the day, and the lesser light to rule the night. Cause the stars also to appear and give light to the earth, the same as with other worlds heretofore created. Call your labors the Third Day, and bring me word.

JEHOVAH: It shall be done, Elohim. Come Michael, let us return again to the earth that we have organized.

MICHAEL: We will return, Jehovah.

JEHOVAH: Michael, we will divide the light from the darkness, and we will call the light "day," and the darkness "night." We will cause the lights in the firmament to appear, the greater to rule the day, and the lesser to rule the night. We will cause the stars also to appear and give light to the earth; the same as with other worlds heretofore created. We will call our labors the Third Day, and return and report.

…

FOURTH DAY

ELOHIM: Jehovah, Michael, return and place seeds of all kinds in the earth that they may spring forth as grass, flowers, shrubbery, trees, and all manner of vegetation; each bearing seed in itself after its own kind. Call your labors the Fourth day, and bring me word.

JEHOVAH: It shall be done, Elohim. Come Michael, let us go down.

MICHAEL: We will go down, Jehovah.

JEHOVAH: Michael, we will place seeds of all kinds in the earth that they may spring forth as grass flowers, shrubbery, trees, and all manner of vegetation. We will call our labors the Fourth Day, and return and report.

…

FIFTH DAY

ELOHIM: Jehovah, Michael, now that the earth is formed, divided and beautified, and vegetation is growing thereon, return and place beasts upon the land: the elephant, the lion, the tiger, the bear, the horse, and all other kinds of animals; fowls in the air in all their varieties, fishes of all kinds in the waters, and insects and all manner of animal life upon the earth. Command the beasts, the fowls, the fishes, the insects, all creeping things, and other forms of animal life to multiply in their respective elements, each after its kind, and every kind of vegetation to multiply it its sphere, that every form of life may fill the measure of its creation, and have joy therein. Call your labors the Fifth Day, and bring me word.

JEHOVAH: It shall be done, Elohim. Come Michael, let us go down.

MICHAEL: We will go down, Jehovah.

JEHOVAH: Michael, now that the earth is formed, divided and beautified, and vegetation is growing thereon, we will place all beasts upon the land: the elephant, the lion, the tiger, the bear, the horse, and all other kinds of animals; fowls in the air in all their varieties, fishes of all kinds in the waters, and insects and all manner of animal life upon the earth. We will command the beasts, the fowls, the fishes, the insects, all creeping things, and other forms of animal life to multiply in their respective elements, each after its kind, and every kind of vegetation to multiply in its sphere, that every form of life may fill the measure of its creation, and have joy therein. We will call our labors the Fifth Day, and return and report.

...

SIXTH DAY

ELOHIM: Jehovah, Michael, is man found upon the earth?

JEHOVAH: Man is not found on the earth, Elohim.

ELOHIM: Jehovah, Michael, let us go down and form man in our own likeness and in our own image, male and female, and put into them their spirits, and let us give them dominion over all things on the face of the earth. We will plant for them a garden, eastward in Eden, and place them in it to tend and cultivate it, that they may be happy, and have joy therein. We will command them to multiply and replenish the earth, that they may have joy in their prosperity. We will place before them the Tree of Knowledge of Good and Evil, and we will allow Lucifer, our common enemy, whom we have thrust out to tempt them, and to try them, that they may know by their own experience the good from the evil. If they yield to temptation we will give unto them The Law of Sacrifice, and we will provide a savior for them, as we counseled in the beginning, that they may be brought forth by the power of the redemption and the resurrection, and come again into our presence, and with us partake of Eternal Life and exultation. We will call this the sixth day, and we will rest from our labors for a season. Come, let us go down.

The problems here lie in the differences between this temple ceremony story of the creation and the story told twice in the *Pearl of Great Price* found in Moses, Chapter 2 and Abraham, Chapter 4. In Moses, almost everything was completed by God. In Abraham, it was "the Gods" who accomplished everything. In the temple ceremony, it was Elohim telling Jehovah and Michael to perform the creation. Why would God give to his prophet Joseph Smith three different accounts of the creation and make them different, and thus confusing and complicated? Moreover, an even greater problem is why God didn't simplify the explanation of the creation in the temple ceremony in the endowment, as He required it to be kept secret.

REASON 51
PROBLEMS WITH TEMPLE SIGNS AND TOKENS

It seems incredible to me that God would require us to learn and memorize various signs and tokens as a requirement to being able to pass the Angels and to enter into the Celestial Kingdom after we die. Nevertheless, this is exactly what is taught in the temple ceremony of the Mormon Church. During the endowment ceremony in the temple, participants are required to receive and demonstrate various signs and tokens that are associated with the Aaronic and Melchizedek Priesthoods. The tokens are different handclasps and the signs are made by different positions of the arms and hands. They are given and demonstrated twice in the endowment ceremony, and are a prerequisite for entering into the Celestial Room in the temple after the Endowment Ceremony is completed. This is supposed to be indicative of what will occur after we die, previous to our entrance into the Celestial Kingdom.

My question is "Why are these even necessary at all?" Whether we obtain the Celestial Kingdom or not should depend entirely on what kind of life we live, and not also depend upon whether we can remember various hand and arm signals ("signs and tokens"). When I was working at the veil in the temple, my responsibility was to make sure those persons who were being presented at the veil really knew the signs and knew the tokens. Most did not and had to be helped by the temple worker on the other side of the veil. If people cannot even remember the tokens that they were given within the hour prior to arriving at the veil, then how are they going to remember them after they die? They won't, and will have to be helped just like at the temple! Therefore, it really doesn't make any sense to me to place such emphasis on these signs and tokens. God knows that most of us will forget them and have to be reminded after we die and are presented at the Celestial Kingdom if we are worthy enough to even get there. Further, some signs given and demonstrated in the temple ceremony are not required at the veil; however, the names associated with the signs and tokens are.

The bottom line is that the rituals within the temple ceremony, as well as the temple ceremony itself, seem to be only worthwhile for members of the Mormon Church while they are participating in the temple ceremony and really seem to have nothing to do with what occurs after we die. Therefore, all of this should not be relevant as to where we end up after we die. Only how we live our lives should be relevant. A just God would only require us to be involved in relevant acts and not those that are confined to Mormon temples—and to such a small percentage of God's spiritual children here upon the earth.

REASON 52
TAKING ONE'S LIFE

In 1984, in Orem, Utah, two brothers, Ron and Dan Lafferty, brutally murdered and killed their brother's wife and her child. It was March of that year that

> Ron recorded on a yellow legal pad what would come to be known as "the removal revelation." He later shared it with [a group he helped create called] the School of the Prophets, to the alarm of its members.
>
> "Thus saith the Lord unto my servants the prophets," Ron wrote. "It is my will and commandment that ye remove the following individuals in order that my work might go forward. For they have truly become obstacles in my path and I will not allow my work to be stopped. First thy brother's wife Brenda and her baby [Erica], then Chloe Low and then Richard Stowe. And it is my will that they be removed in rapid succession."
>
> On the afternoon of July 24, 1984, Ron, 42, and Dan, 36, set out to fulfill the revelation. In a battered green station wagon, they drove to [their brother,] Allen [and his wife] Brenda's, American Fork duplex, carrying with them a sawed-off shotgun, a .30-30 Winchester, a .270 deer rifle, and two pearl-handled knives. They would [end up only using] the knives.
>
> ...Dan said he and his brother were led by God to beat Brenda unconscious, wrap a vacuum cord around her neck until she went limp, and then slit her throat. She was 24.
>
> "I held Brenda's hair and did it pretty much the way they did it in the scriptures," he says proudly. "Then I walked in Erica's room. I talked to her for a minute, I said, 'I'm not sure why I'm supposed to do this, but I

guess God wants you home.'" He then looked away as he slit the 15-month-old baby's throat (Hyde, "1984").

This tragic event was the basis for a book, *Under the Banner of Heaven: A Story of Violent Faith* by best-selling author Jon Krakauer, first published in July 2003, and one that may become a movie.

In the Mormon temple ceremony prior to 1990, members were asked to demonstrate the penalties that would occur to them if they disclosed certain names, signs, and tokens given to them.

> Originally, the penalties included graphic descriptions of the particular ways one's life would be taken in punishment for violating the covenants of non-disclosure. (The same is true of Masonic ritual.) These graphic descriptions were replaced in the 1920s with a generic statement that rather than reveal the signs, tokens, and keywords, an initiate "would suffer my life to be taken." Note that this revision actually shifts the nature of the penalty: instead of a violent punishment falling upon those who disclose secret knowledge, the penalty becomes an affirmation that one will preserve the secret *despite* threats of violence.
>
> All penalties were omitted in the 1990 revision. Elohim still impresses upon initiates the sacred nature of the signs, tokens, and keywords, but without using the word "secrecy"; and initiates still covenant never to disclose them, but no longer at the peril of their lives ("The Garden").

One of the penalties demonstrated during the temple ceremony prior to 1990 on how one's life could be taken was slitting ones throat from ear to ear. It is interesting to me that this part of the temple ceremony, the penalties, were removed after all of the information came out in the Lafferty murders in regard to how the two victims throats were cut and the statement by them that they "did it pretty much the way they did it in the scriptures."

What has troubled me the most though is the fact that when I went through the temple ceremony for the first time in 1966, I was shocked that we were required to demonstrate different ways that our lives could be taken as threats for disclosing what we were being told and shown. Furthermore, that we agreed that if we disclosed the forbidden, "we would suffer our lives to be taken." It seemed so archaic and gruesome at the time. Over the past fifty (50) years, it has become even more so. God would not require our lives to be taken for disclosing something that God knew would eventually be on the Internet for all to view.

REASON 53
BAPTISMS FOR THE DEAD QUESTIONS

Baptisms for the dead are mentioned in the New Testament, 1 Corinthians 15:29 and in more detail in the *D&C*, 124:28–36. Surprisingly, they are missing from the *Book of Mormon*, even though the *BOM* was to restore truths lost in the Bible. Another interesting point is that nowhere in the *Book of Mormon* does it mention baptism for the dead. In fact, it seems to support the opposite position—that those persons living on the Earth who never hear of the laws of God, as stated in the Bible and *BOM*, do not need baptism, for they are just like little children. In Moroni 8:22, it states:

> For behold that all little children are alive in Christ and also all they that are without the law. For the power of redemption cometh on all them that have no law; wherefore, he that is not condemned, or he that is under no condemnation, cannot repent; and unto such baptism availeth nothing.

Recently, the Mormon Church received a lot of criticism for members baptizing persons that died in the Holocaust during World War II. In an article written by Bernard I. Kouchel in 2008, titled "Mormons Hijack Dead or Alive Jewish Souls," we read the following:

> The Church of Jesus Christ of Latter-day Saints (often referred to as the LDS or Mormons) has spent millions of dollars microfilming, indexing and cataloging nearly every document known to man from every country on earth—including millions of Jewish records. Church members are encouraged to find the names of ancestors to baptize by proxy, which they believe gives the dead the opportunity to embrace the faith in the afterlife. They say that those who are dead retain their identity and free will and therefore can either accept or reject the rites performed for them. A hands-on proxy baptism ceremony, called an ordinance, takes place in a Mormon temple, and

includes full immersion to wash away sins and commence church membership. It is supposedly performed, commentators say, for people who had believed in Christ, but had not had a chance to be baptized. To be baptized is to publicly acknowledge one's faith in Christ as Savior and Lord. Originally, the practice was reserved for ancestors of church members, but over the years[,] many other people have been baptized posthumously.

From the founding of their religion in 1830, Mormons have respected Judaism as a religion. Thus in 1994, Jews were outraged when it became known that members of LDS were posthumously baptizing Holocaust victims and other Jewish dead. Many followers of Judaism find the practice highly offensive, something akin to the forced baptism of Jews practiced for centuries in Europe during the Middle Ages. Some see the practice as an implicit bias, an act of intolerance.

A postscript reads:

> In a 1995 agreement, the Church agreed to limit their posthumous baptism practice of Jews—of all Jews, not just Holocaust victims—to only direct ancestors of Mormons. Instead of implementing promises made, the Church has engaged in a course of unfulfilled promises, a record of decisions adopted and then abandoned, and an apparent wish to undo what they have agreed to (Kouchel).

Then in February 2012, it was reported that:

> Mormon church leaders apologized to the family of Holocaust survivor and Jewish rights advocate Simon Wiesenthal after his parents were posthumously baptized, a controversial ritual that Mormons believe allows deceased people a way to the afterlife but offends members of many other religions. Wiesenthal died in 2005 after surviving the Nazi death camps and spending his life documenting Holocaust crimes and

hunting down perpetrators who remained at large. Jews are particularly offended by an attempt to alter the religion of Holocaust victims, who were murdered because of their religion, and the baptism of Holocaust survivors was supposed to have been barred by a 1995 agreement. Yet records indicate Wiesenthal's parents, Asher and Rosa Rapp Wiesenthal, were baptized in proxy ceremonies performed by Mormon Church members at temples in Arizona and Utah in late January (NewsOne Staff).

The whole concept of baptisms for the dead does not make sense to me. Consider that, according to *D&C*, 137:1, 5–8, Joseph Smith saw a vision of his brother, Alvin, (who had not been baptized while alive), in the Celestial Kingdom. These verses state:

> The heavens were opened upon us, and I beheld the celestial kingdom of God, and the glory thereof, ...And [I] marveled how it was that he [Alvin] had obtained an inheritance in that kingdom, seeing that he had departed this life before the Lord had set his hand to gather Israel the second time, and had not been baptized for the remission of sins. Thus came the voice of the Lord unto me, saying: All who have died without a knowledge of this gospel, who would have received it if they had been permitted to tarry, shall be heirs of the celestial kingdom of God. Also, all that shall die henceforth without a knowledge of it, who would have received it with all their hearts, shall be heirs of that kingdom.

Therefore, if God knows what is in the hearts of all those that have died or will die without being baptized and whether they will accept the gospel or not, what is the purpose of doing a baptism for them? Further, if one were to watch the baptisms for the dead being performed in a Mormon temple, they would be disappointed. The baptisms are done at such a fast pace that one has a hard time understanding the baptizer's words, or in knowing who it is they are being baptized for. They would conclude that it does not make sense at all, and would not support a belief in a God that required it.

REASON 54
ENDOWMENTS FOR THE DEAD CONFUSION

Like baptisms for the dead, endowments for the dead also do not seem necessary or applicable for a God with all knowledge. As mentioned in the previous Reason, Joseph Smith saw his un-baptized deceased brother, Alvin, in the Celestial Kingdom, because God knew what was in Alvin's heart. This makes the endowment ceremony for Alvin and everyone else who has died, an unnecessary waste of time.

Further, most of what is done in the temple ceremony by the participants is not applicable to someone that is dead. The first part of the ceremony concerns the washing and anointing of the physical body. Various parts of the physical body are washed and then anointed. Obviously, a person who has died does not have a physical body. Therefore, there is no reason to wash and anoint it, especially because we do not receive a perfect resurrected body until later; and, at that time, it will be perfect, without need of washing and anointing. After the washing and anointing, the participant is clothed in the garment of the Priesthood, which members are required to wear throughout their lives for an earthly protection. Again, there is no need for the garment after one has died.

Then in the endowment ceremony, the participants make numerous covenants with the Lord that can only be kept while a person is living. Promises are made to keep the law of chastity and to not have sex with anyone but your spouse. There is no need for this law of chastity during the time period after you die and before the resurrection, which hasn't occurred yet for most people who have died. This is because people who have died are only spirits and do not have a physical body with which to have sex, so it would appear that they cannot have sex anyway, so this promise would not be applicable.

Participants also promise to keep the Law of Sacrifice, which is to sacrifice all that we posses in our earthly lives to sustain the Kingdom of God upon earth. Again, this would be impossible for someone who is dead. Another promise made in the temple is known as the Law of Consecration, where members agree to consecrate all of their earthly time, talents, and assets, if asked, to the Mormon Church.

Again, once someone is dead, they do not have any earthly possessions or assets to give to the Church.

The penalties for disclosing the sacred parts of the ceremony when used were only concerned with how one's earthly life could be taken. Once a person dies, there is no physical life to be taken; and one would not have the opportunity to disclose anything anyway. This part of the ceremony would be un-applicable and unnecessary for a dead person. In fact, the majority of the endowment ceremony for the dead is only applicable if they are living. Therefore, it is hard to believe that God would require endowments for dead persons who cannot even perform most of what is required in the endowment.

REASON 55
CELESTIAL MARRIAGE PROBLEMS

"Celestial marriage" for a Mormon is to be married in a Mormon temple and sealed for time and all eternity to their spouse. This is a specific requirement under Mormon doctrine to obtain the highest degree of the Celestial Kingdom and become a god. In *D&C*, 132:19–21 we read:

> And again, verily I say unto you, if a man marry a wife by my word, which is my law, and by the new and everlasting covenant, and it is sealed unto them by the Holy Spirit of promise, by him who is anointed, unto whom I have appointed this power and the keys of this priesthood; and it shall be said unto them—Ye shall come forth in the first resurrection…which glory shall be a fullness and a continuation of the seeds forever and ever. Then shall they be gods, because they have no end; … Then shall they be gods, because they have all power, and the angels are subject unto them. Verily, verily, I say unto you, except ye abide my law ye cannot attain to this glory.

Any other marriages upon Earth are not recognized by God and are of no effect or force after we die (*D&C*, 132:15–18). So, what happens to those who live righteous lives upon Earth and are married, but then die without having the opportunity to be married in the Mormon temple in a Celestial Marriage? Well, they can receive the blessings of celestial marriage through others here upon the Earth performing their marriages for them by proxy in the temple. Married members of the Mormon Church who have temple recommends can go to the temple, and in a sealing room, participate in doing sealings for the dead. The reason for doing Celestial Marriages for the dead, like doing baptisms for the dead, is based upon the Mormon belief that we cannot perform these ordinances in the hereafter. In *D&C*, 132:16, we read: "Therefore, when they are out of the world they neither marry nor are given in marriage; but are appointed angels in heaven." This is also stated in the New Testament in Matthew 22:30 which states: "For in the resurrection they neither marry, nor are given in marriage, but are as the angels of God in heaven." (This scripture was not changed by Joseph Smith in his *Inspired Translation* of the New Testament.)

The question that arises is, "What happens to those who do not have the opportunity to be married at all upon Earth?" Apparently, under Mormon doctrine, they can never achieve the highest degree of the Celestial Kingdom and become gods. One example is my niece, who was unfortunate to be born with Down syndrome and who will never marry upon Earth. According to Mormon doctrine, she does not get an opportunity to be married in the hereafter when she receives a perfect resurrected body, which seems unfair to me. The same can be said for all of the children who die before the age of accountability—who, under Mormon doctrine, are free from sin and automatically inherit the Celestial Kingdom. However, because they were not married upon Earth, they cannot become gods. They do not get the chance to be married and have eternal increase. At least nothing has been revealed to any Mormon prophet in answer to these issues.

One answer to the problem given by Mormon authorities is that we don't know and we must rely upon God to make all things right in the hereafter. I agree that God should treat everyone the same. Therefore, everyone should have an opportunity to be married in the hereafter, if they were denied that opportunity while living upon Earth. If that is the case, then there is no need for a temple marriage performed upon Earth for someone who has died, since God will allow it to be done after we die. Again, this is a confusing and ambiguous doctrine that should effect why we would believe in the Mormon God(s).

REASON 56
QUESTIONS ABOUT MORMON RITUALS

Not only the Mormon religion, but also most other Christian religions, require numerous rituals for their members to perform, such as baptism, the sacrament, confessions, tithing, and prayers. The Mormon religion adds the temple rituals of baptism for the dead, the endowment, and temple marriage. Almost all of these rituals are alleged to have originated from Jesus Christ and His Atonement, as recorded in the Bible, *Book of Mormon*, and other scriptures.

In the field of law, a legal analysis includes examining all of the facts and then applying the law to those facts to obtain a legal conclusion. However, sometimes even though the facts seem to fit into the applicable law, the conclusion does not seem to pass the smell test, or in other words, the conclusion just doesn't appear right. Sometimes this is called the common sense test, in that the conclusion just doesn't make sense.

Further, there is law of logic called Occam's razor, which "is a meta-theoretical principle that 'entities must not be multiplied beyond necessity' and the conclusion thereof, that the simplest solution is usually the correct one." These two suggestions, or laws of logic and common sense, may be applied to some of the problems discussed below about the Mormon's beliefs in the various rituals alleged to have been established by God.

Baptism, which is required by most Christian religions—with some requiring total immersion in water like the Mormon religion, and others requiring just sprinkling of water like the Catholic religion—is a ritual that just doesn't make sense. The Mormon doctrine teaches that children are sinless until they reach the age of accountability, which is around eight years old. Therefore, they do not need to be baptized until they reach that age. (See *Book of Mormon*, Moroni 8:5–11.)

However, according to the doctrines of the Mormon religion, baptism to those accountable is essential to being saved and inheriting the Celestial Kingdom to live with God. If one is not baptized, then that person is "damned" or denied the opportunity to live with God. *D&C*, 84:74 states:

> Verily, verily, I [the Lord] say unto you, they who believe not on your words, and are not baptized in water in my name, for the remission of their sins, that they may receive the Holy Ghost, shall be damned, and shall not come into my Father's kingdom where my Father and I am.

One may ask if the foregoing makes sense. Why would God prohibit a person who lived a remarkable life helping others and exhibiting love to all from living with God just because they were not baptized? This belief is not only held by the Mormon religion but also other Christian religions, including the Catholic religion. Why should it make any difference whether someone participates in the ritual of baptism or not if they live their life following the Golden Rule and helping others? The answer given by the Mormon religion and others is that baptism is necessary because God said it was, and it is an act by us that shows God that we believe and acknowledge our sins and our desire to have them removed from us. However, does the ritual of baptism by being immersed in water really have anything to do with washing away our sins and does it really come from God?

The ritual of baptism for the remission of sins (which appears to be a requirement for everyone except little children, whether living or dead, to enter into heaven to live with God) does not seem to be the simplest solution (Occam's law). If there is a punishment affixed to a sin, then the simplest solution is for the person that committed the sin to suffer the punishment. Of course, a person would need to repent of his sins or improve his actions. Otherwise, his sins would keep multiplying faster than he could suffer the punishments. Further, as mentioned above, God (who is omniscient and knows the beginning to the end) would know what is in a person's heart and whether that person's suffering would satisfy the demands of justice, so that person could live with God. This has been previously discussed in other Reasons relating to Joseph Smith's brother Alvin being in the Celestial Kingdom, even though not baptized.

The argument has been made that baptism is just an outward sign or act by someone to acknowledge that they accept Christ and covenant to keep his commandments, which is then reaffirmed every time that person partakes of the sacrament. However, as stated in many scriptures, including *D&C*, 112:29, a person who does not believe and is not baptized, is "damned." Therefore, baptism is more than just an outward sign or act. It is an essential requirement to keep one from being damned. Why would a rational and all-knowing God make this ritual such an essential requirement to keep one from being damned? Again, wouldn't what is in a person's heart and what kind of life they lived upon Earth be the essential requirements to keep from being damned?

The sacrament is another ritual in the Mormon religion. It is not to be partaken of by non-members. Only baptized members of the Mormon Church can partake of the sacrament, eat the bread in remembrance of Christ's body, and drink the water in remembrance of Christ's blood, and then only if they are worthy. In addition, in Mormon doctrine, a person recommits to keep Christ's commandments when they partake of the sacrament. Why can't anyone commit to keep Christ's commandments and remember his atoning sacrifice through what is in their heart and by their actions? What about the billions and billions of people who have lived upon Earth and who currently live upon Earth that do not have the opportunity to partake of the sacrament? Are they somehow less fortunate or denied God's blessings or influence in their lives?

Then there is the requirement to pay tithing to the Mormon Church of one-tenth of one's income. A friend of mine, who is a member of the Mormon Church, earned six figures of income and for many, many years. He paid his tithing of ten percent (10%) of his gross income to the Church, which is a requirement to obtain a temple recommend that allows you to go to the temple. However, one problem that bothered him was the fact that the Church spent millions and millions of dollars constructing new temples throughout the world, which my friend thought was a waste of money. Therefore, he quit paying tithing and began giving ten percent (10 %) of his gross income to high schools to be given to worthy students who couldn't afford to go to college. Should that friend be denied the Celestial Kingdom when his charitable contributions did more for mankind than the previous tithing that he paid?

Another troublesome ritual is that of confession. The Mormon doctrine requires an individual to confess his serious sins and wrongdoings to his Bishop so that appropriate actions can be taken. However, the action taken often varies, depending on the gender of the transgressor and upon the attitude of the Bishop. For example, another friend of mine who had sex outside of his marriage because his wife refused to have sex for over 10 years was excommunicated from the

Church. But another friend's wife who had sex outside of marriage even though her sexual life within the marriage was very good was not excommunicated and got her temple recommend back after only three months of probation because she was a very attractive lady and the Bishop was a very forgiving person.

The ritual of prayer is discussed in Reasons 1 and 2, but it seems that prayer is a personal ritual that can benefit anyone whether they believe in a god or not. Again, God knows what is in a person's heart and what kind of life they have lived upon Earth. Therefore, whether a person participates in any of these rituals or not shouldn't make a difference. If the Mormon God(s) require these rituals, then perhaps one shouldn't believe in the Mormon God(s).

REASON 57
ADAM AND EVE DISCREPANCIES

The book of Genesis in the Old Testament, the books of Moses and Abraham in the *Pearl of Great Price*, 1 and 2 Nephi in the *Book of Mormon*, *Doctrine and Covenants*, Section 29, and the LDS temple endowment ceremony all tell the story of Adam and Eve. Almost every Christian, Jew, and Muslim knows the story, as well as many others in other religions. Although the story differs somewhat in the different Mormon accounts, the main parts are quite similar:

God (or the Gods) creates Adam from the dust of the earth, breathes life into him to become the first man of all men, plants a garden (Eden) for him to dwell in, takes a rib from Adam to create Eve, then tells them not to eat from the Tree of Knowledge. Satan tempts Eve and she eats from the Tree of Knowledge. Adam eats too. They disobey God. Death enters the world and they are cast out. Mankind begins.

In the temple ceremony of the creation, we learned that Adam was Michael, who helped Jesus Christ in the creation of the world prior to his being created as a man upon Earth. We are also told that it was Eve who succumbed to the temptation of Satan and not Adam. Adam only partook of the fruit of the Tree of Knowledge so that he could continue to be with Eve and multiply and replenish the earth. This sounds sexist to me.

So what is wrong with this story? Is this really how God started mankind upon Earth? Actually, there are so many questions about the story that it is hard to know where to begin. The obvious question is how evolution and the existence of life and animals prior to Adam are explained when death did not come to earth until the fall of Adam, according to Mormon doctrine (see *PGP*, Moses 3:7). Some of that is discussed in other Reasons, so it will not be repeated here, where we will only discuss the actual story of Adam and Eve. If Adam was created out of the dust of the earth, why did God need a rib to create Eve? If Adam was Michael who helped Christ create the Earth prior to being born, who was Eve prior to being born and why didn't she participate in the creation? Was Adam more righteous than Eve? Is that why Satan approached Eve first to disobey God and eat the fruit? Why did God command them to "be fruitful, multiply, and replenish the earth" prior to them partaking of the forbidden fruit, when they did not have the capability of doing the same, since they were not as yet mortal and could not have children? Why did Adam have to name every living creature if they were created prior to his existence, apparently by God or the Gods, who would have already been familiar with them? The questions could go on and on; but the final question is, "Why should we believe this story as to how God created the Earth, or how mankind came into existence, when there is so much evidence and facts to the contrary (a lot of which I have seen at dinosaur quarries and museums)? Nevertheless, this is the belief of the Mormon Church and how the Mormon God or Gods created man.

   Some people ask the questions of where the women came from that married Cain and Abel and who were they? Mormon theology explains that Adam and Eve had other children prior to or at the same time as Cain and Abel, some of whom were girls! Therefore, Cain and Abel married their sisters. The problem of incest and of bad genes being passed on is supposedly explained away by accepting the fact that since Adam and Eve were the first persons, their physical bodies were perfect. Therefore, they had no bad genes to pass on, and if their sons married their daughters, there would not be a problem. However, many problems arise from the vast evidence upon Earth that Adam and Eve were not first, and that mankind is much older than just 6,000 years.

REASON 58
MANKIND'S LACK OF OPPORTUNITY TO HAVE THE GOSPEL

President Gordon B. Hinckley, 15th President of the Mormon Church, once estimated that there had been over seventy-five billion people born upon Earth ("Chapter 6"). According to Nathan Keyfitz's calculations, there have been over ninety-six billion people who have lived on Earth (Ramsey).

If we accept the Old Testament, the *Book of Mormon*, and Joseph Smith's revelations as true and accurate records of when the Gospel of Jesus Christ was upon Earth, then less than ten percent of the people who have lived upon Earth have had access to said Gospel. Again, this seems to be extremely discriminatory to over 90 percent (90%) of God's children, because the core teaching of Christians is that a belief in Christ and following His Gospel brings happiness. If a person on Earth does not have said Gospel available, then they are denied that happiness.

Further, there is no historical record other than the Bible and the *Book of Mormon* that indicates that the Gospel of Jesus Christ was available to any culture or people prior to the life of Christ, except the few chosen people of Israel. In addition, the teachings of the prophets in the Old Testament were apparently only available to chosen Israelites who received the teachings from their prophets. What about the millions of people who lived in the areas that today are known as Europe, Asia (including Russia and China), Australia and the Pacific Islands, India and the Near East, and other areas not in the Middle East? These were the various regions of the earth prior to Christ that obviously did not have the teachings of the Old Testament or those of Christ. None of these people had prophets who received revelations from God giving them the teachings that would bring them the happiness promised by the Old and New Testaments. Why wouldn't a universal God speak to "all" of his children upon Earth and give them His word or teachings?

Because we have no record of the Gospel of Jesus Christ being taught to anyone else, we can assume that all of the peoples of China, Russia, India, and most of the rest of the world, for the last 6,000 years, have had no communications from the God in whom members of the

Mormon Church have been taught to believe. Why have all of these nations and their people been discriminated against? When a friend of mine asked a son of one of the members of the First Presidency of the LDS Church this same question, the answer he received was that they were not the valiant or righteous spirit children in the pre-existence when they lived with God. Therefore, they were not blessed to be born in a time or place where they would have the Gospel of Jesus Christ. This is the same answer many members of the Mormon Church have received numerous times throughout their lives from other scholarly members of the LDS Church.

However, this is hard to believe for the reason that we, as spirit children in the pre-existence (according to LDS doctrine) were not exposed to evil, because Satan had already been cast out and we continued to live within the influence of God. So how could we be more righteous or valiant? Those who were not valiant, one third of the spirit children of God, were also cast out with Satan; and the two-thirds that were left were the valiant ones. Would the real God discriminate against 90 percent of His spirit children by not allowing them to have His teachings (Gospel) that would allow them to have the greatest amount of happiness on Earth? Should we still believe in such a God?

REASON 59
LACK OF REVELATIONS SINCE JOSEPH SMITH

After the restoration of the Gospel of Jesus Christ through Joseph Smith and the beginning again of revelations from God or Jehovah, would God again cease revelations? The Mormon religion teaches that Joseph Smith and each president of the Mormon Church thereafter, were called as Prophets by the Lord, Jesus Christ and that the Lord spoke to them directly. Said revelations are contained in the *Doctrine and Covenants*. The *D&C* has 138 Sections. Approximately 108 of the Sections are revelations given to Joseph Smith, between 1828 and 1841, where the Lord (God or Jehovah, all the same entity) is speaking directly to Joseph Smith in the first person.

Some of these sections are extremely small and deal with issues that were not too relevant to the establishment of the Mormon Church. For example, Section 116 names a place in the State of Missouri where Adam will come to visit his people. Section 126, received in 1841, is only about Brigham Young being commended for his labors. Section 136 is a revelation where the Lord speaks to Brigham Young in 1847. The other twenty-nine sections of the *D&C* are visions, epistles, explanations, prayers, declarations, instructions, letters, minutes, and other miscellaneous statements. Furthermore, the Mormon religion teaches that all revelations in the *D&C* came from Jesus Christ and not from His Father, God/Elohim.

There are two Official Declarations at the end of the *Doctrine and Covenants*: the first in 1890, when the Mormon Church ended the sanctioning of polygamy; and the second in 1978, when the Mormon Church eliminated the ban against the blacks from holding the Priesthood. However, neither of the Official Declarations are direct words from the Lord where He is speaking to His Prophet, as were the 109 sections discussed above.

From the last written book of the New Testament (written sometime in the 1st century A.D.) until 1828, there are no recorded revelations from the Lord or God, where He is speaking to his Prophets (or anyone upon Earth), as recorded by any Christian Church. The Muslim religion believes that God (Allah) spoke to the Prophet Mohammed in approximately 700 A.D., as recorded in the

Qur'an, but nothing since then. Mormons believe God spoke to the Prophets in the *Book of Mormon* until 421 A.D.; but nothing has been revealed since then. Finally, from 1847 to the present, there have been no recorded revelations from the Lord, where He is speaking directly to his Prophets.

It is hard to believe in a God that only spoke to His alleged "Church" for a few years over the past two centuries and does not speak directly to them now. It is also hard to believe in a God who would speak directly to Joseph Smith about seemingly trivial matters, and then cease to speak to any Prophet after 1847 through the present, when there have been so many substantial issues and matters. For example, why didn't God speak to the prophets of the Mormon Church during World War I or II, or during other world conflicts, when mass atrocities were taking place? In the Bible and the *Book of Mormon* there are numerous instances where Jehovah warned the prophets about what was going to occur, such as the Great Flood, Sodom and Gomorrah, the Passover, Lehi leaving Jerusalem, etc. Why wouldn't God warn the prophets about the Holocaust or the other mass murders we have witnessed throughout the world? It seems acceptable to believe that God would continuously manifest Himself to His children upon Earth from the beginning to the end and not be an absentee God.

REASON 60
PROBLEMS WITH THE
PEARL OF GREAT PRICE GOD

According to Mormon theology, the God in the *Pearl of Great Price* is also Jesus Christ, before he was born in the flesh upon Earth. In *Mormon Doctrine* by Bruce R. McConkie, page 392, it states:

> Christ is *Jehovah*; they are one and the same Person. ...the God of Israel...revealed himself to Moses and others...[and] to Joseph Smith and Oliver Cowdery.

However, this concept is confusing when reading the *PGP*. For example, in Moses 1:1–3, it states:

> The words of God, which he spake unto Moses at a time when Moses was caught up into an exceedingly high mountain, And he saw God face to face, and he talked with him, and the glory of God was upon Moses; therefore Moses could endure his presence. And God spake unto Moses, saying: Behold, I am the Lord God Almighty, and Endless is my name; for I am without beginning of days or end of years; and is not this endless?

Then in verse 6 we read:

> And I have a work for thee, Moses, my son; and thou art in the similitude of mine Only Begotten; and mine Only Begotten is and shall be the Savior, for he is full of grace and truth; but there is no God beside me, and all things are present with me, for I know them all.

It appears that God (pre-mortal Jesus Christ) talks to Moses about himself, but as a third person. This is somewhat confusing and continues to be confusing through the rest of the book of Moses in the *PGP*. It is further interesting to note that the God of the *PGP* (who Mormons believe is Jesus Christ, as stated above) is not really "without beginning of days." According to Mormon theology, Jesus Christ was the firstborn spirit of God the Eternal Father; therefore, Christ *did* have a beginning of days as a spirit.

Another problem with the God in the *PGP* is in Moses 1:33–35, where it states:

> And worlds without number have I created; and I also created them for mine own purpose; and by the Son I created them, which is mine Only Begotten. And the first man of all men have I called Adam, which is many. But only an account of this earth, and the inhabitants thereof, give I unto you. For behold, there are many worlds that have passed away by the word of my power. And there are many that now stand, and innumerable are they unto man; but all things are numbered unto me, for they are mine and I know them.

Again, God (pre-mortal Jesus Christ) is talking about two different beings, when in fact this God and Jesus Christ are the same being. In chapters 2 through 8 in Moses, the creation is described, as well as God's dealings with Adam down through Noah. Again, the God or Lord of the *Pearl of Great Price* talks about His Son as though He is talking about someone else and not Himself. This is very confusing, but resolved by some explaining that Jesus Christ speaks for both and as both.

The other problem is that there are "innumerable worlds" with innumerable people created by God through the Son; all after Jesus Christ was born as the first spirit child of God the Eternal Father. Because Satan was most likely the second born (see Abraham 3:28), then he would also be the Satan of all these other innumerable worlds and people that were also apparently spirit children of God the Eternal Father. Then we have the one third of the spirits of God the Eternal Father who followed Satan and which apparently would number more than we can comprehend. This seems to make the God of the *Pearl of Great Price* not only confusing, but incomprehensible.

The confusion continues in the Book of Abraham. Here God, or the Lord, speaks to Abraham face-to-face and identifies himself as "Jehovah or the Lord" (see 1:16 and 3:11). We know as Mormons that Jehovah (or the Lord) is in fact Jesus Christ and, with the help of Michael/Adam, under the direction of God/the Eternal Father, created this earth and many others, as is described in the Book of Abraham.

These three are the "Gods" mentioned in chapter 4. However, what is confusing is that "God" and the "Lord" seem to be the same entity and not two different entities. For example, in 3:19 it states:

> And the Lord said unto me: These two facts do exist, that there are two spirits, one being more intelligent than the other; there shall be another more intelligent than they; I am the Lord thy God, I am more intelligent than they all.

Therefore, who is more intelligent that they all, God the Eternal Father or Jesus Christ? Then in verse 27 it states:

> And the Lord said: Whom shall I send? And one answered like unto the Son of Man: Here am I, send me. And another answered and said: Here am I, send me. And the Lord said: I will send the first.

Therefore, The Lord basically is talking to himself and about himself and is sending himself. This is really confusing and lacks the clarity that a loving God would convey and what we would need to help us believe in such a God or Gods.

REASON 61
THE BOOK OF ABRAHAM PROBLEMS

On July 3, 1835, the Prophet Joseph Smith recorded the following, as found in the *HC,* 2:235–36:

> Michael A. Chandler came to Kirtland to exhibit some Egyptian mummies. There were four human figures, together with some two or more rolls of papyrus covered with hieroglyphic figures and devices.

Then on July 5, 1835 the following was recorded:

> Soon after this, some of the Saints at Kirtland purchased the mummies and papyrus, a description of which will appear hereafter, and with W. W. Phelps and Oliver Cowdery as scribes, I commenced the translation of some of the characters or hieroglyphics, and much to our joy found that one of the rolls contained the writings of Abraham, another the writings of Joseph of Egypt.

Joseph Smith translated some of the papyri and published it. It is found as the Book of Abraham in the *Pearl of Great Price*, and is considered by the Mormon Church to be the word of God and scripture. However, a careful reading of the Book of Abraham raises a lot of questions about its authenticity and truthfulness. One problem has already been discussed in a Reason 25 in regard to the reference in the Book of Abraham that there were numerous Gods involved in the creation of the earth. Another problem is the differences between Abraham's rendition of the creation and the chronology of events as it is compared to the creation in the Book of Moses, which is also contained in the *Pearl of Great Price*. If both are revelations from God, then it would be fair to assume that they should be somewhat identical, which they are not. It is also interesting to note that Joseph Smith's *Inspired Translation* of the Book of Genesis in the Old Testament corresponds more with the Book of Moses in the *Pearl of Great Price* than it does with the Book of Abraham.

Another question raised in the Book of Abraham is God's violation of one of His own Ten Commandments. In previous Reasons, we have discussed God ignoring the commandment not to kill. In the Book of Abraham, God also ignores the commandment not to tell a lie. In Abraham 2:22–25, the Lord told Abraham to lie to the Egyptians so that they would believe that Abraham's wife, Sarai, was in fact his sister.

An additional question arises in Abraham 1:21–27, where it indicates that because the Pharaoh was a descendant of Ham and therefore cursed, he could not have the Priesthood. The curse upon the black race and not being allowed to hold the Priesthood is discussed in greater detail in Reason 63. However, the Pharaoh and his descendants were not of the black race, as verified by all of the pictures and murals found in the various tombs of the Pharaohs. So why is this discrepancy or contradiction in the scriptures? Is the curse of Cain through his descendant Ham of not being allowed to hold the Priesthood also upon all white descendants of the Pharaohs, as well as the black race from Africa? These problems or questions evolving from the Book of Abraham add to the dilemma of whether one should believe in the Mormon God or plural Gods, as described in the Book of Abraham.

REASON 62
INCORRECT TRANSLATION OF PAPYRI

The real dispute as to the authenticity of the Book of Abraham (in the *Pearl of Great Price*) didn't begin until the original papyri thought to have been destroyed in the Chicago fire, was discovered in 1976 in the Metropolitan Museum of Art in New York City. It has since been examined by scholars as to the veracity of Joseph Smith's translation of the Egyptian hieroglyphics. One of the best books written on this subject is titled *By His Own Hand Upon Papyrus*, by Charles M. Larson, published in 1985. In his book, Mr. Larson has pictures of the exact Book of Abraham Papyrus Scroll and the un-translated Book of Joseph Papyrus Scroll, both of which came from those found at the Metropolitan Museum. It is the Book of Abraham Papyrus Scroll that Joseph Smith translated, but the Book of Joseph Papyrus was not translated, even though Joseph Smith indicated that he would translate it. (See *HC*, 2:350.)

Mr. Larson makes an interesting point when he asks why the current prophet, seer, and revelator of the Mormon Church hasn't translated the Book of Joseph Papyrus now that it is available again and has been identified as the same papyrus that Joseph Smith identified as the Book of Joseph? In fact, in 1966, Bruce R. McConkie (a General Authority of the Mormon Church) wrote the following in *Mormon Doctrine* on page 97: "But the day shall come when the Book of Joseph shall be restored and its contents shall be known again." Why not in 1967, when the papyrus was re-discovered, or some time since then?

I recommend, to those interested, reading Mr. Larson's book. Here I am only going to state some of his conclusions found on pages 173–75, which are as follows:

> Based on comparisons of the Metropolitan papyri to every available resource, including descriptions contemporary with Joseph Smith of the so-called Abraham and Joseph scrolls, as well as to a number of original translation manuscripts and other notes of the time, the papyrus scroll Joseph Smith represented as containing "the writings of Abraham" was shown to be merely a common pagan funeral papyrus of late date

known as the Book of Breathings. The scroll thought to contain "the writings of Joseph in Egypt" was also indentified as a typical late copy of the Egyptian Book of the Dead. ...Neither scroll ever had anything to do with the biblical patriarchs Abraham or Joseph, except in the mind of Joseph Smith.

...The Book of Breathings scroll that Joseph Smith represented as being the Book of Abraham was prepared between about 50 BC and AD 50 in Thebes for a man named Hor, who was a priest, or purifier, to the Egyptian god Amon at Karnak. It was written in hieratic script, a cursive adaptation of hieroglyphic writing that first appeared around 600 BC—at least a dozen centuries too late to have been used by Abraham.

...Not a single word, thought, or concept from Joseph's Smith's Book of Abraham, including his explanations of his three facsimiles, is in any way related to the subject matter of the common Egyptian funeral texts from which they were supposedly translated.

Further, from The Full Wiki, on the topic of the "Book of Abraham" we read:

Criticism and response

The arguments concerning the Book of Abraham primarily concern the source of the text of the Book of Abraham, Joseph Smith's method of interpretation and his explanations of the meanings of the vignettes. Currently there is little argument concerning the transliteration of the Egyptian writing on the fragments, as evidenced by the broad agreement in the translations by LDS and non LDS Egyptologists. Critics primarily use inerrancy and identification of texts as their primary arguments against the Book of Abraham's authenticity;

- Transliterated text from the recovered papyri and facsimiles published in the Book of Abraham

contain no direct references, either historical or textual, to Abraham. Rather, they parallel other texts from the Egyptian Book of the Dead and Book of Breathings.
- Abraham's name does not appear anywhere in the papyri or the facsimiles.
- Joseph Smith's explanation of the facsimiles and interpretation (as contained in the Book of Abraham text) does not parallel Egyptologists' transliterations or explanations of the text or images on the papyri.
- The Joseph Smith Papyri have been dated to the late Ptolemaic or early Roman period, 1500 years after Abraham's supposed lifetime. Critics feel this is relevant because of Joseph Smith's statement that the papyri were "written by [Abraham's] own hand upon papyrus."
- Anachronisms exist in the Book of Abraham, which indicate that it was not written in Abraham's time.
- The "Egyptian Alphabet and Grammar", also known as the "Kirtland Egyptian Papers", contain an arrangement of correlated characters from the papyri and text from the Book of Abraham that some critics suggest indicates that the Book of Abraham text came entirely from the existing papyrus fragments.

Critics further assert that the "Egyptian Alphabet and Grammar" indicates that Smith did attempt a direct, literal, comprehensive, translation. Critics interpret Smith's statements to mean that the Book of Abraham is a conventional translation of an original handwritten manuscript and not a revelation.

Defense of the book

A number of theories have been presented in defense of the official LDS Church position that the work is a revelation from God, through Joseph Smith, which tells a true story of actual events from the life of Abraham;

- Joseph Smith interpreted the documents by revelation, rather than a standard "translation" of text from one language to another, in a process similar to his translation of the Bible.
- The facsimiles in Egyptian funerary scrolls may have been a mnemonic device.
- The facsimiles were not penned by Abraham, but by a Jewish redactor many centuries later.
- The facsimiles represent a corrupted version of a document originally written by Abraham, with Joseph Smith giving the interpretation of the original document.
- There are other messages and meanings embedded in the text along with the Egyptologist's translations that are unknown to us, and could be where Joseph Smith found his message and interpretation.
- The papyri may be copies of an original which was written personally by Abraham.
- The remaining papyrus fragments are only part of the complete original papyri, or the fragments may have been a starting point for reconstruction. Critics argue that Facsimile No. 1 matches the vignette in the existing papyrus and that there is a direct textual reference to it in the Book of Abraham.

Why would God have his prophet Joseph Smith translate ancient papyrus when God knew that eventually scholars would discover the fraud? Moreover, why wouldn't God have a modern-day prophet, seer, and revelator translate the Book of Joseph papyri to silence the critics of the Book of Abraham? After careful study and analysis of the Book of Abraham in the *Pearl of Great Price* and the critic's concerns, I should be convinced that the Book of Abraham did not come from God, but was written by a brilliant man who had written other religious texts also, to wit: a man named Joseph Smith.

REASON 63
CHANGES FOR BLACKS
AND THE PRIESTHOOD

In the 1960's, when I was playing basketball and baseball at Brigham Young University, we did not have any black players at all on our teams. In fact, there were very few blacks even attending BYU. There was also a lot of civil unrest going on in the country, and we would experience some of it when we traveled to play in other states. At that time, the Mormon Church did not allow blacks to hold the Priesthood; therefore, they could not function in the Church in leadership positions or attend the temple to receive their endowments.

Discrimination against the black race of people was an extremely sore blemish on the Mormon Church. It was a stance that I and other members of our basketball and baseball teams did not agree with or support. The Mormon Church's position is based upon many revelations given to the Church, but some of the first are found in the *Pearl of Great Price*. In the Book of Moses, after Cain slew Abel, he was cursed by the Lord and "the Lord set a mark upon Cain" (Moses 5:40). Cain and his descendants became known as the Canaanites or people of Canaan. In Moses 7:8 and 22, it states:

> For behold, the Lord shall curse the land with much heat, and the barrenness thereof shall go forth forever; and there was a blackness came upon the children of Canaan, that they were despised among all people. ...And Enoch also beheld the residue of the people which were the sons of Adam; and they were a mixture of all the seed of Adam save it was the seed of Cain, for the seed of Cain were black, and had not place among them.

Then in the Book of Abraham, discussed in previous Reasons, we are told that the blacks cannot hold the Priesthood. In Abraham 1:21 and 27 we read:

> Now this King of Egypt was a descendant from the loins of Ham, and was a partaker of the blood of the Canaanites by birth. ...Now, Pharaoh being of that lineage by which he could not have the right of

Priesthood, notwithstanding the Pharaohs would fain claim it from Noah, through Ham, therefore my father was led away by their idolatry.

Joseph Smith's gave his view of the Negro race in the *HC*, 5:217, where he stated, "Elder Hyde inquired the situation of the negro. I replied, they came into the world slaves, mentally and physically." Then the second prophet and president of the Mormon Church, Brigham Young, in a speech he gave as the Governor of Utah in Joint Session of the Legislature on February 5, 1852, stated the following:

> What is that mark? you will see it on the countenance of every African you ever did see upon the face of the earth, or ever will see. Now I tell you what I know; when the mark was put upon Cain, Abels [*sic*] children was in all probability young; the Lord told Cain that he should not receive the blessings of the priesthood nor his seed, until the last of the posterity of Able [*sic*] had received the priesthood, until the redemption of the earth. If there never was a prophet, or apostle of Jesus Christ spoke it before, I tell you, this people that are commonly called negroes are the children of old Cain. I know they are, I know that they cannot bear rule in the priesthood, for the curse on them was to remain upon them, until the residue of the posterity of Michal [*sic*] and his wife receive the blessings, the seed of Cain would have received had they not been cursed; and hold the keys of the priesthood, until the times of the restitution shall come, and the curse be wiped off from the earth, and from Michals [*sic*] seed ("Brigham Young Address" 2).

So, from the 1830s until 1978, the Mormon God, through his prophets, denied African blacks the right to hold the Priesthood in the Mormon Church. Then God changed his mind and gave the black race the right to hold the Priesthood. President Spencer W. Kimball, the prophet of the Mormon Church in 1978, stated in a Declaration found at the end of the *Doctrine and Covenants* that "all worthy male members of the Church may be ordained to the Priesthood without regard for race or color." Finally, a sensible decision! Prior to that, it was hard to accept the position that the spirit children of God who were born into the black race were less valiant in the pre-existence and therefore were born black and without the same opportunities given to whites in the Mormon Church.

REASON 64
EXISTENCE OF KOLOB AND THE THRONE OF GOD

Another interesting discussion about God in the *Pearl of Great Price* is found in Abraham 3:1–4, where the Lord teaches Abraham about astrology and the stars that are closest to where God resides. Specifically, it states as follows:

> And I Abraham, had the Urim and Thummin [two special stones call seer stones given from time to time by the Lord to chosen prophets to be used in receiving revelations or translating ancient languages], which the Lord my God had given unto me, in Ur of the Chaldees; And I saw the stars, that they were very great, and that one of them was nearest unto the throne of God; and there were many great ones which were near unto it; And the Lord said unto me: These are the governing ones; and the name of the great one is Kolob, because it is near unto me, for I am the Lord thy God: I have set this one to govern all those which belong to the same order as that upon which thou standest. And the Lord said unto me, by the Urim and Thummim, that Kolob was after the manner of the Lord, according to its times and seasons in revolutions thereof; that one revolution was a day unto the Lord, after his manner of reckoning, it being one thousand years according to the time appointed unto that whereon thou standest. This is the reckoning of the Lord's time, according to the reckoning of Kolob.

This discussion goes on with a face-to-face conversation between Abraham and the Lord in Abraham 3:5–17. Below are only verses 10–11, 13, and 16:

> And it is given unto thee to know the set time of all the stars that are set to give light, until thou come near unto the throne of God. Thus I, Abraham, talked with the Lord, face to face, as one man talketh with another; and

he told me of the works which his hands had made; ...And he said unto me: This is Shinehah, which is the sun. And he said unto me: Kokob, which is star. And he said unto me: Olea, which is the moon. And he said unto me: Kokaubeam, which signifies stars, or all the great lights, which were in the firmament of heaven. ...If two things exist, and there be one above the other, there shall be greater things above them; therefore Kolob is the greatest of all the Kokaubeam that thou hast seen, because it is nearest unto me.

Apparently, the words "Shinehah," "Kokob," "Olea," "Kokaubeam," and "Kolob" have some significance in the Egyptian language, because the astrology lesson was given to Abraham so that he could declare the same to the people in Egypt when he went there (verse 15). Joseph Smith goes on to explain a "facsimile" from the Book of Abraham (No. 2). In the explanation found there, he states: "Fig. 1. Kolob, signifying the first creation, nearest to the celestial, or the residence of God." Can we take from this that Kolob was in fact God's first creation and is the closest object or planet to where God resides?

What I don't understand though is why God talks about Kolob rather than where God actually resides. Wouldn't it be a greater benefit to mankind to know and understand where God lives, rather than knowing about the planet *next to* God's home? Furthermore, it doesn't make sense why the comparison is made between the revolutions of Kolob being 1,000 years to Earth's one single day. Perhaps it is only to make the argument that the creation of the earth took 6,000 years rather than 6 days, so as to reconcile the creation story in Genesis, Moses, and the LDS temple endowment.

In visiting the Museum of the Rockies in Bozeman, Montana, I viewed a video on the cosmos made up of pictures taken from the Hubble telescope in outer space. It showed galaxies millions of light years away and stars many times larger than the sun, where a revolution around those stars would be greater than that of Kolob. If God created all of the stars in the Universe and all the infinite number of galaxies in the cosmos, then what did the Gods that existed before our God create?

Although this conversation on astrology between the Lord and Abraham is interesting, it seems to add to the confusion about the length of time for the creation of the heavens and the earth, and how at odds this is with the scientific facts that have been discovered about the Universe and the creation of the Earth. Moreover, why even mention Kolob as being near God's home and not reveal more about the actual throne of God?

REASON 65
GOD CREATING OTHER WORLDS WITHOUT NUMBER

In the *Pearl of Great Price*, Moses 1:33–35 we read:

> And worlds without number have I created; and I also created them for mine own purpose; and by the Son I created them, which is mine Only Begotten. And the first man of all men have I called Adam, which is many. But only an account of this earth and the inhabitants thereof, give I unto you. For behold, there are many worlds that have passed away by the word of my power. And there are many that now stand, and innumerable are they unto man; but all things are numbered unto me, for they are mine and I know them.

Then in Moses 7:29–30, the Lord is talking with Enoch about the remaining people upon the earth, after the Lord took the righteous people of the 'City of Enoch' into heaven. Enoch declares that the Lord "wept" and then Enoch said to the Lord:

> How is it that thou canst weep, seeing thou are holy, and from all eternity to all eternity? And were it possible that man could number the particles of the earth, yea, millions of earths like this, it would not be a beginning to the number of thy creations;

What is interesting about these passages of scripture are the enormous consequences created by their message. From them, we learn that "millions of earths" are only a small fraction of all of the earths like ours that God has created. Further, because all of the worlds without number were created by the Son, they would have been created after God, the Eternal Father had his first spiritual child, Jesus Christ, in the pre-existence. All of us are also spiritual children of God; but God must have had so many spiritual children that he needed to create "worlds without number" for them to populate even before this earth was created for us.

Although many worlds have "passed away," there are many other worlds or earths that now stand, and their existence may even parallel our earth's existence to some degree. Why is it such a secret as to what has transpired on these other earths, when that could be helpful and beneficial to our existence here upon this earth? In addition, because God created these "worlds without number" by his son, Jesus Christ, then is Christ also the God and Savior of those earths? This doesn't seem possible, because many of these other worlds have ceased to exist. Those spirit children who lived and died there would have been back in heaven before Jesus Christ even came to this earth to die, save mankind, and be resurrected.

Then there is the problem of the first "man of all men" being Adam, who was chosen to dwell upon our earth and not one of the "innumerable others." Apparently, Adam had to wait for many earths or worlds to pass away before our earth was created, so he could be born here. The other earths would have to have been populated by spirits that were born after Adam, because Adam was the first "man of all men." Apparently, Jesus Christ, although involved in creating all of the "innumerable others," also had to wait to come to our earth to be crucified and resurrected.

Why did Jesus Christ come to our earth and not to another? According to the verses in Moses 7:32–36, the people on this earth have been more wicked than the people on the other earths created and populated by God. Those verses state:

> The Lord said unto Enoch: Behold these thy brethren...in the day I created them; and in the Garden of Eden, gave I unto man his agency. ...but behold, they are without affection ... and in my hot displeasure will I send in the floods upon them. ...Behold, I am God; ...Wherefore, I can stretch forth mine hands and hold all the creations which I have made; and mine eye can pierce them also, and among all the workmanship of mine hands there has not been so great wickedness as among thy brethren.

Apparently, Jesus Christ was sent to our earth to perform the infinite and eternal atonement because we were the most wicked. That is not saying much about the people on this earth, when one considers that there are billions and billions of other earths with "centillion" of God's spirit children inhabiting them. However, why was Adam, the first "man of men" sent here as well? Further, why don't we know more about all of these other worlds and their inhabitants? Does all of this make sense? Or does it seem somewhat embellished by those writing the alleged scriptures? Does it create much of an incentive to believe in the Mormon God(s)?

REASON 66
GOD'S CENTILLION SPIRIT CHILDREN

As has been mentioned in previous Reasons, all of mankind born upon Earth are literal spirit children of God, the Eternal Father. It is estimated that there have been at least approximately eighty billion (80,000,000,000) people born upon this earth as of 2008. Therefore, based upon the War in Heaven and one third of God's spiritual children choosing not to stay with God and Jesus Christ, this would mean that there are a least another forty billion (40,000,000,000) spirit children of God the Father residing with Lucifer. Both of these numbers are obviously increasing each year that Earth remains in existence.

The LDS Church further teaches that God the Father has also created other worlds (innumerable to man) and inhabited those worlds with His spirit children (*PGP*, Moses 1:27–35, as stated in Reason 65). This would increase God the Father's spirit children that have dwelt upon earths or are currently dwelling upon other earths to an astronomical number and that would only be two-thirds of God's spiritual children, because one third would be the spirit children residing with Lucifer.

Further, in regard to these other worlds that are inhabited, in *D&C,* 76:22–24, we read:

> And now, after the many testimonies which have been given of him, this is the testimony, last of all, which we give of him: That he lives! For we saw him, even on the right hand of God; and we heard the voice bearing record that he is the Only Begotten of the Father—That by him, and through him, and of him, the worlds are and were created, and the inhabitants thereof are begotten sons and daughters of God.

This scripture also verifies the Mormon position that the "innumerable worlds," created by God through Jesus Christ, were populated by the spirit children created by God the Eternal Father. So how many spiritual children does God the Eternal Father have, taking into account not only the ones inhabiting all of the worlds, but the additional one third, who were cast out with Satan after the War in

Heaven? If you are just looking for a very large number, a googol is the number 1 followed by 100 zeroes. That is one of the largest numbers that actually has a name. A centillion (10^{103}) is the largest standard named number. If we assume then that there are at least a centillion other worlds, each with at least 80 billion spirit children of God (having dwelled thereon or dwelling thereon currently), and then add an additional one half of that number to represent the one third cast out with Satan, then the number of God's spirit children does in fact become "innumerable."

What makes this concept of centillion spirit children of God so hard to believe or even comprehend is that, according to the scriptures, each one of us is supposed to be important to God. He is supposed to be involved in our lives, such as hearing and answering prayers. How can one feel even a little significant in the eyes of God if one is less than a grain of sand on a beach of sand that extends beyond a comprehensible distance? Would it not be easier and of more comfort to believe in a God or Gods that are more connected to us than what is described above?

REASON 67
GOD'S FIRST BORN, SECOND BORN, ETC.

We have discussed the fact that Jesus Christ was the firstborn spirit child of God the Eternal Father, which is supported by numerous scriptures in all four of the "Standard Works," or books of scripture of the Mormon Church. Who was the second born? Some believe that it was Lucifer or Satan. In *D&C*, Section 76, Joseph Smith and Sidney Rigdon had a vision where they saw God and Jesus Christ and described the kingdoms or glories of heaven. They also saw Lucifer, as recorded in verses 25–27, where we read:

> And this we saw also, and bear record, that an angel of God was in authority in the presence of God, who rebelled against the Only Begotten Son whom the Father loved and who was in the bosom of the Father, was thrust down from the presence of God and the Son, And was called Perdition, for the heavens wept over him—he was Lucifer, a son of the morning. And we beheld, and lo, he is fallen! Is fallen, even a son of the morning!

Then in the *PGP*, Moses 4:1, we read:

> And I, the Lord God, spake unto Moses, saying: That Satan, whom thou has commanded in the name of mine Only Begotten, is the same which was from the beginning, and he came before me, saying—Behold, here am I, send me, I will be thy son, and I will redeem all mankind, that one soul shall not be lost, and surely I will do it; wherefore give me thine honor.

Bruce R. McConkie, in *Mormon Doctrine*, page 192, states: "The *devil*…is a spirit son of God who was born in the morning of pre-existence." It was Jesus Christ, the firstborn, and Lucifer (Satan), who presented plans to God, the Eternal Father in regard to our earth life. Therefore, if Satan was not the second born, he at least had an almost-equal status to Jesus Christ for God, the Eternal Father to even consider his plan of salvation.

Who the third, fourth, and so forth born as spirit children to God, the Eternal Father are, would only be speculation; but in Abraham 3:19, 22–23, we are told the following:

> And the Lord said unto me: These two facts do exist, that there are two spirits, one being more intelligent than the other; there shall be another more intelligent than they; I am the Lord thy God, I am more intelligent than they all. ...Now the Lord shown unto me, Abraham, the intelligences that were organized before the world was; and among all these there were many of the noble and great ones; And God saw these souls that they were good, and he stood in the midst of them, and he said: These I will make my rulers; for he stood among those that were spirits, and he saw that they were good; and he said unto me: Abraham, thou are one of them; thou wast chosen before thou wast born.

Apparently, there were different classes of intelligences and different classes of spirits in the pre-existence. Perhaps the spirits who were born first would have had more time to become a "noble and great one." The intelligences apparently were not created and have existed co-eternally with God. In *D&C*, 93:29, it states: "Man was also in the beginning with God. Intelligence, or the light of truth, was not created or made, neither indeed can be." Joseph Smith explained further:

> I am dwelling on the immortality of the spirit of man. Is it logical to say that the intelligence of spirits is immortal, and yet that it had a beginning? The intelligence of spirits had no beginning, neither will it have an end. ...There never was a time when there were not spirits; for they are co-equal (co-eternal) with our Father in Heaven (Smith, J. Fielding *Teachings* 353).

It is safe to conclude then that, in Mormon theology, all of the intelligences that have existed co-eternally with God were used by God when He created our spirits. Then our intelligences became part of our spirit, as children of God. One question would be how God decided which intelligence went with which spirit. However, based upon God's teaching, as stated above, certain spirits became "chosen spirits" in the pre-existence and therefore were chosen to be rulers upon Earth. Those spirits apparently had greater intelligences and were chosen as such by God. This leads us to our problem with the hierarchy of spirit children born to God in the pre-existence.

If we are not His rulers here upon Earth, then we can assume that we do not have chosen intelligences of spirits and are pre-destined to just be average spirits. Did the order in which we are born spiritually to God make a difference in where and when we came to Earth? If this is the case, then do we not have justification in blaming our co-eternal intelligence for our plight here upon Earth? Or blaming the order that God produced us as a spirit child of His? Perhaps then, we should reconsider whether we should believe in this kind of a God.

REASON 68
THE ABSENCE OF A HEAVENLY MOTHER

Absent from Mormon theology (and in fact, in all of the Christian religion's theologies) as to "God" or "the Godhead" is a Heavenly Mother. We don't know why. We do know, according to Mormon doctrine, that for us to become a God and have eternal increase of spirit children in the hereafter, a man has to be married to a woman in the Temple and be sealed for time and all eternity. *D&C*, 132:19–20 states:

> And again, verily I say unto you, if a man marry a wife by my word, which is my law, and by the new and everlasting covenant, and it is sealed unto them by the Holy Spirit of promise, by him who is anointed, unto whom I have appointed this power and the keys of this priesthood; and it shall be said unto them—Ye shall come forth in the first resurrection; …and shall inherit thrones, kingdoms, principalities and powers…to their exaltation and glory in all things, as hath been sealed upon their heads, which glory shall be a fullness and a continuation of the **_seeds_** forever and ever. Then shall they be gods, because they have no end; therefore shall they be from everlasting to everlasting, because they continue; then shall they be above all, because all things are subject unto them. Then shall they be gods, because they have all power, and the angels are subject unto them.

Based on this, there would be a Heavenly Mother for our spirit children if we become a God. Furthermore, as discussed in Reason 22, God the Eternal Father was once a man like us and became a God and had spiritual children. Therefore, it would probably be safe to assume that he had to abide by the same eternal laws (which included temple marriage) in order to become a God and have spirit children. In the Mormon Hymn Book, there is a hymn titled "O My Father," wherein one of the verses refers to the idea that truth and reason would suggest that we have a mother in heaven. But this is only one of a few places where this topic is even discussed.

The question would not be whether God, the Eternal Father has a wife and whether we have a Heavenly Mother or not, but whether He has more than one wife. Therefore, perhaps there is more than one Heavenly Mother and the centillion spirit children who were born to God have different mothers. If so, how many Heavenly Mothers would be needed to give birth to centillion spirit children?

In addition, it seems extremely sexist and inappropriate to exclude our Heavenly Mothers from involvement in our earthly existence. Our earthly mothers are the ones with whom we share our feelings and inadequacies and therefore it would seem logical for us to be praying to our Heavenly Mother or Mothers for help and assistance with our earthly problems.

Then, there is the absence of our Heavenly Mother in our creation and the creation of the Earth. In all of the scriptural references and the temple ceremony concerning the creation of the earth and mankind, there is no mention of our Heavenly Mother or her involvement. The only entities mentioned are male: to wit, God the Eternal Father (Elohim), Jesus Christ (Jehovah), and Michael (Adam). Wouldn't God reveal to us, his spirit children, the fact that we have a Heavenly Mother and that she is also involved in our earthly existence? But this is not the case!

REASON 69
WAR IN HEAVEN INCONSISTENCIES

In Reason 67, we discussed different classes of intelligences in the pre-existence, and some who were chosen to be rulers upon Earth. Continuing with Abraham 3:24–28 in the *Pearl of Great Price*, we read:

> And there stood one among them that was like unto God, he said unto those who were with him: We will go down, for there is space there, and we will take of these materials, and we will make an earth whereon these may dwell; And we will prove them herewith, to see if they will do all things whatsoever the Lord their God shall command them; And they who keep their first estate [the pre-existence (see Jude 1:6)] shall be added upon; and they who keep not their first estate shall not have glory in the same kingdom with those who keep their first estate; and they who keep their second estate [earth life] shall have glory added upon their heads for ever and ever. And the Lord said: Whom shall I send? And one answered like unto the Son of Man: Here am I, send me. And another answered and said: Here am I, send me. And the Lord said: I will send the first. And the second was angry, and kept not his first estate; and, at that day, many followed after him.

It is written in the Bible in Revelation 12:7–17, in the *BOM* in 2 Nephi 2:16–18, in the *D&C* in Section 29:36–38, and in the *PGP* in Moses 4:1–6, that there was a War in Heaven before the Earth was created. During the War in Heaven, Satan or Lucifer, who was also a spirit child of God, the Father (as was Jesus Christ) made a different proposal to the Father as to the plan for mankind upon Earth. To wit, Satan wanted the power and honor and Jesus Christ proposed that the glory be given to God, the Father forever. Based upon the different proposals, Satan was cast out of heaven and convinced one third of the hosts of heaven to go with him.

As was mentioned in Reason 66, the number of hosts of heaven who would have gone with Satan would have been astronomical, in the trillions or greater, depending on how many other earths that God, the Father created through Jesus Christ and inhabited them with his spirit children. (See *PGP*, Moses 1:31–42.) Therefore, to allow the expulsion of one third of your spirit children from your presence, and therefore deny them the opportunity to come to an earth, seems to be a huge mistake to me. It is hard to imagine that God would not have been more persuasive to His spirit children or more intuitive as to their spiritual needs so that He might have prevented such a large loss of his spirit children to the "dark side." The argument could be made that, even in the War in Heaven, all of God's spirit children had free agency, or the freedom to choose what they felt was the right choice. However, it is difficult to believe that an all-knowing and all-powerful God would make the mistake of not teaching His spirit children the ability to choose the path that would bring them the most happiness and progression.

If we as mortal parents on Earth lose one third of our children to the "dark side," we believe we have failed and made many mistakes that caused said result. In fact, we are commanded to teach our children correct principles so that when they grow up they won't depart therefrom. President David O. McKay, Prophet of the Mormon Church, made a statement that seemed to indicate that no success in life could compensate for failure in the home by not teaching your children.

One might argue that there had to be sin or evil upon the Earth so that mankind could be tested to see if they would follow God. Therefore, Satan needed to be cast out of heaven and given the power to tempt mankind and lead them astray. This doesn't quite make sense though, because one of the eternal laws is "opposition in all things" (2 Nephi 2:11–19 in the *BOM*). Therefore, good and evil have always been present, even in the pre-existence in the War in Heaven. Apparently, there was an opposition to the plan of Jesus Christ in the pre-existence, the one offered by Lucifer. Lucifer's plan was apparently an evil plan, because it resulted in the expulsion of Lucifer or Satan and of one third of God's children from God's presence. Therefore, there must have been an evil influence present there in order to influence Satan to rebel against God. The conclusion, that good and evil are eternal laws co-existing with God, seems to make sense.

Further, if God was perfect in the pre-existence and would have raised His spirit children perfectly, why did He not raise all of His spirit children with the desire to do good and resist evil, and therefore prevent losing one third of His spirit children? If God also knew everything, the beginning from the end, He would have known about the rebellion and the loss of his spirit children, just like he knew of the loss of millions to the flood at the time of Noah. Both of these events seem to be mistakes that cost the physical death of millions, but the spiritual death of centillions, because the spirits who were cast out can never obtain a physical body, nor will they return to God's presence, and will therefore suffer spiritual death (*D&C*, 29:36–45). Is it not a mistake to allow so many of your children to perish and be condemned to an eternal existence with Satan?

We also read in Revelation 12:7–9:

> And there was war in heaven: Michael and his angels fought against the dragon; and the dragon fought and his angels, And prevailed not; neither was there place found any more in heaven. And the great dragon was cast out, and that old serpent, called the Devil, and Satan, which deceiveth the whole world: he was cast out into the earth, and his angels were cast out with him.

Then in *D&C*, 29:36–37, it states:

> And it came to pass that Adam, being tempted of the devil—for, behold, the devil was before Adam, for he rebelled against me, saying, Give me thine honor, which is my power; and also a third part of the hosts of heaven turned he away from me because of their agency; And they were thrust down, and thus came the devil and his angels.

Therefore, one third (1/3) of the hosts of heaven followed Satan. If we believe the other scriptures quoted herein regarding the inhabitation of innumerable other worlds by God, the Eternal Father with his spirit children, then there must have been one third of God's centillion spirit children who followed Satan. How could that be? How could one third of the spirit children raised by God, the Eternal Father, choose to follow Satan and be condemned, and not choose to have an earthly existence? This just does not make sense and is another reason for the erosion of my belief in the Mormon God.

REASON 70
PERFECT GOD LOSES ONE THIRD OF HIS CHILDREN

As discussed in the previous Reason, God, the Eternal Father lost one third of His centillion spirit children in the pre-existence to Satan, apparently because Satan had more influence and was a more persuasive personality than God. This does not compute, because God, the Eternal Father is not only perfect, but has all of the power, glory, and knowledge. God stated in the *Pearl of Great Price*, Abraham 3:19:

> And the Lord said unto me: These two facts do exist, that there are two spirits, one being more intelligent than the other; there shall be another more intelligent than they; I am the Lord thy God, I am more intelligent than they all.

Further, God is omniscient, which means that He has unlimited knowledge. As stated by Bruce R. McConkie in *Mormon Doctrine* at page 545:

> God knows all things (2 Ne. 9:20; D. & C. [*sic*] 38:1-2; 88:7-13); possesses "a fullness of truth, yea, even of all truth (D. & C. [*sic*] 93:11, 26); "has all power, all wisdom, and all understanding" (Alma 26:35); is infinite in understanding (Ps. 147:4-5); [and] comprehends all things (Alma 26:35; D. & C. [*sic*] 88:41).

Then, Joseph Smith stated in his *Lectures on Faith* at page 54:

> [W]ithout the knowledge of all things, God would not be able to save any portion of his creatures; ... and if it were not for the idea existing in the minds of men, that God had all knowledge, it would be impossible for them to exercise faith in him.

Therefore, because God, the Eternal Father has all wisdom, knowledge, and understanding, it seems inconceivable that He would not be able to teach at least most of his spirit children the benefits of following His plan for redemption using Jesus Christ rather than Satan. In this way, they would also have the knowledge to make the decision in the pre-existence to follow God. A spirit child would be crazy and stupid to choose to follow Satan, knowing that said choice would condemn them to eternal misery. God would have to have given his spirit children the knowledge of the consequences of their decision; otherwise, the choice or exercise of their free agency would not have been fair for a lack of said knowledge.

In *D&C*, 68:25, Mormons are taught that if they do not teach their children to understand the Gospel of Jesus Christ, that "the sin be upon the heads of the parents." Mormons are further taught that if they *do* teach their children the correct principles of the Gospel, that when the children grow older, they will not depart therefrom. Because God, the Eternal Father, has all knowledge and power, He most certainly would have taught His spirit children in the pre-existence the true and correct principles of the following Him. This way, one third of his children would not have departed from Him and followed Satan. Therefore, it is extremely hard to accept that God would have lost one third of his spirit children to an inferior Satan, who did not possess all knowledge and all power.

REASON 71
SATAN, LUCIFER, OR THE DEVIL PROBLEMS

Satan, Lucifer, or the Devil was one of God, the Eternal Father's spirit children. He was also perhaps the second born spiritual child after Jesus Christ, because it was Satan who was allowed to also present a plan to God along with Jesus Christ for the redemption of mankind. We do know that Satan was born in the morning of the pre-existence (*D&C*, 76:25–26). Therefore, he probably was one of the great intelligences that existed before the Earth was created. He was

> an angel of God who was in authority in the presence of God, who rebelled against the Only Begotten Son whom the Father loved and…was thrust down from the presence of God and the Son. (*D&C*, 76:25)

"He became a devil, having sought that which was evil before God" (*BOM*, 2 Nephi 2:17).

If Satan was a "liar from the beginning," (*D&C*, 93:25) and "sought…evil," then there must have been evil *before* Satan. This would mean that evil has also been present forever and that there may have been previous Satans. Further, we know from the Mormon temple ceremony that when Satan was in the Garden of Eden tempting Eve, that he was confronted by Jehovah. Satan defended his actions by stating that he was just doing that which had been done in other worlds. Apparently, Satan had done the tempting in other worlds, or there were other Satans doing the same thing.

However, what seems amazing is that Satan was able to convince one third of God the Eternal Father's centillion spirit children to also rebel against their spiritual Father. He got them to become his angels who will eventually

> go away into everlasting fire, prepared for them; and their torment as a lake of fire and brimstone, whose flame ascendeth up forever and ever and has no end. (2 Nephi 9:16)

I don't know if this indicates that Satan had an unbelievable persuasive personality in the pre-existence, or that one third of God's spirit children were just not very bright. Either way, it just seems like a good story that may not be true.

Furthermore, there is the mission of Satan "to deceive and to blind men, and to lead them captive at his will" (*PGP*, Moses 4:4) and to get man to "worship [him]" (Moses 1:12). Satan also founded his own church, as stated in the *BOM*, 1 Nephi 13:6:

> And it came to pass that I beheld this great and abominable church; and I say the devil that he was the founder of it.

In fact, Nephi goes on to say in 1 Nephi 14:10:

> Behold there are save two churches only; the one is the church of the Lamb of God, and the other is the church of the devil; wherefore, whoso belongeth not to the church of the Lamb of God belongeth to that great church, which is the mother of abominations; and she is the whore of all the earth.

This is quite a bold statement, because it would apparently include everyone who does not believe in Christ, which would be the majority of people upon the Earth. Therefore, we have this great battle going on upon the Earth between God and Satan for the souls or spirits of mankind. Did Satan obtain his evil ways from the influence of another Satan that existed prior to Jesus Christ and is he the Satan referred to in our scriptures? When God, the Eternal Father, was living upon an Earth, who was the Satan for that earth to attempt to influence people to rebel against God? And if there have always been good and evil influences in the eternities, why did God, the Eternal Father, have to create a spirit child that would become Satan or the Devil?

There are just too many unanswered questions about Satan and why his Father and our Father allows Satan to do what he apparently does here upon the Earth. It is just as reasonable to assume that influences for evil co-exist with influences for good and have been around forever.

We all like to blame Satan for our mistakes and wrong doings, just like Bill Cosby who said, "The Devil made me do it." But the story of Satan from the beginning of the War in Heaven to his final battle with God after the Millennium is just too much for me to accept and constitutes part of a story that someone made up.

REASON 72
QUESTIONS ABOUT THE PRE-EXISTENCE

A son of a member of the First Presidency of the Church was asked by someone I know as to why over 90% of God's spiritual children who lived here upon the Earth never had the opportunity to hear the Gospel. The man answered that it was because they were not valiant in the pre-existence. How could a spirit child not be valiant in the pre-existence? His or her father was perfect (God, the Eternal Father); his or her mother was perfect (God's wife); and his or her oldest brother was also perfect and a God (Jesus Christ). As a spirit, he or she did not have a physical body; so there were no temptations of the flesh. Apparently, the test of being valiant was whether the spirit accepted what was told to them by God. But why wouldn't a spirit believe what God, being perfect and full of truth, told him or her? One's level of being valiant would only be a mental or spiritual activity. Moreover, because the spirits lived with God, their Father and were taught by Him, it doesn't appear that there would be any reason to disagree with the truth.

We are not talking about the one third of God's spirit children that followed Satan, but the two-thirds that followed Jesus Christ's plan for redemption. These spirit children lived with God, the Eternal Father and Jesus Christ for millions of years before they were born upon the Earth. We know we were with God, the Eternal Father and Jesus Christ in the pre-existence for a very long time, because we were spiritually born before the Earth was created, and the Earth is believed to be at least 200 million years old.

However, Mormons believe that we all had free agency in the pre-existence and that God had instituted laws for us to follow there (J. Fielding Smith, *Teachings* 354). Apparently, our life in the pre-existence was one of being taught and schooled. I am not quite sure what laws we would have to have followed, because in our spirit form, we did not have to know or follow physical laws or be subjected to physical temptations. It would have been purely a teaching of the mind over millions of years. So, how could we not be valiant? What would we have had to do to be non-valiant? Our teacher was our Father in heaven, one who had all knowledge and all power to teach us what we needed to know in order to progress. Of course, we had the agency to learn or not, and to follow the laws that were instituted or not. Again, why would a spirit child of a perfect Father in Heaven, who had the ability to teach us what we needed to know and learn, not be valiant? It just does not compute that (90%) percent of God's spirit children would not have been valiant enough to have been born upon the Earth at a time and place so that they would have been exposed to the Gospel of Jesus Christ.

REASON 73
AMBIGUITY OF THE CREATORS OF THE EARTH

The creation of the Earth is described in the Bible in Genesis 1 & 2; in the *Pearl of Great Price,* Moses 2 & 3 and Abraham 4 & 5; in the *Doctrine and Covenants,* 77:12; and in great detail in the LDS endowment ceremony in the Mormon temples. Numerous parts of these various accounts are different from each other. I am only going to discuss the differences between Abraham 4, Genesis 1 (as stated by Joseph Smith in his *Inspired Translation* of the Old Testament), and the temple endowment ceremony.

The specific message of Abraham, Chapter 4 is that "the Gods [plural], organized and formed the heavens and the earth." However, in the comparison between Genesis 1 of the Old Testament and Genesis 1 of Joseph Smith's inspired translation, found in the book *The Complete Joseph Smith Translation of the Old Testament,* we find that the specific message is that "I, God" (singular) created the heaven and the earth (Wayment). Then in the endowment ceremony, where the story of the creation is portrayed, we find that Elohim, or the Father of Jesus Christ, commands Jehovah (Jesus Christ) and Michael (pre-existent Adam) to go down and create the earth. So there are three different accounts of the creation, all contained in the scriptures or revelations given to the Mormons.

It could be argued that the "Gods" referred to in Abraham 4, Jehovah and Michael (Jesus Christ and Adam respectively) are, in fact, one and the same. However, that brings up the idea that Adam was a God before he came to the Earth. This Adam-God theory has been argued by non-Mormons, but has been discounted by the Mormon Church. In *Mormon Doctrine,* at page 18, McConkie states:

> There is a sense, of course, in which Adam is a god. But so also, in the same sense, are Abraham, Isaac, and Jacob; Moses and all the ancient prophets; Peter, James, and John; and all the righteous saints of all ages [Joseph Smith, Brigham Young, etc.], including those of both high and low degree.

So many of the spirit children of God, the Eternal Father may become gods; but were they the gods that participated in the creation of the Earth? According to the temple endowment ceremony, Adam or Michael was one such god. We do not know for sure how Jesus Christ became a God before he came to the Earth. But because his plan was accepted by God, the Father, and he appeared to many prophets in the Old Testament and in the *Book of Mormon* as a God before he was born, apparently, he became a God in the pre-existence. However, nowhere do we find support in the scriptures for the idea that Adam was also a God before he was born.

Then, we have the absence of our Heavenly Mother in the creation or organization of the earth. As mentioned in previous reasons, for any of us to become a god, among other things, we have to be sealed in the temple to our spouse (husband or wife). If we are both righteous enough, then the man will become a god and the woman will become a Heavenly Mother and offspring (or spirit children) will be created or born to that union. If that union is necessary to create spirit children, then it seems reasonable to assume that the same union would be necessary to create an earth for the offspring to inhabit. However, we do not have any scriptural references to any involvement of Elohim's wife, Jehovah's wife, or the wife of Michael, who would have been Eve.

This ambiguity of who in fact was involved in the creation of the Earth is just another example of problems with the Mormon God or Gods in whom we were taught to believe.

REASON 74
PROBLEMS WITH MAN BEING THE FIRST FLESH ON EARTH

In the *Pearl of Great Price*, Moses 3:7, it states:

> And I, the Lord God, formed man from the dust of the ground, and breathed into his nostrils the breath of life; and man became a living soul, the first flesh upon the earth, the first man also.

The Lord is referring to Adam, who, according to the chronology of the Bible, was born approximately 6,000 years ago. The above scripture basically says that there cannot be any animal or flesh older than Adam, because he was the first of both. In further support of the position that there was no death for man or any animal before Adam, we read in *BOM*, 2 Nephi 2:22:

> And now, behold, if Adam had not transgressed he would not have fallen, but he would have remained in the garden of Eden. And all things which were created must have remained in the same state in which they were after they were created; and they must have remained forever, and had no end.

This topic is further discussed in *Doctrines of Salvation* by Joseph Fielding Smith, vol. 1, at pages 107–20. It is therefore a basic Mormon belief that there was no death upon Earth prior to the fall of Adam. (See Moses 6:48; Alma 12:23–24, and *D&C*, 29:42). How can this be? Do we completely ignore the physical evidence upon the Earth that there was death here before the fall of Adam? Didn't the death and decay of animals and plants for millions of years upon Earth create the vast deposits of oil that have and will be found? And what about all of the skeletons of animals and humans found that are older than 6,000 years?

There are many explanations offered by Mormons as to how Moses 3:7 could be true. One belief is that God created the Earth from parts of other earths that had animals like dinosaurs that died there and did not exist on this Earth, or that God was only speaking about the Garden of Eden area when death was discussed, or many other explanations, none of which seem plausible or believable. The big question would be if those other explanations are true, "Why hasn't God, through his prophets, told us about that process?" and why is it not part of the temple ceremony on the creation?

The bottom line is that someone is wrong. If God created man only 6,000 years ago and death was not upon Earth prior thereto, then all of the scientists and archeologists are wrong. If there was death before Adam, then the *Pearl of Great Price* is wrong. Again, why would God not reveal to his prophets a simple answer to how this scripture Moses 3:7 could be true? We do know that God has not revealed the answer to this dilemma. Therefore, we are in darkness as to knowledge that seems important to know.

REASON 75
NON-BELIEF IN DINOSAURS

My sweet mother was a college graduate with a B.A. and a M.A. and taught school for 25 years. She was raised in the Mormon faith, a devout member, and a temple worker in the Salt Lake City Temple for many years. Based upon what she had been taught in the Mormon Church (discussed in the previous Reason) and in the temple endowment ceremony, she did not believe in dinosaurs. The source of her belief was the Mormon doctrine discussed in the previous Reason that there was no death before Adam and Eve ate the forbidden fruit and brought mortality upon the Earth. Therefore, there could not be any animal older than Adam and Eve because there was no death of man or animals upon the Earth prior to that time.

My mother and I had numerous conversations on this subject. Even though I reminded her of the dinosaur quarry and park in Vernal, Utah that I had visited, where one could actually see the dinosaur bones still embedded in the Earth, she would not change her belief. The Mormon God or Gods were always right in my mother's mind; and it didn't matter what evidence or physical facts that I could produce. Her mind would not be changed. A Mormon is taught to believe, no matter what; and she sincerely believed that dinosaurs never existed upon the Earth prior to Adam and Eve.

When I was in New Zealand in 1967, as a missionary for the Mormon Church, my companion and I taught the missionary lessons to a Brother Jensen, whose wife was already a member of the Mormon Church. He agreed to be baptized into the Church if we could explain to him why the Church did not believe that dinosaurs were older than Adam and Eve. He relied upon Moses 3:7 in the *Pearl of Great Price*, cited in the previous reason as a basis for his belief that the Mormon theology did not believe in dinosaurs. I sent a letter to Elder Harold B. Lee of the Counsel of the Twelve Apostles, a friend of my father and grandfather, requesting help in answering Brother Jensen's concern. Elder Lee was kind enough to answer my letter, but only indicated that neither he nor the Church knew where dinosaurs came from or whether they were on Earth prior to Adam. For some, it seems to be acceptable to just believe something based entirely upon faith, even when the physical evidence is directly against said belief. This was the position of my dear mother and the position of many other faithful members of the Mormon Church. I have wondered for many years why I cannot have this kind of belief and why I cannot just ignore the facts and evidence surrounding the existence of dinosaurs before man.

I keep asking the question of why such an important fact or answer would be left out of the revelations given to the prophets of God, especially when there are people like Brother Jensen, who would join the Church if the answer was available. Some argue that it is another example of why we need to just exercise faith, believing that some time the answer will be given. This just isn't enough for me. I cannot believe something when the facts and evidence are so enormously contrary to that belief.

I have visited the "Museum of the Rockies," in Bozeman, Montana many times, where there are remnants of numerous bones and skulls of the dinosaur called Tyrannosaurus Rex. In fact, there is an entire skeleton of a "T-Rex" there, which is made up of approximately sixty percent (60%) of the original bones of that dinosaur found in Montana. Even though Elder Lee indicated that the Mormon Church did not know the answer regarding whether dinosaurs existed on the Earth, wouldn't it be better if the official position of the Mormon Church was that it was a possibility? Then intelligent people, like my sweet mother, would not have to take a position directly opposed to factual existing evidence. Why wouldn't a loving and kind God give to His children on Earth revelations, through His prophets, containing the answers to these kinds of questions?

REASON 76
A VENGEFUL OLD TESTAMENT GOD

Although Christians, Jews, and Muslims all believe in the God of the Old Testament, to one degree or another, the Mormon faith even goes further by stating that the God of the Old Testament is in fact Jesus Christ before He was born in the flesh (see *BOM*, Ether 3). Therefore, the God that caused the flood killing millions of people including innocent children, the God that killed the first born of the Egyptians, and the God that covenanted with Abraham and disregarded the rest of the human race at that time, was in fact Jesus Christ, according to Mormon doctrine.

The God of the Old Testament is vastly different from the Jesus Christ of the New Testament. The Law of Moses given by the Old Testament God to the Israelites allowed for revenge "an eye for an eye" (Leviticus 24:20), killing adulterers and homosexuals (Leviticus 20:10–13), giving restrictions on what kind of meat could be eaten (Leviticus 11), and numerous other restrictions and laws found in the books of Leviticus and Deuteronomy. The Old Testament God was also a god of violence and war against the enemies of Israel, also explained in Reason 16.

In contrast, the God of the New Testament did away with the laws of Moses and preached "turning the other cheek" and "loving your enemies," as found in Matthew 5, 6 and 7 and in *BOM*, 3 Nephi 13, 14 and 15. One has to ask, "Why would the same God, Jesus Christ, be so different in his relationship with the human race?" "Is the scripture in 1 Nephi 10:18 that God "is the same yesterday, today, and forever,' just a myth?"

It appears that the God of the Old Testament (Jehovah, who is Jesus Christ according to the LDS Church) is a god of vengeance, murder, and discrimination. The first great act of vengeance and murder took place during Noah and the flood, as discussed in the next Reason. Another mass killing of thousands by God in the Bible was the destruction of Sodom and Gomorrah, found in Genesis 18 and 19. God warned the Prophet Abraham that He was going to destroy Sodom and Gomorrah because of their wickedness; but Abraham pled with God to save the cities. God and Abraham negotiated the number of righteous people required in the cities to save them and finally agreed on ten. However, God's angels could only find one righteous person, Abraham's nephew Lot, and therefore God caused fire and brimstone to come from heaven and destroyed the two cities, including all men, women, and innocent children. It is interesting to note that in Ezekiel 16:48–50, God accuses Jerusalem of being worse than Sodom, but does not destroy Jerusalem.

One of the worst atrocities performed by God in the Old Testament was the killing of thousands of firstborn sons of the Egyptians, in order to allow Moses to lead the Israelites out of bondage in Egypt. In Exodus 12:12, God tells Moses that He is going to kill "all the firstborn in the land of Egypt," both humans and animals. Then in Exodus 12:29–30, the Bible states:

> And it came to pass, that at midnight the LORD smote all the firstborn in the land of Egypt, from the firstborn of Pharaoh that sat on his throne unto the firstborn of the captive that was in the dungeon; and all the firstborn of cattle. And Pharaoh rose up in the night, he, and all his servants, and all the Egyptians; and there was a great cry in Egypt; for there was not a house where there was not one dead.

The LDS Church acknowledges the existence of Moses and the softening of the heart of Pharaoh, as well as Moses leading the children of Israel out of Egypt, the parting of the Red Sea, and the additional Egyptians being killed there. These are all mentioned in the Church's scriptures (*BOM*, 1 Nephi 17:23–32; 2 Nephi 3:10; Alma 36:28; and *D&C*, 105:27 and 136:22).

The Book of Joshua in the Bible has many accounts where God commands the Israelites to completely exterminate "anything that breathes," including women and children, in the cities in the land that the Israelites are supposed to inherit. The Prophet Joshua and the following Prophets who directed the Israelites, did in fact kill men, women, and innocent children in different cities that they invaded, like Jericho, Ai, the territory of the Danites, and many others. They were also commanded by God to completely destroy entire communities of different sects so that the Israelites would not be taught their abominable practices (Deuteronomy 20:16–18). These groups included the Hittites, Amorites, Canaanites, Perizzites, Hivites and Jebusites.

The following are some of the many additional accounts from the Bible where either God or His Prophets, following His command, kill thousands of people, including some innocent children:

Moses and the idolaters at Mt. Sinai	Exodus 32:26–29
Elijah and the prophets of Baal	I Kings 18
Elisha and the small boys	2 Kings 2:23–24
Men of Beth-shemesh and the Lord's ark	1 Samuel 6:19–20
Amalek and children and infants	1 Samuel 15:2–3
Uzzah and the ark of God	2 Samuel 6:3–7
Men, women, and little children	Ezekiel 9:5–7

The God of the Old Testament killed some of his spiritual offspring, including innocent children, in an arbitrary manner for not being righteous enough while they are upon the Earth; but allowed others to live who were also unrighteous. It makes no sense to kill the unrighteous, or those of a different religion or belief, as recorded in the Old Testament, but to do nothing about the wickedness inflicted upon mankind by numerous historical figures, including, but not limited to, Genghis Khan, Hitler, Stalin, and others. Lastly, there is no possible explanation as to why the Old Testament God would kill innocent children. It should be mentioned that, according to the Mormon religion, children under the age of 8 are not accountable for their sins and therefore are still sinless and innocent in the sight of God and have no need to repent (see Moroni 8:5–22 and *D&C*, 68:24–28). Would God do all of these things to His spiritual children after He created the earth for them to live upon?

REASON 77
NOAH AND THE FLOOD
INCONSISTENCIES

Almost everyone has heard the story of Noah and the flood that is found in Genesis, Chapters 6–9 in the Old Testament of the Bible. This story is authenticated for Mormons because it is referred to in the *Book of Mormon* in Alma 10:22, which states:

> Yea, and I say unto you that if it were not for the prayers of the righteous, who are now in the land, that ye would even now be visited with utter destruction; yet it would not be by flood, as were the people in the days of Noah, but it would be by famine, and by pestilence, and the sword.

It is also mentioned in the *Pearl of Great Price*, Moses 8:30 in a revelation given to Joseph Smith in 1831. Based on this, Mormons cannot say that the flood and the transportation of all the animals in the ark is just a story, but must believe that it actually occurred.

In Genesis, because of wickedness, God decided to wipe mankind from off the face of the earth. God commanded Noah to build an ark and then caused a flood that killed all of the inhabitants on Earth, including all men, women, and innocent children, except for the eight people on the ark. Henry M. Morris, in his book, *The Biblical Basis for Modern Science*, estimates that, according to his scientific calculation, the total number of human beings on Earth at the time of the flood that would have been killed was over three billion people. Why would the God who created these people, His spirit children, allow them to come to earth and multiply and then destroy them? Because it is believed by most religions that God knows the beginning from the end, He knew that he would have to kill all of these people—men, women, and innocent children—and start over with His creations.

Many comedians, including Bill Cosby and Ricky Cervais, have given humorous accounts of Noah being called by God to build an ark and then commanded to gather pairs of all of the animals to transport inside, while the entire world and its inhabitants are destroyed by a flood. They, like so many others, cannot believe that the story is true. One of the reasons that this story is so hard to believe as being true is based upon the omniscience of God. As stated in previous Reasons, God is omniscient, which means that He has unlimited knowledge. To reiterate, *Mormon Doctrine*, page 545 states:

> God knows all things (2 Ne. 9:20; D. & C. [sic] 38:1-2; 88:7-13); possesses "a fullness of truth, yea, even of all truth (D. & C. [sic] 93:11, 26); "has all power, all wisdom, and all understanding" (Alma 26:35); is infinite in understanding (Ps. 147:4-5); [and] comprehends all things (Alma 26:35; D. & C. [sic] 88:41).

Based upon God's omniscience, God obviously knew that the spirit children he allowed to come to Earth at the time of Noah were going to be wicked and that He would have to destroy them with a flood. This seems like an admission of failure by God in how He allowed the spirit children to come to Earth. People can only be so wicked; and there are innumerable instances since Noah's time where people upon Earth seemed to have been just as wicked as the people at the time of Noah. Nevertheless, none of them have been destroyed by flood.

Further, why would God place those spirits upon Earth at the time of Noah when God knew that He was going to destroy them with a flood? God knows all things from the beginning to the end as to what will happen upon Earth (1 Nephi 9:6 and Acts 15:18). So why would God plan to have a flood to destroy his people when He already knew that it was going to happen? Why not just distribute those spirits who were going to be wicked over the 6,000 years of the Earth's existence, so that He would not have to destroy all of the men, women, and children?

This brings up another issue as to why the story of Noah and the flood just doesn't make sense. According to the *BOM*, Moroni 8:5–15, children do not need to be baptized, because they cannot sin until they reach the age of accountability. Obviously, all of the children at the time of Noah were still sinless and did not need to be destroyed. Nevertheless, God destroyed everyone, including the innocent children. Is the story of Noah just another made-up story? If it is, then doesn't that cast doubts upon the Mormon beliefs?

REASON 78
MOSES AND THE PASSOVER KILLINGS

Another story in the Bible tells about Moses appearing before the Pharaoh of Egypt to obtain the release of the Israelite people from Egyptian rule. This entire story of Moses was made into a movie titled *The Ten Commandments* (which ironically is showing on a local TV channel at the same time I am writing this Reason). The Passover has been a sacred holiday for the Jewish religion for centuries. The account of the Passover is found in Exodus, Chapter 11 in the Old Testament of the Bible. After Moses brings down various plagues upon Egypt, the Pharaoh still does not soften to let the Israelite people go. Starting with verses 4–5, we read:

> And Moses said, Thus saith the LORD, About midnight will I go out into the midst of Egypt: And all the firstborn in the land of Egypt shall die, from the firstborn of Pharaoh that sitteth upon his throne, even unto the firstborn of the maidservant that is behind the mill; and all the firstborn of beasts.

Then in Exodus, Chapter 12, the Lord commands the Israelites to kill a lamb for each house and put its blood on their outside doorposts so that when the Lord sees it He will pass by the house and not allow the plague to kill the firstborn therein. In verse 29, it states:

> And it came to pass, that at midnight the Lord smote all the firstborn in the land of Egypt, from the firstborn of Pharaoh that sat on his throne unto the firstborn of the captive that was in the dungeon; and the firstborn of cattle.

So God killed all the firstborn children of everyone who lived in Egypt, some of whom would obviously be innocent children.

Again, Mormons have to accept this story as a true account of events that occurred, because Joseph Smith's *Inspired Translation* of the Bible does not change anything in Exodus 12 except verse 33. Joseph Smith adds the following phrase, which authenticates the validity of some children being killed: "We have found our firstborn all dead; therefore, get ye out of the land, lest we die also." Some of the firstborn may not have all been children, but it would be safe to assume that at least some of them were. How can someone believe that God would kill innocent firstborn children just because the Pharaoh would not let the Israelite people leave Egypt?

There is a story in the *Book of Mormon* where the Nephites are being held captive in bondage by the Lamanites and cannot escape. It is almost the same circumstance that existed in Egypt at the time of Moses. However, the God in the *Book of Mormon* took a different approach in solving the problem. We read in Mosiah 22 the story about said deliverance of the Nephites from the bondage of the Lamanites. In that story, King Limhi and his people and Ammon and his people consulted among themselves as to how to escape from the Lamanites. The Nephites were outnumbered and could not prevail by the sword.

A man named Gideon came up with a plan to provide the Lamanite guards at a particular pass with an abundance of wine, so they would get drunk and pass out. All of the Nephite people, together with their gold, silver, precious things, and with their flocks and herds, got together that night and departed out of the bonds of the Lamanites while the guards were drunk. They journeyed many days in the wilderness and finally arrived in the land of Zarahemla, where they were welcomed by other Nephites. When the Lamanites found out that the Nephites had escaped, they sent an army into the wilderness after them and pursued them for two days, but then lost the Nephites' tracks.

So why does the God in the *Book of Mormon* lead the Nephites to freedom by the strategy of getting the Lamanite guards drunk, but the God of the Israelites has to kill the firstborn of all the Egyptians to accomplish the same thing? This terrible act of murdering the firstborn of the Egyptians (which would include many innocent children), when other means would have been available to God to help the Israelites escape, is another reason to question whether the story is true or just a fabrication, which would definitely effect my disbelief of that kind of God.

REASON 79
TWO SETS OF COMMANDMENTS GIVEN TO MOSES

When Moses and the Israelites reached the wilderness of Sinai after leaving Egypt, Moses again talked with the Lord upon the sacred mountain of Sinai (Exodus 19). Then in Exodus 31:18 we read:

> And he gave unto Moses, when he had made an end of communing with him upon mount Sinai, two tables of testimony, tables of stone, written with the finger of God.

While Moses was talking with the Lord, his brother Aaron and the Israelites made a golden calf and worshipped it, which angered the Lord, so the Lord told Moses to go down from the mountain. Exodus 32:19 states:

> And it came to pass, as soon as he came nigh unto the camp, that he saw the calf, and the dancing: and Moses' anger waxed hot, and he cast the tables out of his hands, and brake them beneath the mount.

Thereafter, Moses had about 3,000 Israelite men slain who chose not to be with the Lord (see Exodus 32:28).

It is assumed by most Christians that the first tablets contained the Ten Commandments, along with the second tablets also, based upon Exodus 34:1 which states:

> And the Lord said unto Moses, Hew thee two tables of stone like unto the first: and I will write upon these tables the words that were in the first tables, which thou brakest.

However, Joseph Smith was inspired by God to explain that there was a difference between the first tablets and the second set, as in his translation of the Old Testament he changed Exodus 34:1–2 to read as follows:

And the Lord said unto Moses, Hew thee two other tables of stone like unto the first, and I will write upon them also the words of the law, according as they were written at the first on the tables which thou brakest; but it shall not be according to the first, for I will take away the priesthood out of their midst; therefore, my holy order and the ordinances thereof shall not go before them; for my presence shall not go up in their midst, lest I destroy them. But I will give unto them the law as at the first, but it shall be after the law of a carnal commandment; for I have sworn in my wrath that they shall not enter into my presence, into my rest, in the days of their pilgrimage. Therefore do as I have commanded thee; and be ready in the morning, and come up in the morning unto Mount Sinai, and present thyself there to me in the top of the mount.

The language of the first tablets of Ten Commandments is found in Exodus 20:2–17; the language of the second tablets of Ten Commandments is found in Deuteronomy 5:6–22. According to Bruce R. McConkie in *Mormon Doctrine*, page 783: "The two accounts differ in only one major respect and that is in the reason assigned for honoring the Sabbath Day." In Exodus, the Sabbath was to draw attention to the period of rest following the six days of creation. In Deuteronomy, it was to commemorate the deliverance from the Egyptians.

Therefore, the question is, "Why would God write his commandments on the first two tablets of stone, have Moses break them, have Moses kill 3,000 men, then write his commandments again on the second two tablets of stone and change the language and reason for observing the Sabbath Day? Then as Joseph Smith asserts, why would God take away any language having to do with the priesthood from the first tablets based upon Moses breaking the first? As stated in other Reasons herein, God is omniscient and knows everything that has or will happen upon Earth. He knew that the Israelites would build and worship a golden calf and therefore would not be able to have the first set of tablets, therefore requiring God to write a second set of tablets. Does this make sense for an omniscient God to have to write His commandments twice and change one of them? This seems to be very similar to Noah and the flood, where God also knew what was going to occur, but still caused events that didn't need to be done. For example, sending millions of His spiritual children to Earth knowing they were going to die in the flood. Is Moses' story of the Ten Commandments another fabricated one that is not true?

REASON 80
JOSHUA AND THE INVASION OF THE PROMISED LAND

The Book of Exodus goes on after the Ten Commandments to tell the story of Moses and the Israelites wandering in the wilderness for 40 years, allowing all the wicked to die. Then Moses dies and the Israelites are finally allowed to enter the Promised Land, which is the land around the River Jordan.

The Israelites are then led by Joshua. The book of Joshua in the Old Testament relates numerous accounts of the Lord instructing Joshua to invade the Promised Land and destroy cities and kill men, women, and children. One such example is the assault on the city of Jericho, where the wall fell down pursuant to God's instructions. Then in Joshua 6:21, we read:

> And they utterly destroyed all that was in the city, both man and woman, young and old, and ox, and sheep, and ass, with the edge of the sword.

Innocent people, including children, were murdered just because they were at the wrong place at the wrong time.

Then Joshua destroyed all the inhabitants of the city Ai, pursuant to God's commands (Joshua 8:26–27). Then all the "souls" in Makkedah and in Libnah and in Lachish and in Gezer and Eglon and Hebron and Debir and on and on are also destroyed (Joshua 10:28–43). In fact, God even killed some of the people himself by causing great stones to be cast down from heaven, killing more than the Israelites did by the sword (Joshua 10:11). Joshua took the whole land, killing everyone in all of the cities, because the "LORD...harden[ed] their hearts, that they should come against Israel in battle" (Joshua 11:18–21).

This carnage and total annihilation of hundreds of thousands of people who lived in the Promised Land—and had lived there for centuries—does not facilitate an increase of belief in the Mormon God(s). As has been mentioned in other reasons, the Mormon God, or Jesus Christ, seems to consistently kill people, including innocent children, rather than accomplish His goals by other means. Surely,

Joshua and the Israelites could have settled in some other place where cities were not already built, and, with the help of an all-knowing God, even convert the desert into a habitable land.

There is no evidence in archeological findings in the Middle East that would support a theory that all available land was being occupied by people at the time of the exodus and that there was absolutely no other land where the Israelites could have settled. If one looks at the area today, there is still land not occupied, or with evidence of *ever* being occupied. An all-powerful and all-knowing God, one who had performed the miracles just 40 years earlier in Egypt and of manna in the wilderness, could obviously have helped the Israelite people find wells and cultivate land to occupy, without all of the killings and destruction. Should the Mormon God really be one who does what is written in the Old Testament?

REASON 81
JOB AND THE BET BETWEEN GOD AND SATAN

I had always believed that the book of Job found in the Old Testament was just a story, and not really scripture. To me, it was one of the parts of the Bible that Mormons believe was not translated correctly (according to the Eighth Article of Faith of the Mormon Church), and therefore not from God. However, a few years ago, when I read Joseph Smith's *Inspired Translation* of the Old Testament, I realized that Joseph did not exclude the book of Job, but actually changed some of it. This would verify that at least Joseph Smith and God, who was inspiring him, believed that the book of Job *was* true.

How can a story be true when it tells of the Lord and Satan making a bet about Job? Job was a successful man upon Earth, with great flocks and assets. The bet was whether Job could remain faithful to God if he lost his assets and health. God apparently allowed Satan to have control of Job's assets so that he lost them. Then Satan and God spoke again, and God bragged that Job was still faithful. Satan then suggested that if Job's health was affected that Job would curse God. Therefore, God allowed Satan to smite "Job with sore boils from the sole of his foot unto his crown," (Job 2:7) in order to test Job's faith. Job cursed the day he was born, wished for death, and questioned God about his afflictions. Nevertheless, in the end, Job persevered and was rewarded by God and given twice as much as he had had before (see Job 3–42).

Why does the story of Job seen like fiction? First of all, because it is contrary to the plan of Jesus Christ presented in the pre-existence, which states that man would have free agency to choose for himself, and neither God nor Satan would force them to do anything. Second, God would not let Satan afflict a man upon Earth just to win a bet or to make a point. Third, God is omniscient and knew beforehand what Job would do, so the tests given to Job were of no benefit to God, because He already knew what the result would be. Fourth, God would not allow such afflictions upon a man just to show Satan that Satan didn't know what he was talking about. Fifth, Satan was cast out of heaven. So why would God or Jesus Christ be talking with Satan or having any communication with him at any time? This makes no sense.

It is also interesting that the subject of Job is absent from Bruce R. McConkie's book *Mormon Doctrine*.

For the above reasons, I disagree with Joseph Smith that the book of Job is a true story about a person who actually lived and existed upon the Earth. A story where God allowed Satan to interfere with a man's life, regardless of that man's agency, is not a story of an omniscient and merciful God.

REASON 82
DIFFERENCES IN SAME VERSES OF SCRIPTURE

In 2004, the entire manuscripts of the *New Translation* of the Old and New Testaments by Joseph Smith were published (Jackson). I believed that it would be a worthwhile project to compare those "inspired translations" with the King James Version of the Old and New Testaments of the Bible and the quotations of the Old and New Testament found in the *Book of Mormon (BOM)*.

A total of approximately five hundred and twenty-nine (529) verses from the Old and New Testament in the King James Version (KJV) of the Bible were compared with approximately the same number of their corresponding verses in the *Book of Mormon*. Then the same verses were compared with the Joseph Smith Translation (*JST*) of the King James Version (KJV) of the Bible. (Hereinafter, the abbreviations will be used: KJV, *BOM*, and *JST*.)

The following is a summary of those comparisons. If there were only punctuation differences between the verses though, then the verses were considered the same:

1. There were two hundred and thirty-six (236) verses where the *BOM* verses were identical to the KJV verses and where the *JST* made no changes to the verses.

2. There were ninety-five (95) verses where the *BOM* verses were different from the KJV verses, but the *JST* made no changes to the verses.

3. There were sixty-seven (67) verses where the *BOM* verses were different from the KJV verses and the *JST* verses were identical to the *BOM* verses.

4. There were one hundred and six (106) verses where the KJV, *BOM,* and *JST* verses were all different from each other and with most of them different in a substantial and material way.

5. There were twenty-five (25) verses where the KJV and *BOM* verses were identical, but the *JST* changed the verses; and many were different in a substantial and material way.

6. Therefore, there were a total of two hundred and thirty-four (234) verses where the *JST* verses were different from the *BOM* verses and most in a substantial and material way.

7. There were three hundred and three (303) verses that were the same in the *BOM* and *JST* and were different from the verses in the KJV.

8. There was only fifty-seven percent (57%) of the verses compared that were the same in the *JST* and *BOM*.

9. There were numerous verses in the *JST* where the punctuation was more similar to the punctuation in the corresponding verse in the KJV than to the punctuation in the corresponding verse in the *BOM*, although the verses were considered the same in our comparison.

10. There were two (2) entire verses that were in the KJV and *JST*, but could not be found in the *BOM*.

11. There were a total of over 1,670 changes or differences in words between the *BOM* verses and the corresponding verses in the *JST*.

(EXAMPLES TAKEN FROM COMPARISONS)

OLD TESTAMENT

KJV	BOM	JST
Isaiah 49:9–11, 16	1 Nephi 21:9–11, 16 (verses almost identical to KJV)	Made no changes

KJV	BOM	JST
Isaiah 48:1 Hear <u>ye</u> this, O house of Jacob <u>which</u> are called by the name of Israel, and are come forth out of the waters of Judah, <u>which</u> swear by the name of the Lord, and make mention of the God of Israel, <u>but</u> not in truth, nor in righteousness.	1 Nephi 20:1 Hearken **and** hear this, O house of Jacob, **who** are called by the name of Israel, and are come forth out of the waters of Judah, **or out of the waters of baptism; who** swear by the name of the Lord, and make mention of the God of Israel, **yet they swear** not in truth nor in righteousness.	No changes to KJV made

The main difference in Verse 1 is the addition of "or out of the waters of baptism" in the *BOM* that was not in the KJV. This clarifying phrase

> demonstrates that baptism was an Old Testament doctrine and practice, although the word baptism does not occur in the Old Testament. Hence the sectarian world believes that the ordinance of baptism was introduced as a practice in the Christian Era by John the Baptist. (Gorton 84).

However, the ordinance of baptism occurs many times in the *BOM* (2 Nephi 31:4–12, Mosiah 18: 8–18, and Alma 5:62). It is taught in the doctrine of the Mormon religion that baptism has existed since the time of Adam (*PGP*, Moses 6:64–67). This phrase: "or out of the waters of baptism" was not found in the KJV of Isaiah. However, the phrase *is* found in the *BOM*. It would seem reasonable and appropriate to find it also in the *JST*; but for whatever reason, we do not find it there.

KJV	BOM	JST
Isaiah 51:1 Hearken <u>to</u> me, ye that follow after righteousness, <u>ye that seek the Lord:</u> look unto the rock whence ye are hewn, and to the hole of the pit whence ye are digged.	**2 Nephi 8:1** Hearken **unto** me, ye that follow after righteousness. Look unto the rock **from** whence ye are hewn, and to the hole of the pit **from** whence ye are digged.	**Isaiah 51:1** Hearken **unto** me, ye that follow after righteousness, *ye that seek the Lord:* look unto the rock **from** whence ye **were** hewn, and to the hole of the pit **from** whence ye are digged.

The *BOM* verse deletes the phrase "ye that seek the Lord"; but the *JST* leaves it in. Both the *BOM* and *JST* verses add "from" to the KJV; and the *JST* changes the "are" in both the KJV and *BOM* to the past tense "were."

KJV	BOM	JST
Isaiah 2:21 To go into the clefts of the rocks, and into the tops of the ragged rocks, for fear of the Lord, and <u>for</u> the <u>glory</u> of his <u>majesty,</u> when he ariseth to shake terribly the earth.	**2 Nephi 12:21** To go into the clefts of the rocks, and into the tops of the ragged rocks, for **the** fear of the Lord **shall come upon them** and the **majesty** of <u>his **glory**</u> **shall smite them,** when he ariseth to shake **terrible** the earth.	**Isaiah 2:21** To go into the clefts of the rocks, and into the tops of the ragged rocks, for **the** fear of the Lord **shall come upon them**; and the **majesty** of *the Lord* shall smite them, when he ariseth to shake terribly the earth.

The *BOM* verse adds substantial language that not only alters the meaning of the KJV verse, but expands it as well. The *JST* verse also has most of the additional language added in the *BOM* verse, but leaves out "his glory" and replaces it with "the Lord," which does seem to change the meaning.

KJV	*BOM*	*JST*
Isaiah 13:8 And they shall be afraid: pangs and sorrows shall take hold of them: <u>they shall be in pain as a woman that travaileth:</u> they shall be amazed one at another; their faces shall be as flames.	**2 Nephi 23:8** And they shall be afraid; pangs and sorrows shall take hold of them; they shall be amazed one at another; their faces shall be as flames.	**No changes to KJV made**

The example of a woman in labor in the KJV verse is deleted in the *BOM* verse; but the *JST* does not make this change.

NEW TESTAMENT

KJV	BOM	JST
Matthew 5:14 <u>Ye are</u> the light of the <u>world</u>. A city that is set on <u>an</u> hill cannot be hid.	**3 Nephi 12:14 Verily, verily, I say unto you, I give unto you to be** the light of **this people**. A city that is set on **a** hill cannot be hid.	Matthew 5:14 *Verily, verily, I say unto you, I give unto you to be* the light of *the world.* A city that is set on *a* hill cannot *be hid.*

Most of the changes made to the KJV verse that are in the *BOM* verse are in the *JST* verse as well. However, "this people" is not changed in the *JST* and instead uses the same words, "the world" as the KJV verse.

| Matthew 5:19 Whosoever therefore shall break one of these least commandments, and shall teach men so, he shall be called the least in the kingdom of heaven: but whosoever shall do and teach them, the same shall be called great in the kingdom of heaven. | **3 Nephi 12:19 And behold, I have given you the law and the** commandments **of my Father, that ye shall believe in me, and that ye shall repent of your sins, and come unto me with a broken heart and a contrite spirit. Behold, ye have the commandments before you, and the law is fulfilled.** | Matthew 5:19 *Whosoever therefore shall break one of these least commandments, and shall teach men so to do*, he shall *in no wise be saved* in the kingdom of heaven: but whosoever shall do and teach *these commandments of the law until it be fulfilled,* the same shall be called great *and shall be saved* in the kingdom of heaven. |

All three verses are worded differently and have different meanings.

232

The Foundation for Apologetic Information and Research (FAIR, found at fairmormon.org) has numerous articles responding to criticism of Mormon religious views or other Mormon issues. In regard to the comparison of the Isaiah passages found in the *Book of Mormon* with the Joseph Smith Translation of Isaiah, critics claim that if the *JST* was an accurate translation, it would match the supposedly more 'pure' Isaiah text possessed by the Nephites. In response to this criticism FAIR concludes:

> The purposes of the Book of Mormon and JST translations were not identical. The LDS do not believe in one fixed, inviolate, "perfect" rendering of a scripture of doctrinal concept. The Book of Mormon likely reflects differences between the Nephite textual tradition and the commonly known Biblical manuscripts. The JST is a harmonization, expansion, commentary, and clarification of doctrinally important points.
>
> ...The Joseph Smith Translation (JST) is better thought of as an "inspired commentary" rather than a "translation" ("Relationship," *FairMormon*).

This conclusion avoids the concept that both the *BOM* and the *JST* are believed to be the "word of God" given to a Prophet, and therefore should be the same. God's revealed word is supposed to be the same at the time of Joseph Smith as it was at the time of Isaiah. If it is supposed to be the same revelation given to both Prophets, then it would be identical even when given to two different prophets at two different times. God would not alter his word and a perfect God would not make mistakes.

REASON 83
NEW TESTAMENT BOOK OF REVELATION DIFFICULTIES

As Mormons, we believe that the Bible is the word of God as long as it is translated correctly (see Eighth Article of Faith, *Pearl of Great Price*). We also believe that Joseph Smith was a prophet of God and that his translation of the New Testament mentioned in the previous Reason was inspired of God. Therefore, we would believe that the Book of Revelation found in the New Testament and Joseph Smith's *Translation* would also be the word of God. However, the question arises as to why a God who possesses all knowledge and sent us here upon Earth to learn about Him, to worship Him, and keep His commandments would give us a revelation that is so confusing. The book of Revelation found in the New Testament is hard to understand and does not have a reasonable interpretation.

Joseph Smith made hundreds of changes to the KJV of the Book of Revelation in his *Inspired Translation* of the New Testament. One of the main changes was in verse 1 of chapter 1, where Joseph Smith changed "The Revelation of Jesus Christ, which God gave unto him," to "The Revelation of John, a servant of God, which was given unto him of Jesus Christ." Significant changes were also made by Joseph Smith to 1:3–7, and he completely omitted 12:5. However, Joseph Smith's *Inspired Translation* is just as confusing, hard to understand, and without a reasonable interpretation as is the King James Version.

From the World Heritage Encyclopedia, we read the following:

> The **Book of Revelation**...is the final book of the New Testament. ...The Book of Revelation is the only apocalyptic document in the New Testament canon, though there are short apocalyptic passages in various places in the Gospels and the Epistles.
>
> ...In terms of being prophetic, the author of *Revelation* uses the words: *prophecy, prophesy, prophesying, prophet,* and *prophets* twenty-one times in these various

forms throughout the text. No other New Testament book uses these terms to this extent.

> ...*Revelation* has a wide variety of interpretations, ranging from the simple message that we should have faith that God will prevail (*symbolic interpretation*), to complex end time scenarios (*futurist interpretation*), to the views of critics who deny any spiritual value to Revelation at all.
>
> In the early Christian era, Christians generally understood the book to predict future events, especially an upcoming millennium of paradise on earth. In the late classical and medieval eras, the Church disavowed the millennium as a literal thousand-year kingdom. With the Protestant Reformation, opponents of Roman Catholicism adopted a historicist interpretation, in which the predicted apocalypse is believed to be playing out in church history. A Jesuit scholar countered with preterism, the belief that Revelation predicted events that actually occurred as predicted in the 1st century. ...In the 19th century, futurism (belief that the predictions refer to future events) largely replaced historicism among conservative Protestants."

The *World Heritage Encyclopedia* goes on the offer some criticism of the book of Revelation:

> Nineteenth-century agnostic Robert G. Ingersoll called Revelation "the insanest of all books." Thomas Jefferson omitted it, along with most of the Biblical canon, from the Jefferson Bible, and wrote that at one time he considered it as "merely the ravings of a maniac, no more worthy nor capable of explanation than the incoherencies of our own nightly dreams." Friedrich Engels claimed that the Book of Revelation was primarily a political and anti-Roman work.
>
> Martin Luther changed his perspective on Revelation over time. In the preface to the German translation of

Revelation that he composed in 1522, he said that he did not consider the book prophetic or apostolic, since "Christ is neither taught nor known in it." But in the completely new preface that he composed in 1530, he reversed his position and concluded that Christ was central to the book. He concluded, "As we see here in this book, that through and beyond all plagues, beasts, and evil angels, Christ is nonetheless with the saints and wins the final victory.

George Bernard Shaw described the book of Revelation as "a curious record of the visions of a drug addict." (Phelan 119)

My criticism is both with the book of Revelation and the fact that as Mormons we believe it to be the word of God. Why would God give us such a revelation and not just explain to us in very simple words, language, and terms what is going to happen in the future regarding the earth and the apparent battle between good and evil, or Jesus Christ and Satan? Moreover, why wouldn't God reveal to Joseph Smith, when he was "inspired" to translate the New Testament, additional revelations as to the meaning of the book of Revelation? Its "visions of a drug addict," described above by George Bernard Shaw, should at least relate to something we could all understand.

REASON 84
NEW TESTAMENT RECORDS NOT PRESERVED

Why were the original manuscripts of the books of the New Testament not preserved by God like the gold plates for the *Book of Mormon* were preserved by God? What we have today for Mormons is the "King James Version of the New Testament" of the Bible, which was a translation by a group of scholars in the early seventeenth century who based their rendition on previous written Greek texts. The main Greek text relied upon by the scholars who produced the King James Version was produced and published by a Dutch scholar, Desiderius Erasmus in approximately 1516. According to Bart D. Ehrman in his book, *Misquoting Jesus*, at pages 78–80:

> Erasmus went to Basel [Switzerland] in search of suitable manuscripts that he could use as the basis of his text. He did not uncover a great wealth of manuscripts, but what he found was sufficient for the task. For the most part, he relied on a mere handful of late medieval manuscripts. ...It appears that Erasmus relied heavily on just one twelfth-century manuscript for the Gospels and another, also of the twelfth century, for the book of Acts and the Epistles—although he was able to consult several other manuscripts and make corrections based on their readings. For the book of Revelation he had to borrow a manuscript from his friend the German humanist Johannes Reuchlin; unfortunately, this manuscript was almost impossible to read in places, and it had lost its last page, which contained the final six verses of the book. In his haste to have the job done, in those places Erasmus simply took the Latin Vulgate and translated its text back into Greek, thereby creating some textual readings found today in no surviving Greek manuscript. And this, as we will see, is the edition of the Greek New Testament that for all practical purposes was used by the translators of the King James Bible nearly a century later. ...Erasmus's editions (he made

> five, all based ultimately on this first rather hastily assembled one) became the standard form of the Greek text to be published by Western European printers for more than 300 years. Numerous Greek editions followed. ...All these texts, however, relied more or less on the texts of their predecessors, and all those go back to the text of Erasmus, with all its faults, based on just a handful of manuscripts (sometimes just two or even one—or in parts of Revelation, none!) that had been produced relatively late in the medieval period. ...All these subsequent editions...go back to...some rather late, and not necessarily reliable, Greek manuscripts.

It is a well know fact and accepted by all Bible scholars that we do not have today, nor did they have when the KJV was translated, any of the originals of any of the books of the New Testament, but only copies that were made, in most instances, centuries after the events actually happened. Mr. Ehrman goes on at page 82 to state:

> These editions, as I have already noted, became the basis for the editions of the Greek New Testament that were then reproduced time and again by the likes of Stephanus, Beza, and the Elzevirs. These editions provided the form of the text that the translators of the King James Bible eventually used.

Throughout this book, Ehrman gives numerous examples of changes and errors, both intentional and unintentional, which are in the present-day Bibles, including the KJV, when they are compared to the existing ancient Greek manuscripts. These errors exceed 250,000! There would probably be even more errors if the present day Bibles were compared to the original books of the New Testament.

We do have Joseph Smith's *Inspired Translation* of the New Testament, but as discussed in previous Reasons, there are problems with that as well. If God wanted us to have His true and correct word, then it seems logical that He would have preserved it. Because we know that the original manuscripts of the New Testament were not preserved, then we could conclude that it is not God's word. Today we have the Dead Sea Scrolls, Nag Hammadi ancient documents, and others that date back to the time that the New Testament books were written. Somehow they were preserved to come forth in modern times so that they could be used and authenticated. However, we have no original manuscripts of books in the New Testament that were written at the time of Christ. Why not? Especially when Joseph Smith allegedly had the original "gold plates" from which the *Book of Mormon* was written.

REASON 85
NEW TESTAMENT NOT WRITTEN AT THE TIME IT HAPPENED

This brings us to another question as to why the books of the New Testament (especially the four Gospels of Matthew, Mark, Luke and John) were not written at the time that the events occurred. Why didn't Jesus have one of his disciples or apostles actually write down the events of His life as it happened and record the exact words of His sermons? We do have that in the *Book of Mormon*. For example, the great sermon of King Benjamin found in Mosiah chapters 2–5 was written exactly at the time it was spoken. Mosiah 2:8 states:

> And it came to pass that he began to speak to his people from the tower; and they could not all hear his words because of the greatness of the multitude; therefore he caused that the words which he spake should be written and sent forth among those that were not under the sound of his voice, that they might also receive his words.

Then in 3 Nephi 23:4–13, when Jesus Christ appeared to the people in the Americas right after his crucifixion, He stated as follows:

> Therefore give heed to my words; write the things which I have told you. ...Behold other scriptures I would that you should write, that ye have not. And it came to pass that he said unto Nephi: Bring forth the record which ye have kept. ...and [Nephi] laid them before him. ...Verily I say unto you, I commanded my servant Samuel, the Lamanite, that he should testify unto this people. ...And Jesus said unto them: How be it that ye have not written this thing, that many saints did arise and appear unto many and did minister unto them? And...Nephi remembered that this thing had not been written. ...Jesus commanded that it should be written; therefore it was written according as he commanded.

These original written records written at the time of Christ and the records written by the prophet Nephi 600 years before Christ were preserved until 400 years after Christ when the prophet Mormon abridged them. Then, Mormon and his son Moroni wrote an abridgement of all of the records. Those written abridgements were preserved until 1827, when Joseph Smith received them as the gold plates and translated them into the *Book of Mormon*. So at least Joseph Smith had the original manuscripts written by Mormon and Moroni, who had the manuscripts written at the time the events occurred! Therefore, at least the *Book of Mormon* is not based upon manuscripts that were written hundreds of years after the events!

In God's wisdom and knowledge, He could have made the same request to his apostles in Jerusalem to write down records as the events and sermons occurred. God would have known that the original manuscripts written at the time of the events and sermons of Jesus Christ would be invaluable, just like the gold plates given to Joseph Smith in proving to mankind that they were in fact God's words. Then, like the *Book of Mormon* gold plates, God could have made sure that the original manuscripts were preserved concerning Jesus Christ and His ministry. However, this did not happen. In fact, we do not have evidence that the Apostles actually wrote down anything or kept any records at the time of Jesus' ministry and life upon Earth! Why not? Wouldn't an all-knowing God make sure that these important teachings and revelations were written down at the time they occurred and then preserved for future generations?

REASON 86
THE GOD IN JOSEPH SMITH'S TRANSLATION OF BIBLE

As mentioned in previous Reasons, Joseph Smith wrote an *Inspired Translation* of both the Old and New Testament of the Bible (*JST*). Did Joseph Smith clarify in his inspired version of the Old Testament who the God of this earth was? Did he explain the relationship between God the Eternal Father and His son, Jesus Christ? Was the God of the Old Testament in *JST* still a God that destroyed His children by the flood and murdered innocent children? Did Joseph Smith clarify the differences in the stories of Jesus Christ contained in the four Gospels in the New Testament?

The answer to all of the above questions is "No!" In Genesis, Chapter 1 of the *JST*, it specifically states that "I, God" was the one who created the earth, the sun and the moon, divided the light from darkness, divided the waters, and created the plants and animals. But then "God," in Genesis 1:26, states to Jesus Christ, "Let us make man in our image." Again, there is confusion as to who God is in the creation when the *JST* is compared to the book of Abraham in the *Pearl of Great Price,* and in the Mormon temple endowment ceremony.

In the *JST*, although expanded, God still has Noah building an ark and putting two "of every living thing of all flesh…of fowls…of every creeping thing of the earth" into the ark (*JST* 8:25–6). Then God still kills by the flood all of mankind except for Noah and his family: all of the animals, fowls, and every creeping thing on the earth (*JST*, Genesis 6:39–45). God still kills all of the firstborn children in Egypt at the time of Moses (*JST*, Exodus 12:33), destroys the people living in the Promised Land through Joshua just because they fought for their land against the invading Israelites (*JST*, Joshua 11:20), and still meets with Satan regarding Job (*JST*, Job 2:1).

The *JST* of the Old Testament does not resolve the problems discussed in previous Reasons regarding the confusion of the Godhead and the problems about which God is involved with mankind and the earth. Further, the *JST* of the New Testament basically mirrors the four Gospels and fails to clarify the differences as to what actually occurred during the ministry of Jesus Christ. One would expect that God would inspire Joseph Smith to resolve the confusion about God in the Old Testament and about Jesus Christ in the New Testament when he translated the Bible; but such was not the case.

REASON 87
DIFFERENCES IN THE
NEW TESTAMENT GOSPELS

We mentioned in previous Reasons that Mormons believe that the Bible is the word of God as long as it is translated correctly. They also believe that the *Book of Mormon* is the word of God (Eighth Article of Faith), that Joseph Smith was a prophet of God, and that his translation of the New Testament (*JST*) was inspired of God. The four gospels of Matthew, Mark, Luke, and John found in the New Testament are the canons of scripture recognized by Christians that describe the life of Christ and his ministry here upon Earth. However, the problem is that these four Gospels were written decades after Christ died by individuals that were not even present when Christ was alive. Further, the four Gospels are full of discrepancies and contradictions. Some of them are as follows:

1. The birth of Jesus is only found in two of the Gospels: Matthew and Luke. In Luke 2:1–4, it states that there was a taxing or census decreed by the Roman emperor, Caesar Augustus, so that everyone in the entire Roman Empire had to go to the city of their ancestral home. However, in the records of Caesar Augustus kept by the Romans, there is no mention of this. This seems odd, because it was something that had to be completed by everyone. Further, Joseph went to Bethlehem "because he was of the house and lineage of David" (Luke 2:4). However, David lived a thousand years before Joseph. It is hard to imagine that everyone in the Roman Empire would be required to go to the city where their ancestors lived a thousand years before they did (basically the same in the *JST*.)

2. In Matthew 2:1, it states that "Jesus was born in Bethlehem of Judaea in the days of Herod the king." However, in Luke 2:1–6, Jesus was born "when Cyrenius [Quirinius] was governor of Syria" (not changed in *JST*). However, Cyrenius did not become governor of Syria until ten years *after* the death of Herod (see the works of Roman historian Tacitus and Jewish historian Josephus).

3. In Matthew 2:14, Joseph takes Jesus and Mary to Egypt after Jesus' birth because Herod was going to kill all the children around Bethlehem. However, in Luke 2:39, they returned to Nazareth

directly after the birth. Further, there are discrepancies as to whether Jesus is from Nazareth or from Bethlehem (not changed in *JST*).

4. Both Matthew and Luke give the genealogy of Jesus or his family line. Both trace Jesus' lineage through Joseph, even though Joseph is not the father of Jesus (because Jesus was born of his virgin mother, Mary). Therefore, the only genealogy of Jesus' lineage that would matter would be that of Mary. Nevertheless, neither Mathew nor Luke gives Mary's genealogy or lineage. Further, there are several obvious differences in the genealogies as given in Matthew 1 and Luke 3, plus differences between Matthew 1:8 and 1 Chronicles 3:10–12 regarding Joram being the father of Uzziah (Ozias). In Chronicles, Joram was the great-great-grandfather of Uzziah and not the father, so three generations were skipped in Matthew. (The wording was changed in *JST*, but not the genealogy. Joseph Smith, being "inspired of God," also skipped the three generations and furthermore did not make any changes to all of Chapter 3 in 1 Chronicles, which listed the three missing generations.)

5. Bart D. Ehrman, in his book, *Jesus, Interrupted*, at pages 29–52 discusses the above contradictions in the Gospels, as well as the following problems or contradictions:

a. What did the voice at Jesus' baptism say? (Substantial differences as to whom the voice was addressing in Matthew, Mark, and Luke and not corrected in *JST*.)

b. Where was Jesus the day after he was baptized? (Matthew, Mark, and Luke tell of Jesus immediately leaving for the wilderness to be tempted by the Devil; but in John, after the baptism of Jesus, Jesus is seen by John the Baptist the very next day and then starts gathering his disciples. This was not corrected in *JST*.)

c. Who is for Jesus and who is against him? (Matthew 12:30 and Mark 9:40 differ and the difference was not corrected in *JST*.)

d. What really happened at the trial before Pilate? (In Mark, the trial was very rapid, Jesus said almost nothing, and was flogged after trial was over. However, in John 18:28 through 19:14, the trial is a lot longer, Jesus says quite a lot, and is flogged in the middle of the trial. These problems were not corrected in *JST*.)

e. Why are the resurrection narratives different? (Numerous differences in all four Gospels are not corrected in *JST*.)

Therefore, a problem that we have as Mormons is that Joseph Smith did not resolve these discrepancies and contradictions in his "*Inspired Translation*" of the Gospels. Why wouldn't the Mormon

God inspire Joseph Smith to correct the problems and mistakes in the New Testament when God told Joseph Smith to do the *Inspired Translation* in the first place?

REASON 88
MIRACLES THEN, BUT NONE NOW

What happened to miracles? The Old Testament, New Testament, and *Book of Mormon* have recorded numerous miracles. A few examples are:

OLD TESTAMENT

1. Moses and the plagues of Egypt, parting the Red Sea, and receiving manna from heaven
2. Joshua causing the walls of Jericho to fall down
3. Daniel in the lions' den
4. Elijah and the fire from heaven

NEW TESTAMENT

1. Jesus changing water into wine and feeding the multitudes
2. Jesus healing deaf, dumb and sick
3. Jesus raising the dead
4. Jesus calming the sea and walking on water

BOOK OF MORMON

1. The brother of Jared has sixteen stones touched by the Lord to provide light
2. Lehi, father of Nephi, is given compass directors to travel in the wilderness
3. Lehi, son of Helaman, collapses the prison walls and is encircled by fire
4. Ammon and his brethren convert the Lamanites with miracles

In Mormon 9:9 & 20, it discusses God and miracles:

> Do we not read that God is the same yesterday, today, and forever? ...And if there were miracles wrought then [by Christ and his apostles], why has God ceased to be a God of miracles and yet be an unchangeable Being?

> And behold, I say unto you he changeth not...and he ceaseth not to be God, and is a God of miracles.

Then in Moroni 7:35–37, we have recorded the following:

> [H]as the day of miracles ceased? Or have angels ceased to appear unto the children of men? Or has he withheld the power of the Holy Ghost from them? Or will he, so long as time shall last, or the earth shall stand, or there shall be one man upon the face thereof to be saved? Behold I say unto you, Nay; for it is by faith that miracles are wrought; and it is by faith that angels appear and minister unto men; wherefore, if these things have ceased wo be unto the children of men, for it is because of unbelief, and all is vain.

Because God is unchangeable and a God of miracles always, we can only conclude that the lack of recorded miracles since the end of the Bible and the *Book of Mormon* is because we do not have faith and because of our unbelief. Nevertheless, there were many angels and ancient prophets who appeared to Joseph Smith, so at least he had the faith and belief. However, no angelic visitations since Joseph Smith have taken place. Are we to believe that for the last (almost 200) years that the Mormons have lacked faith and do not believe? This does not seem accurate. The Mormon Church has flourished and grown since Joseph Smith. There *should* be numerous written scriptural accounts of miracles, but we have none.

While serving a mission for the Mormon Church in New Zealand in 1966–68, I met several Polynesian members of the church who related to me supposed various miracles of healings and raising of the dead performed by the Apostles of the church. However, none of them have been written down and given to us as scripture. The Bible and the *Book of Mormon* contain the experiences of prophets and righteous people and the miracles that they performed or witnessed. Why don't we have the same recorded experiences of the prophets and righteous people who have lived in the past 200 years? In my opinion, they have had enough faith and belief to perform and witness miracles. The written scriptures of said miracles would be a tremendous benefit to spreading the Gospel of Jesus Christ and verifying the truthfulness of the Mormon religion. Again, we do not have them. If God is the same yesterday and today, then there should be written accounts of miracles that can and would be canonized as scripture.

REASON 89
VISIONS THEN, BUT NONE NOW

The *Doctrine and Covenants* and the *History of the Church* written by Joseph Smith are full of visions received from 1820 to 1844. Both the Bible and the *Book of Mormon* also have numerous accounts of visions. Following are just a few of said visions:

OLD TESTAMENT

1. Abraham's vision of his posterity
2. Isaiah's vision concerning Judah and Jerusalem
3. Ezekiel's visions of four creatures and wheels and God's glory
4. Isaiah's visions of the Messiah, gathering of Israel, and the latter days

NEW TESTAMENT

1. The transfiguration of Christ and appearance of Moses and Elias
2. The vision of the angel Gabriel to Zacharias and Mary
3. Paul's vision on the road to Damascus
4. All of the visions of John in the book of Revelation

BOOK OF MORMON

1. Lehi and Nephi's vision of the Tree of Life
2. Nephi's vision of the Americas and restoration of the gospel
3. Nephi's vision of the coming of Christ to the Americas
4. Samuel the Lamanite's vision of the destruction of the Nephites

DOCTRINE & COVENANTS AND HISTORY OF THE CHURCH

1. Joseph Smith's first vision when he saw God and Jesus Christ
2. Joseph Smith's vision of seeing the Angel Moroni and the gold plates
3. Three witnesses are shown gold plates by an angel
4. Joseph Smith and Oliver Cowdery see the Lord standing on paved gold

5. Moses, Elias, and Elijah appear to Joseph Smith and Oliver Cowdery
6. John the Baptist gives the Aaronic Priesthood to Joseph and Oliver and then Peter, James, and John give them the Melchizedek Priesthood
7. Joseph Smith and Sidney Rigdon's vision where they saw the three degrees of glory in heaven
8. Joseph Smith's vision of the celestial kingdom and the "blazing throne of God, whereon was seated the Father and the Son."

The only recorded vision that we have in canonized scripture in the Mormon Church since Joseph Smith's time is found in the 138th Section of the *Doctrine and Covenants.* In that Section, Joseph F. Smith, the sixth President and Prophet of the church, had a vision in 1918 of the spirit world and the preaching of the Gospel there. Therefore, in almost 160 years, we have had only one vision received by a prophet or apostle of the Lord. (There are numerous talks given by General Authorities in General Conference since Joseph Smith, which some claim constitutes visions, but none have been canonized as scripture). The two declarations regarding polygamy and giving the Blacks the Priesthood are written and recorded in the *D&C*, but again, not as canonized scripture.

As mentioned in the previous Reason and Reason 11, God is the same yesterday and today and we should receive visions all of the time like in the time of Joseph Smith. The fact is that we don't, and that none of them have been written and recorded as scripture. Why doesn't God continually give visions to us through prophets and apostles? Moreover, if He does, then why are they not written down and given to us as scripture like in the past, so we can benefit from them?

REASON 90
CHRIST'S ALLEGED PERFECT LIFE

As Mormons, we believe that Jesus Christ was perfect while upon the earth and led a perfect life without sin. In the *Book of Mormon*, 3 Nephi 12:48, Jesus Christ states: "Therefore I would that ye should be perfect even as I, or your Father who is in heaven is perfect." Then in *Teachings of the Prophet Joseph Smith*, compiled by Joseph Fielding Smith, on page 187 it states: "None ever were perfect but Jesus." In Hebrews 4:14–15, we read:

> Seeing then that we have a great high priest, that is passed into the heavens, Jesus the son of God, let us hold fast our profession. For we have not an high priest which cannot be touched with the feeling of our infirmities; but was in all points tempted like as we are, yet without sin.

Then in 1 Peter 2:21–22: "Christ also suffered...who did no sin, neither was guile found in his mouth." Also, in 2 Corinthians 5:21, we read:

> For he hath made [the Christ] to be sin for us, who knew no sin; that we might be made the righteousness of God in him.

(These verses were not changed by Joseph Smith in his *Inspired Translation* of the New Testament.)

Nevertheless, did Jesus Christ actually lead a perfect life upon Earth? Or did he in fact sin? A sin is defined as a violation of God's commandments. One of those commandments states: "Thou shall not steal." Theft or stealing is taking something that does not belong to you and then depriving the owner of the use thereof. Christ did steal in the story found in Matthew 8:28–34, which was modified by Joseph Smith in his *Inspired Translation* to state as follows:

> And when he was come to the other side, into the country of the Gergesenes, there met him a man possessed with devils, coming out of the tombs,

exceeding fierce, so that no man could pass by that way. And, behold, he cried out, saying, What have we to do with thee, Jesus, thou Son of God? Art thou come hither to torment us before the time? And there was, a good way off from them, a herd of many swine, feeding. So the devils besought him, saying, If thou cast us out, suffer us to go into the herd of swine. And he said unto them, Go. And when they were come out, they went into the herd of swine; and, behold, the whole herd of swine ran violently down a steep place into the sea, and perished in the waters. And they that kept them fled, and went their way into the city, and told everything which took place, and what was befallen the possessed of the devils.

It is apparent from this story that Jesus did not own the herd of swine. Yet, by his power, the devils entered the swine and then the swine were killed. Is this not in violation of the law and commandment to not take something that belongs to another and destroy it? Therefore, isn't this a sin?

Matthew 21:17–19 in Joseph Smith's *Inspired Translation* tells the story of Christ and a fig tree:

And when he saw a fig tree in the way, he came to it, and there was not any fruit on it, but leaves only. And he said unto it, Let no fruit grow on thee henceforward for ever. [*sic*] And presently the fig tree withered away. And when the disciples saw this, they marveled and said, How soon is the fig tree withered away!

This same story is told in Mark 11:12–14; but in those verses, it indicates that Christ was hungry and that is why he went to the fig tree. One of the commandments given to Moses was not to covet anything that is thy neighbor's. A common law in any society is to refrain from destroying property that is not yours. It appears that both of these laws were violated by Christ destroying the fig tree.

Then, there is the story of Christ cleansing the temple found in Matthew 21:12–13 and Mark 11:15–17, where Christ "overthrew the tables of the moneychangers, and the seats of them that sold doves," and "cast out them that sold and bought" in the temple. Again, this is a violation of a commandment and a law to not steal or destroy something that is not yours. The argument of Christians is that the temple was Christ's, but the tables and other items were not.

Under our modern laws of civil obedience, the above incidents would be prosecuted as violations of the law for disturbing the peace, theft, and criminal mischief. Therefore, perhaps Jesus Christ was not perfect and did in fact commit some small and minor sins. Further, during his short existence upon Earth of thirty-three (33) years, he may not have had the opportunity to withstand other potential violations of the commandments that always surface.

Although the acts of Jesus Christ in the *Book of Mormon* as related in Reason 35 occurred after his crucifixion but before his resurrection, the destruction of so many cities and the murder of so many people upon Earth (including innocent children) could be interpreted as sins committed upon the earth.

Lastly, Christ was not married; or at least we have no known revelation or recording of such. As everyone knows, one of the hardest tasks in life is maintaining a marital relationship without losing one's temper or having unholy thoughts. Therefore, the Christian and Mormon doctrine that Christ is without sin may not be entirely true. If he did sin, then perhaps he was not the God that we thought he was.

REASON 91
IS THE ATONEMENT REALLY NECESSARY?

The main religious concept of the Mormon Church (and for that matter, all of Christianity) is the atonement of Jesus Christ. The Third Article of Faith in the Mormon Church states:

> We believe that through the Atonement of Christ, all mankind may be saved, by obedience to the laws and ordinances of the Gospel.

The term "saved" or "salvation" however, has a different meaning to Mormons as compared to some other Christian denominations. The first part of our salvation is unconditional and consists of the mere fact that we all will be resurrected when our spiritual body is reunited with a perfected physical body. This is available for everyone who comes to Earth regardless of what kind of life they led while being mortal. Apparently, this gift of the resurrection is based upon the atoning sacrifice of Christ when he freely gave his life on the cross, and is considered by most Christians to be free or by "grace." In 1 Corinthians 15:21–22, it states:

> For since by man came death, by man came also the resurrection of the dead. For as in Adam all die, even so in Christ shall all be made alive.

The original sin of Adam and Eve transgressing God's commandments in the Garden of Eden was forgiven through Jesus Christ atoning for the same, as indicated in the Second Article of Faith of the Mormon beliefs: "We believe that man will be punished for their own sins and not for Adam's transgression."

However, mankind really had nothing to do with this unconditional salvation, because the transgression of Adam was not something that anyone else upon the earth did. And the forgiveness of it was again something that no one on earth merited, other than Adam. Apparently, Jesus Christ was the only one who could resolve this problem. Moreover, none of us had any responsibility for it in the first place.

The second part of salvation or obtaining the Celestial Kingdom of God, according to Mormon theology, is conditional upon our faith, repentance, baptism, and obedience to God's commandments to the end of our mortal life. Also included is the repentance of our sins and mistakes, which, according to Mormon doctrine, can only be resolved through and by the atonement of Jesus Christ. However, everyone will not obtain this second part of salvation.

Some members of the Mormon Church have a difficult time with the concept of the atonement. This is the religious idea that Jesus, in the garden of Gethsemane, took upon himself all of the sins of the world that occurred both before He lived upon Earth and those that occurred thereafter. This suffering by Jesus Christ apparently took place in the space of a few hours, where allegedly he suffered for all of the sins in our behalf. The rituals of baptism, the sacrament, and confession and repentance of sins all relate in some way to this atonement.

If there is an eternal law of justice that requires a person to suffer for his or her sins, and we live forever after we die, then it appears that there would be sufficient time for each of us to suffer for our own sins, so that eventually we could become clean and live with God. The idea that one physical man (in such a short time in the Garden of Gethsemane) could suffer for the sins of over eighty billion people does not make sense. There is the argument that Jesus, being the Son of God in both the spiritual and physical sense, had the capacity to suffer for all of our sins in that short time.

Some claim that we do not have the capacity to suffer for our sins no matter how long we live in the eternities. However, if the suffering for these sins created physical pain (which apparently caused Jesus to bleed at every pore) and did not kill him, then God *could* require the same of us. How many people in the history of the world have suffered excruciating pain for a longer period of time than just a few hours, and pain that almost caused their physical death? One need only recall all of the torture that has occurred in the past, including for religious reasons. There were also those who suffered and died in the Holocaust and in other historical genocides and atrocities. In all of these, we find similar suffering that continued for substantial periods of time exceeding a few hours. The explanation that we cannot understand the suffering that Christ went through, because His suffering could only be accomplished by a God, appears to be a self-fulfilling concept.

The belief in the atonement also seems to be a circular argument. God creates humanity and His commandments and if we break them it is a sin, which requires justice or punishment (suffering) for the sin. However, God does not allow a way for us to meet the demands of justice and suffer for our own sins, but creates a plan where His Son is the only one capable of suffering for our sins. It seems a lot simpler to create a plan whereby we are responsible for all of our own actions and must suffer the consequences and punishment that is required under eternal laws. Apparently though, according to the Christian belief, we are not given that choice, thus the atonement is required only because the plan created by God requires it.

The above problems with the atonement and the fact that the entire scenario was planned and resolved by God without giving us the free agency or choice to suffer for ourselves creates doubts in my mind as to why the atonement was necessary. This is so problematic for me and for others with whom I have discussed this issue.

REASON 92
THIS LIFE SHOULD NOT DETERMINE ETERNITY

The purpose of this earth life, according to Mormon theology, is twofold: First, we have the opportunity to receive a physical body so that after we die, we can be resurrected and united with our spiritual body, as a perfect being for eternity. Secondly, we are tested while on Earth to see how well we can keep God's commandments; and if we sin and make mistakes, then whether we can truly repent of the same. In the *Book of Mormon*, Alma 34:32–34 we read:

> For behold, this life is the time for men to prepare to meet God; yea, behold the day of this life is the day for men to perform their labors. And now, as I said unto you before, as ye have had so many witnesses, therefore, I beseech of you that ye do not procrastinate the day of your repentance until the end; for after this day of life, which is given us to prepare for eternity, behold, if we do not improve our time while in this life, then cometh the night of darkness wherein there can be no labor performed. Ye cannot say, when ye are brought to that awful crisis, that I will repent, that I will return to my God. Nay, ye cannot say this; for that same spirit which doth possess your bodies at the time that ye go out of this life, that same spirit will have power to possess your body in that eternal world.

Therefore, what we do during this short period of time called mortality, which only lasts (on average) from 60 to 80 years, apparently determines our lives for the rest of eternity, or forever! Somehow, this just doesn't seem fair! How we perform here upon Earth has a lot to do with when, where, and how we are born and how long we are here. I am aware of some examples of this unfairness.

A close friend of mine who was only 30 years old was on a work assignment in another state, away from home for over a month, when he was placed in a compromising circumstance that he was unable to withstand. He was married with children and had led a decent life.

However, a beautiful, sexy young woman hit on him at a hotel bar and he yielded and went back to her room. While they were involved in having sex, he had a heart attack and died. There was no time to regret his actions and no time or opportunity to repent of his sin.

Another female friend of mine was sexually abused by her stepfather from the time she was 10 until she was 14 years old. As a result of her abuse, she developed a serious problem with her sexuality. After being married, she continued to allow other men, including her counselor and therapist, to have sex with her. She then died a short time later.

Are these people penalized for eternity because of mistakes they made upon Earth, even though the majority of their lives were involved in helping other people? There are also billions of people who have lived upon Earth who, because of where and when they were born, did not even have a chance to hear the Gospel of Jesus Christ, let alone live according to God's commandments. Is their eternal life determined solely upon their short earth life existence (because they cannot repent after death)?

Why would God have a plan that only allows a very few of his spirit children the opportunity to hear and follow his Gospel while living on Earth and then condemn others for eternity because they did not? Although, as mentioned in Reasons 42 and 53, Joseph Smith taught that some people could still make it to the Celestial Kingdom based upon their capacity to accept the Gospel on Earth *if* they had the chance. Nevertheless, those billions who are assigned to the Terrestrial Kingdom for eternity may have lived a different life had they tarried on earth for a few hundred years. One's life of forever, being based upon such a short time period of earth life that is so diverse for so many people, does not seem to be fair. Nor does it support a belief in the Mormon's "Plan of Salvation" that was supposed to have been instituted by a just and kind God.

REASON 93
CONFUSION IN THE SECOND COMING

Jesus taught that the Son of Man was soon to arrive from heaven in judgment of mankind—with those who followed the laws of the Gospel being rewarded, and those who did not, being punished (see Matthew 25:31–46). He also taught that this judgment would come in the lifetime of his disciples. In Mark 9:1 he states:

> And he said unto them, Verily I say unto you, That there be *some of them* that stand here, which shall not taste of death, till they have seen the kingdom of God come with power. (Emphasis added.)

Then in Mark 13:30–37, after he describes the signs of Christ's coming to judge, he states:

> Verily I say unto you, that this generation shall not pass, till all these things be done. Heaven and earth shall pass away: but my words shall not pass away. But of that day and that hour knoweth no man, no, not the angels which are in heaven, neither the Son, but the Father. Take ye heed, watch and pray: for ye know not when the time is. For the Son of Man is as a man taking a far journey, who left his house, and gave authority to his servants, and to every man his work, and commanded the porter to watch. Watch ye therefore: for ye know not when the master of the house cometh, at even, or at midnight, or at the cockcrowing, or in the morning: Lest coming suddenly he find you sleeping. And what I say unto you I say unto all, Watch.

According to Mormon doctrine, the above passages of scripture are interpreted to refer to the apostle John, who was told by Jesus that he would not taste death until Christ would come again, as is stated in John 21:21–23. Therefore, the Second Coming was not imminent. However, this does not make sense for a few reasons. First of all, the above passages of scripture refer to "some of them" and "this generation" who will be alive and see the Second Coming. It does not limit it to just one person. Secondly, the book of John was not written by the apostle John and was written many years *after* the book of Mark (Ehrman *Jesus, Interrupted* 104–12). Thirdly, both the books of Mark and John were written after Paul had died and the Christians knew that the Second Coming had not occurred, as predicted by Jesus and Paul. Fourthly, Jesus, in the above passages, specifically tells his followers to watch and be prepared. He was not talking to people who would be living thousands of years after his (Jesus') death.

It is interesting to note that Jesus states above in the scripture from Mark that the Father knows when the end will come, but that the Son does not know. This would contradict the belief that God, the Son, also knows the beginning from the end, as stated in the *Pearl of Great Price*, Abraham 2:8: "My name is Jehovah, and I know the end from the beginning; therefore my hand shall be over thee."

Then in the 24th Chapter of Matthew, Christ tells his disciples the signs of His Second Coming and the end of the world. Although it appears that a lot of signs need to take place before the end of the world, the Apostle Paul thought the end was close at hand. In 1 Thessalonians, which was the Apostle Paul's letter to the church of the Thessalonians, he exhorts them to "stand fast in the Lord" (3:8) and to love one another and keep the commandments that were given to them so that they would be caught up with the Lord when He came in glory. Paul states in 4:13–18 and 5:23 the following:

> But I would not have you be ignorant, brethren, concerning them which are asleep, that ye sorrow not, even as others which have no hope. For if we believe that Jesus died and rose again, even so them also which sleep in Jesus will God bring with him. For this we say unto you by the word of the Lord, that we which are alive and remain unto the coming of the Lord shall not prevent them which are asleep. For the Lord himself shall descend from heaven with a shout, with the voice of the archangel, and with the trump of God: and the dead in Christ shall rise first: Then we which are alive and remain shall be caught up together with them in the clouds, to meet the Lord in the air: and so shall we ever be with the Lord. Wherefore comfort one another with these words.

> And the very God of peace sanctify you wholly; and I pray God your whole spirit and soul and body be preserved blameless unto the coming of our Lord Jesus Christ.

Ehrman explains it better in *Jesus Interrupted*, when he states on pages 263–65 the following:

> So taught the early Jewish apocalypticists, and so taught Jesus. The Kingdom of God was soon to appear with the coming of the Son of Man. …This was also the teaching of the apostle Paul and, so far as we can tell, of all the earliest Christians. One key difference between Paul and Jesus is that Paul believed that Jesus himself would bring this kingdom when he returned in glory (I Thessalonians 4–5). Moreover, for Paul the resurrection at the end of the age has already in some sense begun. This is one reason Jesus' resurrection was so significant for Paul. Since the resurrection is to occur at the end of the age, and since Jesus has already been raised, that shows we are living at the end of the age. This is why Paul speaks of living in the end times.
>
> …What happens when this expected end doesn't happen? What happens when the apocalyptic scenario that Jesus expected to occur in "this generation" never comes? When Paul's expectation that he will be alive at the second coming of Christ is radically disconfirmed by his own death?

Ehrman further explains:

> When the end does not come, people who want to remain faithful to the original vision of Jesus and his disciples have to grapple seriously with the fact that an essential element of that vision appears to have been wrong. Of course the faithful would not claim that Jesus was wrong. More likely, he was misunderstood. And so there begins a long and significant process of

reinterpretation, in which the original message comes to be transformed into a less tactile, less tangible, less easily disconfirmed view (265).

It is true that Joseph Smith changed some, but not all, of the above scriptures in his *Inspired Translation* of the New Testament. However, he leaves us with the same confusion, as discussed in the next Reason. As Mormons, we believe in the above scriptures from the Bible as to the Second Coming of Jesus Christ. But the fact that it has not occurred yet, and that the scriptures are so ambiguous, supports disbelief in the same.

REASON 94
JOSEPH SMITH'S SECOND COMING CONFUSION

If the confusion as to the timing of the Second Coming was only evident in the Bible, then an argument could be made that the words of Jesus and Paul have in fact been misinterpreted. However, we have the same problem occurring with Joseph Smith and the revelations in the *Doctrine and Covenants*, which seem to indicate that Joseph Smith and the early Mormons also believed that the Second Coming was close at hand and would occur in their lifetimes. *D&C*, 34:7 states:

> For behold, verily, verily, I say unto you, the time is soon at hand that I shall come in a cloud with power and great glory.

This phrase or one similar is found tens of times in the *D&C*, along with many other scriptures, exhorting the early members of the Mormon Church to watch and pray and be prepared for the Second Coming of Christ.

In his *History of the Church,* Joseph Smith spoke about the timing of the Second Coming of Christ and a revelation that he received in regard to the same. In Volume 5 at page 336, Joseph Smith states in April 1843 the following:

> Were I going to prophesy, I would say the end [of the world] would not come in 1844, 5, or 6, or in forty years. There are those of the rising generation who shall not taste death till Christ comes.

This is very similar to Jesus' statement in Mark 9:1 quoted in the previous Reason. However, just as in the time after Jesus made that statement, after Joseph Smith made his statement, Christ did not come, and all of the rising generation passed away before the Second Coming. Joseph Smith went on to say in the *HC,* 5:336 (similar text found in *D&C*, 130:14–17):

> I was once praying earnestly upon this subject, and a voice said unto me, "My son, if thou livest until thou are eighty-five years of age, thou shalt see the face of the Son of Man." [The following is found only in the *Doctrine and Covenants*: "therefore let this suffice, and trouble me no more on this matter."] I was left to draw my own conclusions concerning this; and I took the liberty to conclude that if I did live to that time, He would make His appearance. But I do not say whether He will make his appearance or I shall go where He is. I prophesy in the name of the Lord God, and let it be written—the Son of Man will not come in the clouds of heaven till I am eighty-five years old.

Joseph Smith would have turned eighty-five in 1890; but now, at least 120 years later, the Son of Man still has not come. Joseph Smith made a further statement in *D&C*, 130:12–13:

> I prophesy, in the name of the Lord God, that the commencement of the difficulties which will cause much bloodshed previous to the coming of the Son of Man will be in South Carolina. It may probably arise through the slave question. This a voice declared to me, while I was praying earnestly on the subject, December 25th, 1832.

It appears that Joseph Smith (in 1832) thought the coming of the Son of Man would follow the "difficulties in South Carolina," but we know that that did not happen as well.

So why did the Lord add to the confusion as to when the Second Coming was to occur by the revelations given to Joseph Smith? Why is there the continued secrecy of the timing of the Second Coming? If Christ is going to come a second time, why not let us know when? All of us procrastinate; but if we knew that Christ was coming the second time in the year 2025, perhaps we would do something about all of the evil that is going on in the world presently!

REASON 95
BATTLE OF GOG AND MAGOG CONFUSION

Bruce R. McConkie, on pages 324–25 in *Mormon Doctrine*, under the title, "God and Magog," mentions that Christ's Second Coming will be while the great battle of Armageddon is taking place during the war between Israel and "God and Magog." This is a name given to the nations that will be fighting against Israel or "the remnant of the Lord's chosen seed." Apparently, "At the Second Coming, all the nations of the earth are to be engaged in battle, and the fighting is to be in progress in the area of Jerusalem and Armageddon." (*See also* Revelation 16:14–21 and Zechariah, Chapters 11–14.)

Furthermore, the 38th and 39th chapters of Ezekiel in the Old Testament give a lot of detail about this great war. In those chapters, it states that it will

> take place "in the latter years"; that it will be fought in the "mountains of Israel," against those who have been gathered to their ancient land of inheritance. ...Gog and Magog shall come "out of the north parts" in such numbers as "to cover the land" as a cloud; that the Lord will then come, and [with] fire and brimstone descend upon the armies; that the forces of Gog and Magog will be destroyed (McConkie 325).

Joseph Smith, in his *Inspired Translation* of the Old Testament, did not change anything in the 38th and 39th chapters of Ezekiel or in the 11th, 12th, and 13th chapters of Zechariah. So we can assume that the Lord did not want them altered. Furthermore, the only change made by Joseph to Revelation 14 was in verse 7. So Armageddon must be a literal war, or battle that is going to take place.

What troubles me is why God would have the Lord wait until the war against "His chosen seed" Israel is in progress before coming? If the Lord is coming the second time with all power and destruction, then why let people kill each other before the Lord kills them? This makes no sense. Further, with all of the different means of modern technological warfare available, millions of people could be killed in a very short period of time. The real question is, "Why have a battle or war at all when God knows that He is going to intervene and solve the problem by killing most of mankind himself (see *JST*, Matthew 24)?" Again, the question comes to mind as to why God has a chosen people that have to be engaged in a war with non-Israelites. In today's population, this would be a battle between billions of non-chosen people with a few million chosen people. In addition, the non-chosen people would have the greater nuclear arsenal to totally annihilate the chosen people.

Apparently, there will also be another battle with Gog and Magog (those nations that are against God's plans and purposes) at the end of the Millennium, which will be the final battle of the Great God led by Michael or Adam against Satan, which is discussed in Reason 97 hereafter. However, these types of confusing and unbelievable scriptures and prophecies are extremely hard to believe.

REASON 96
MILLENNIUM INCONSISTENCIES

According to Mormon doctrine, the Millennium refers to the 1,000-year period that commences just after the Second Coming of Christ to the Earth. During this time:

> Christ will reign personally upon the earth; ...the earth will...receive its paradisiacal glory; ... corruption, death and disease will cease; and...the kingdom of God on earth will be fully established in all its glory, beauty, and perfection. (McConkie 492)

In *D&C*, 43:29–31 and 29:11, we read respectively what the Lord said in revelations to Joseph Smith:

> For in mine own due time will I come upon the earth in judgment, and my people shall be redeemed and shall reign with me on earth. For the great Millennium, of which I have spoken by the mouth of my servants, shall come. For Satan shall be bound, and when he is loosed again he shall only reign for a little season, and then cometh the end of the earth.

> ...For I will reveal myself from heaven with power and great glory, with all the hosts thereof, and dwell in righteousness with men on earth a thousand years, and the wicked shall not stand.

Who are the lucky spirits who will be born upon the Earth at the time when Satan will be bound and can't tempt man and when Christ will be present? Apparently, there will be additional billions of people born during the Millennium, who won't have to deal with Satan and will not die, but be "changed in the twinkling of an eye" (*D&C*, 43:32). Why were you and I so unfortunate to be born now rather than then? Moreover, how unlucky were all the spirits who were born during the Dark Ages, or during the atrocities discussed in other Reasons rather than during the Millennium?

D&C, 101:22–34 discusses how life will be during the 1,000-year Millennium period: Christ will be seen by all; corruptible things will be consumed; things shall become new; there will be no "enmity"; man can ask and get anything; Satan shall not have any power; there will be no sorrow; people will live until very old and then will not die, just experience a quick change into glory; and all things will be revealed. If we knew in the pre-existence what it was going to be like, all of us would have chosen to be born during the Millennium!

However, it doesn't compute that it would take 1,000 years to destroy the wicked. It only took God or Christ a day to destroy all of the wicked living in the Americas after His crucifixion, as recorded in the *Book of Mormon* in 3 Nephi and discussed in Reason 35. Additionally, if Satan is bound after the wicked are destroyed, then what is the purpose of living upon Earth during the Millennium? It seems that it will not be the same test that you and I have living now. At this point, our test is to see if we can keep God's commandments, when evil, sin, and temptation are everywhere and Christ is not here, like He *will be* during the Millennium. How hard would it be to believe in God and keep His commandments during the Millennium, when Christ has returned and is there and Satan is not?

Lastly, why would God discriminate so much in regard to His spirit children as to who would be allowed to live during the Millennium? Again, based upon God's knowledge of everything and having power over everything, there just doesn't appear to be a purpose for a 1,000-year Millennium period. God could accomplish everything that needed to be done in a short period of time. The remaining spirit children, who would still need to come to earth to gain a physical body, could also accomplish that in a very short period of time. Their eternal glory and kingdom would already have been determined, because they were chosen to be born during the Millennium when they will not be tempted to do evil. These are additional problems in belief in the Mormon God(s).

REASON 97
JUDGMENTS OF GOD ISSUES

Through out the history of mankind, there have been numerous famines, plagues, floods, pestilences, earthquakes, tornadoes, wars, and fire and brimstone raining from heaven. According to *Mormon Doctrine* by Bruce R. McConkie, at pages 404–05:

> all these and infinitely more are sent of God upon men who forsake him and his laws. (Lev. 26; Deut. 28; 29; 30; 3 Nephi 8, 9, 10; D. & C. [*sic*] 43:25; 63:32–33; 88:88–91).

Further,

> these judgments come upon peoples and nations to punish them for their rebellion. ...[A]lso a righteous minority group may be called upon to suffer with those who are receiving a just reward for their unholy deeds (Chase 168).

Besides all of God's judgments that He has and will invoke upon mankind, there will also eventually be a final judgment. In Mormon doctrine, after all spirit children have had a chance to come to Earth, and when all mankind has died by the end of the Millennium, there will be a final judgment. In 2 Nephi 9:15–16 we read:

> And it shall come to pass that when all men shall have passed from this first death unto life, insomuch as they have become immortal, they must appear before the judgment-seat of the Holy One of Israel; and then cometh the judgment, and then must they be judged according to the holy judgment of God. And assuredly, as the Lord liveth, for the Lord God hath spoken it, and it is his eternal word, which cannot pass away, that they who are righteous shall be righteous still, and they who are filthy shall be filthy still; wherefore, they who are filthy are the devil and his angels; and they shall go away into

everlasting fire, prepared for them; and their torment is as a lake of fire and brimstone, whose flame ascendeth up forever, and ever and has no end.

Then in Alma 41:3–6 we read:

> And it is requisite with the justice of God that men should be judged according to their works; and if their works were good in this life, and the desires of their hearts were good, that they should also, at the last day, be restored unto that which is good. And if their works are evil they shall be restored unto them for evil. Therefore, all things shall be restored to their proper order, every thing to its natural frame—mortality raised to immortality, corruption to incorruption—raised to endless happiness to inherit the kingdom of God, or to endless misery to inherit the kingdom of the devil, the one on one hand, the other on the other—The one raised to happiness according to his desires of happiness, or good according to his desires of good; and the other to evil according to his desires of evil; for as he has desired to do evil all the day long even so shall he have his reward of evil when the night cometh. And so it is on the other hand. If he hath repented of his sins, and desired righteousness until the end of his days, even so he shall be rewarded unto righteousness.

What bothers me about the judgments of God is that God decides or knows whether people are going to repent or not. Based on this, He kills them, as mentioned above and in other Reasons, before they have a chance to live longer and perhaps repent. If God already knows what is in our hearts and whether we are going to repent or not upon the Earth, then what is the purpose of a final judgment? God already knows or has decided where each of us will be in the eternities and it may not matter what works we performed upon the Earth if we did not have the right heart.

This is also mentioned in Reason 42, describing the Prophet Joseph Smith seeing his brother in the Celestial Kingdom, even though his brother had not been baptized and had not heard or received the Gospel of Jesus Christ. Joseph's brother's judgment was based upon his heart and what he would have done had he tarried upon Earth and not died so young. It is argued that even though God already knows, *we* need to be told what our judgment is, based on the thoughts and actions we did upon the Earth, or what God knows was in our hearts. Will we not know ourselves what was in our hearts, when we did what we did upon Earth? Again, why should we be judged for such a short period of time we were on Earth, when we will live forever after our death and resurrection, and then have a chance to learn a lot more and to progress in our understanding?

REASON 98
DEATH AND THE SPIRIT WORLD QUESTIONS

As members of the Mormon Church, we understand that God, the Father, is literally the father of our spirit body that was created through an unknown process between God (our Heavenly Father) and our Heavenly Mother in the pre-existence prior to coming to the Earth. Our spirit body, which is separated from our physical body at death, has the same form and resemblance as our physical body (See *Book of Mormon*, Ether 3:7–17).

Therefore, as we begin our journey at the time of our death, we are a spirit being in the likeness of our physical body and resembling the same. The Prophet Joseph Smith stated that:

> All spirit is matter, but is more fine or pure, and can only be discerned by purer eyes. We cannot see it, but when our bodies are purified, we shall see that it is all matter (*HC*, 5:393).

In one of the volumes of the *Journal of Discourses* of the Mormon Church, it explains that our spirit body retains the five senses of the physical body, to wit: sight, touch, smell, taste, and hearing, but with a greater capacity (Moody 71). In addition, our thoughts, movement, and communications are also enhanced beyond our current understanding. So even though we are dead and have no physical body prior to being resurrected, we still can function with our senses.

Where do we go then as spirits immediately upon our physical death? This answer can be found in the *BOM*, Alma 40:11–14, where we read:

> Now, concerning the state of the soul between death and the resurrection—Behold, it has been made known unto me by an angel, that the spirits of all men, as soon as they are departed from this mortal body, yea, the spirits of all men, whether they be good or evil, are taken home to that God who gave them life. And then shall it come to pass, that the spirits of those who are righteous are

received into a state of happiness, which is called paradise, a state of rest, a state of peace, where they shall rest from all their troubles and from all care, and sorrow. And then shall it come to pass, that the spirits of the wicked, yea, who are evil—for behold, they have no part nor portion of the Spirit of the Lord; for behold, they chose evil works rather than good...and these shall be cast out. ...Now this is the state of the souls of the wicked, yea, in darkness, and a state of awful, fearful looking for the fiery indignation of the wrath of God upon them; thus they remain in this state, as well as the righteous in paradise, until the time of their resurrection.

The resurrection, as evidenced by the story of Christ's resurrection, is defined in the scriptures and the doctrine of the Mormon Church as the time when one's spirit body and physical body are reunited again after death into a perfect form (a creation of an immortal soul) to live forever (Alma 11:42–45 and Chapter 40). Apparently, there are different times for mankind's resurrection. The first person resurrected was Jesus Christ, as alleged in the New Testament (1 Corinthians 15:23); also, some of the righteous that had died prior to Christ, were resurrected with Him at that time as well. The main first resurrection does not start until the Second Coming of Christ. The second resurrection begins at the end of the Millennium, the 1,000-year period that starts with the Second Coming of Christ.

The Lord further explains the different resurrections to the Prophet Joseph Smith in Sections 76 and 88 of the *Doctrine and Covenants*. Apparently, at the time of Christ's resurrection, or shortly thereafter, many of the ancient prophets and righteous people who had already died were resurrected as well, and received Celestial bodies and are heirs to the Celestial Kingdom (see also *D&C*, 133:54–55 and Matthew 27:52–53). Then there will be two great resurrections: one for the just and one for the unjust. Within these two, there is an order in which the dead will come forth.

At the time of Christ's Second Coming, those spirits who will be receiving Celestial bodies and inheriting the Celestial Kingdom will be resurrected at what is called the "Morning of the First Resurrection," and they will meet the Lord at that time. In the afternoon of the First Resurrection, or after the Lord has begun the Millennium (the 1,000 years that the Lord will reign upon Earth), those spirits who have accepted the Gospel in Spirit Prison and whom will be receiving Terrestrial bodies and inheriting the Terrestrial Kingdom, will be resurrected. At the end of the Millennium, the Second Resurrection begins for those spirits who are unjust and will be receiving Telestial bodies and inheriting the Telestial Kingdom. Finally, in the later part of the Second Resurrection, those spirits who have obtained a knowledge of the divinity of Christ through the Holy Ghost and then have openly rebelled against Christ and have become Sons of Perdition, will be resurrected, but will be cast out to dwell with Satan and his angels. Why so many different times for resurrection?

The division of spirits, which takes place at the time of death, has been going on for at least 6,000 years, as explained by Joseph Smith in *Teachings of the Prophet Joseph Smith*, compiled by Joseph Fielding Smith, on page 219. In this division, some go to a place called "Paradise" and some (the wicked) go to a place called "Sprit Prison." So, what have the billions of people who have died been doing in Paradise or in Spirit Prison while waiting to be resurrected? Moreover, why do the righteous who are assigned to Paradise have to wait to be resurrected? These spirits are limited in what they can do without physical bodies; but then, as stated above, they can communicate and associate with each other. One would imagine that they would be able to continue to learn and assimilate knowledge and therefore change themselves; although there is confusion in regard to whether they can repent based upon the scripture found in Alma 34:33–35 which states:

> And now, as I said unto you before, as ye have had so many witnesses, therefore, I beseech of you that ye do not procrastinate the day of your repentance until the end; for after this day of life, which is given us to prepare for eternity, behold, if we do not improve our time while in this life, then cometh the night of darkness wherein there can be no labor performed. Ye cannot say, when ye are brought to that awful crisis, that I will repent, that I will return to my God. Nay, ye cannot say this; for that same spirit which doth possess your bodies at the time that ye go out of this life, that same spirit will have power to possess your body in that eternal world.

Why would God have all of these spirit children of His wait for thousands of years to be resurrected, judged, and assigned to a kingdom, when He already knows what is in their hearts and where they will be assigned? If there is life after death, a judgment, and a resurrection, why would that process be so long and this complicated?

REASON 99
NECESSITY OF MISSIONARIES IN THE SPIRIT WORLD

Joseph Smith taught that, contrary to most Christian beliefs, the destiny of man is not irretrievably fixed at his death. We are not made either eternally happy or eternally miserable at that time. Just because someone dies without the knowledge of God or the Gospel of Jesus Christ, they still may have an opportunity to accept Christ and his Plan of Salvation and be delivered from being cast out. (See *Teachings of the Prophet Joseph Smith*, compiled by Joseph Fielding Smith, page 219.) This takes place in Spirit Prison during the time immediately after our death. Furthermore, Joseph Smith states at page 179:

> The Saints have the privilege of being baptized for those of their relatives who are dead, whom they believe would have embraced the Gospel, if they had been privileged with hearing it, and who have received the Gospel in the spirit, through the instrumentality of those who have been commissioned to preach to them while in prison.

This is also alluded to in the New Testament in 1 Peter 3:18–20 which states:

> For Christ also hath once suffered for sins, the just for the unjust, that he might bring us to God, being put to death in the flesh, but quickened by the Spirit: By which also he went and preached unto the spirits in prison; Which sometime were disobedient, when once the long suffering of God waited in the days of Noah.

The most enlightening revelation concerning the Spirit World and the missionary work that allegedly takes place there, was given to President Joseph F. Smith in a vision in 1918, when he was the prophet and president of the Mormon Church. This is recorded in Section 138 of the *Doctrine and Covenants* and accepted as doctrine of the Church. President Smith was pondering over 1 Peter 3:18–20 mentioned above and also 1 Peter 4:6, which states:

> For for this cause was the gospel preached also to them that are dead, that they might be judged according to men in the flesh, but live according to God in the spirit.

Thereafter, he received the following vision, beginning with verse 11 and continuing with excerpts from other verses:

> As I pondered over these things which are written, the eyes of my understanding were opened, and the Spirit of the Lord rested upon me, and I saw the hosts of the dead, both small and great. And there were gather together in one place an innumerable company of the spirits of the just, who had been faithful in the testimony of Jesus while they lived in mortality; [those in Paradise] ...They were assembled awaiting the advent of the Son of God into the spirit world, to declare their redemption from the bands of death. ...While this vast multitude waited and conversed, rejoicing in the hour of their deliverance from the chains of death, the Son of God appeared, declaring liberty to the captives who had been faithful; And there he preached to them the everlasting gospel, the doctrine of the resurrection and the redemption of mankind from the fall, and from individual sins on conditions of repentance. But unto the wicked he did not go, and among the ungodly and the unrepentant who had defiled themselves while in the flesh, his voice was not raised; Neither did the rebellious who rejected the testimonies and the warnings of the ancient prophets behold his presence, nor look upon his face. Where these were, darkness reigned, but among the righteous there was peace; ...But his ministry among those who were dead was limited to the brief time intervening between the crucifixion and his resurrection; And I wondered ...how it was possible for him to preach to those spirits and perform the necessary labor among them in so short a time. And as I wondered, my eyes were opened, and my understanding quickened, and I perceived that the Lord went not in person among the wicked and the disobedient who had rejected the truth, to teach them;

> But behold, from among the righteous, he organized his forces and appointed messengers, clothed with power and authority, and commissioned them to go forth and carry the light of the gospel to them that were in darkness, even to all the spirits of men; and thus was the gospel preached to the dead.

Therefore, according to this vision, there will be missionary work after we die. Some of the spirits who are assigned to Paradise will be going to those spirits assigned to Spirit Prison and teaching them the Gospel of Jesus Christ. Apparently, this missionary work that Jesus Christ participated in at the time of his death, offers a means by which those spirits in Spirit Prison may join other spirits in Paradise. But how does this take place? Many of us who were missionaries for the Mormon Church remember how much we had to learn and how difficult it was to preach the Gospel to others. However, in the Sprit World, it appears to be a simple task.

First of all, Jesus Christ personally appeared there. That event would have been recorded by whatever recording devices there are in the Spirit World. Based upon the technology we have today of recording events and sharing them via the Internet or other mediums, it would be safe to assume that the spiritual technology is far superior to what we have now. Therefore, through this technology, the spirits in Spirit Prison would be able to personally see the appearance of Jesus Christ in the Spirit World and review His life and teachings on the Earth. It would not take any leap of faith to believe and know that Jesus Christ was the Son of God and that His Gospel was true. Further, there would be no debate as to whether we lived after we died, because we would definitely know that truth at that time! So the missionary work would be fairly simple and of short duration, because it would not be necessary to do it on a one-to-one basis. The spirits in Spirit Prison could all view or be exposed to the relevant recordings and make their decision or choice to accept the Gospel or not.

Those spirits in Sprit Prison who want to change, will apparently have the opportunity to repent and become heirs of the Celestial Kingdom. However, this seems to be contrary to what is stated in the *Book of Mormon*, Alma 34:33–34:

> And now, as I said unto you before, as ye have had so many witnesses, therefore, I beseech of you that ye do not procrastinate the day of your repentance until the end; for after this day of life, which is given us to prepare for eternity, behold, if we do not improve our time while in this life, then cometh the night of darkness wherein there can be no labor performed. Ye cannot say, when ye are brought to that awful crisis, that I will repent, that I will return to my God. Nay, ye cannot say this; for that same spirit which doth possess your bodies at the time that ye go out of this life, that same spirit will have power to possess your body in that eternal world.

So can a spirit assigned to Spirit Prison (based upon an unrighteous life upon the Earth) actually repent of their Earthly sins and have those sins removed so that they can inherit the Celestial Kingdom?

This process would seem like it would be *more* difficult to accomplish in the Spirit World. For example, if someone had been promiscuous and immoral in their sexual life, or had become addicted to alcohol or drugs due to their upbringing and circumstances while upon the Earth, they would not have the opportunity in the Spirit World to show that they had really repented. This is because they would not have the opportunity to succumb to those sins or to repent of them, due to the lack of having a physical body. However, as mentioned in other Reasons, we have the revelation given to Joseph Smith in *D&C*, Section 137, where he saw his brother, Alvin, who had died, residing in the Celestial Kingdom. The Lord told Joseph Smith:

> Thus came the voice of the Lord unto me, saying: All who have died without a knowledge of this gospel, who would have received it if they had been permitted to tarry, shall be heirs of the celestial kingdom of God; Also all that shall die henceforth without a knowledge of it, who would have received it with all their hearts, shall be heirs of that kingdom; For I, the Lord, will judge all men according to their works, according to the desire of their hearts. And I also beheld that all children who die before they arrive at the years of accountability are saved in the celestial kingdom of heaven (7–10).

So why would there be any reason to do missionary work in the Spirit World prior to the resurrection, when the Lord has already determined what is in an individual's heart, and whether they will inherit the Celestial Kingdom or not?

One may also wonder why any spirit would reject the Gospel of Jesus Christ in the Spirit World at that time. They would know then that the account of Jesus Christ was true and that the only way to enter into the presence of God would be by accepting His Gospel. All they would have to do is repent by admitting their mistakes made upon the Earth and express their desire to thereafter live according to the principles of the Gospel. This is a lot easier than having to do it during one's lifetime.

Therefore, there does not appear to be any necessity for missionary work in the Spirit World. Even if there were, it would not take much time to accomplish it all. Furthermore, we have to wonder what we will be doing the rest of the time, prior to being resurrected, if it will not take much time to teach all of the spirits in Spirit Prison. There are so many unanswered questions concerning the Spirit World after death, that it makes it difficult to believe in the same.

REASON 100
GOD'S LANGUAGE USED TO COMMUNICATE WITH MAN

It has always been interesting to me the way that God communicated with the Prophets, including Joseph Smith. One would think that God, who is omniscient and knows everything (including what is in a man's heart), would be simple and direct in His communications with man. The *Doctrine and Covenants* is full of passages where God is speaking to Joseph Smith in revelations given from 1829–44, where the language is far from simple and direct. For example, in Section 6, verses 2–3, God states:

> Behold, I am God; give heed unto my word, which is quick and powerful, sharper than a two-edged sword, to the dividing asunder of both joints and marrow; therefore give heed unto my words. Behold, the field is white already to harvest; therefore, whoso desireth to reap, let him thrust in his sickle with his might, and reap while the day lasts, that he may treasure up for his soul everlasting salvation in the kingdom of God.

This exact same statement is also made in Sections 11:2–3; 12:2–3; and 14:2–3. What does it mean? Someone has to interpret the passage. Many have interpreted it to indicate that it refers to missionary work and bringing other souls to the Gospel of Jesus Christ within the LDS Church (see Alma, Chapter 26 in the *Book of Mormon*).

One only needs to read the various scriptures to know that God has not spoken to us through his prophets in simple language on many of the important issues. For example, God could put it in very simple terms in regard to the Godhead by saying:

> I am God the Father, and my firstborn son in the spirit world was Jesus Christ, who is also a God with me and acts for me in regard to mankind and to the earth. The Holy Ghost is the third member of the Godhead and is also involved in dealing with mankind; but we are all separate beings.

Also, when it is Jesus Christ speaking to the prophets, he could have said, "I am Jesus Christ, the Son of God, speaking for my Father." This would prevent confusion by saying he is "God the Father." In Reason 31, "The Confusing Godhead in the Book of Mormon," there are numerous examples of the ambiguous way in which God has communicated with man and the confusion caused by the language used.

Another prime example is the Book of Isaiah, which appears not only in the Old Testament, but also in numerous passages in the *Book of Mormon*. Why are the statements of Isaiah, as to what God told him, so mysterious and not understandable? I have read the Book of Isaiah many times without ever understanding it. I have also read books written by General Authorities of the Mormon Church that try to explain what Isaiah meant. If the scriptures are really God's word to mankind, then wouldn't they be simple and understandable so that everyone would have the benefit of what God has said to man?

Even in the New Testament, there are numerous examples of Jesus speaking in parables or making statements that even his Apostles at that time did not understand (see Matthew, Chapters 13 and 15). Again, the question is, "Why does God want to make it so difficult to know what He is saying to mankind?" If we are to follow His word, then should not His word be in a form that all can understand?

REASON 101
STILL NO ANSWER TO PRAYERS

I have been working on this book for a few years now. During that time, while writing the different Reasons, I have continually prayed, asking God for guidance and wisdom in regard to what was being written and whether it was true or not. A prior year, I wrote another book titled, *Will the Real God Please Stand Up?* In that book, I discuss the God of the Mormon Church, the God of the Catholic and Protestant Churches, the God of Judaism, the God of Islam, the God or Gods of Hinduism and Buddhism and Sikhism, the Gods of Primal-Indigenous religions, and the Gods of the Chinese and Japanese religions. While writing that book, I also continually prayed for guidance and wisdom to help me find the truth about God. Nevertheless, my prayers have never been answered at all during the past years. I continue to wonder why. I continue to wonder and have numerous questions about Mormonism and whether to believe in the Mormon God or Gods, when there are so many reasons not to.

Should we quit believing then? Alternatively, should we just believe, as referred to in the song "I Believe," from the musical *The Book of Mormon* (because that is what we have been taught)? There may be no logical or rational reason to continue to believe, because there is no empirical or factual evidence to support the beliefs. However, beliefs are important, especially regarding how we should live our lives. Mormonism has numerous practices about how we should raise our families and treat other people. These beliefs we should continue to hold, and always try to live the "Golden Rule" of treating other people the way that we want them to treat us.

Further, it makes sense that we should continue believing our current beliefs in the Mormon religion until we can find a set of beliefs to replace them. To just adopt a non-belief system will not help us to be happy and enjoy our lives. To maintain those beliefs that we have as Mormons that work and make us better people seems to be a better approach. When, and if, we can find a set of beliefs that are more compatible to our mindset and do not raise so many questions and problems, then we should probably adopt them.

No matter what we do, we should never quit reading, researching, inquiring, and even praying about life and God, in hopes of finding some knowledge, some peace of mind, and hopefully a more compatible set of beliefs! We should always have an open and inquisitive mind, and remember that we have obtained just a small fraction of all the available knowledge that exists everywhere. Life can be exciting when we search for knowledge, have new experiences, and realize and accept that we have only scratched the surface in finding answers to the questions about our immense Universe, about Gods, and about our existence here upon the Earth!

Works Cited

"A Facsimile from the Book of Abraham, No. 2." *The Book of Abraham* in *The Pearl of Great Price*, The Church of Jesus Christ of Latter-day Saints, 1988, pp. 36–37. *LDS.org*, lds.org/scriptures/pgp/abr/fac-2. Accessed 29 Aug 2018.

"Abdul Hamid." *Wikipedia* 13 Aug 2018, *Wikimedia Foundation, Inc.*, en.wikipedia.org/wiki/Abdul_Hamid_I. Accessed 31 Aug 2018.

"Apocalypse of John." *World Heritage Encyclopedia.* Project Gutenberg Self-Publishing Press, self.gutenberg.org/articles/eng/Apocalypse_of_John#cite_note-4. Accessed 31 Aug 2018.

"Archeology and the Book of Mormon," *Wikipedia*, 21 August 2018, *Wikimedia Foundation, Inc.*, en.wikipedia.org/wiki/Archaeology_and_the_Book_of_Mormon#cite_note-irr.org/smith-82. Accessed 29 Aug 2018.

"Book of Abraham," *The Full Wiki*, 19 Aug 2010, thefullwiki.org/Book_of_Abraham. Accessed 31 Aug 2018.

"Chapter 6: Computers and Family History Research." *Introduction to Family History Teacher Manual: Religion 261 (2012).* Intellectual Reserve, Inc., pp. 26–28, *LDS.org*, lds.org/manual/introduction-to-family-history-teacher-manual-religion-261/chapter-6-computers-and-family-history-research. Accessed 29 Aug 2018.

"Church History." *Times and Seasons*, vol. 3, no. 9, March 1, 1842, pp. 706–10. *Centerplace.org*, centerplace.org/history/ts/v3n09.htm. Accessed 29 Aug 2018.

"Declaration of Faith Issued by the Richmond Conference in 1887." *QuakerInfo.com*, 23 July 2008, quakerinfo.com/rdf.shtml. Accessed 24 Aug 2018.

"Ebola virus disease." *Wikipedia*, 23 Aug 2018, *Wikimedia Foundation, Inc.*, en.wikipedia.org/wiki/Ebola_virus_disease#2013%E2%80%932016_West_African_outbreak. Accessed 24 Aug 2018.

"Everyday Disciples: John Wesley's 22 Questions." *Discipleship Ministries*, 2018, umcdiscipleship.org/resources/everyday-disciples-john-wesleys-22-questions. Accessed 24 Aug 2018.

"Genetics and the Book of Mormon." *Religion-wiki*, FANDOM, religion.wikia.com/wiki/Genetics_and_the_Book_of_Mormon #cite_ref-2. Accessed 28 Aug. 2018.

"Genetics and the Book of Mormon." *Wikipedia*, 29 May 2018, en.wikipedia.org/wiki/Genetics_and_the_Book_of_Mormon. Accessed 28 Aug. 2018.

"History of Joseph Smith (Continued)." *Times and Seasons*, vol. 3, no. 11, April 1, 1842, pp. 748–49. *Centerplace.org*, centerplace.org/history/ts/v3n11.htm. Accessed 29 Aug 2018.

"History of science and technology in China" *Wikipedia*, 10 July 2018, en.wikipedia.org/wiki/History_of_science_and_technology_in_China. Accessed 24 Aug 2018.

"Josephus on Jesus." *Wikipedia*, 28 Aug 2018, *Wikimedia Foundation, Inc.*, en.wikipedia.org/wiki/Josephus_on_Jesus. Accessed 28 Aug. 2018. His works can be found here: en.wikipedia.org/wiki/Josephus#Works.

"List of causes of death by rate." *Wikipedia*, 13 Aug 2018, en.wikipedia.org/wiki/List_of_causes_of_death_by_rate#Developed_vs._developing_economies. Accessed 24 Aug 2018.

"Mass crimes against humanity and genocides: Atrocities since World War 11," Ontario Consultants, *Religious Tolerance*, 1 Jan. 2001, religioustolerance.org/genocide4.htm. Accessed 31 Aug 2018.

"Primary Accounts of Joseph Smith's First Vision of Deity," *The Joseph Smith Papers*, josephsmithpapers.org/site/accounts-of-the-first-vision. Accessed 29 Aug 2018.

"Question: What about the revelation John Taylor received on September 27, 1886?" *Mormon Fundamentalism, Modern Polygamy and Mormon Fundamentalism*, mormonfundamentalism.com. Accessed 26 Aug 2018.

"Relationship of the Joseph Smith Translation of the Bible to the Book of Mormon," *FairMormon.org*, fairmormon.org/answers/Mormonism_and_the_Bible/Joseph_Smith_Translation/Relationship_to_the_Book_of_Mormon. Accessed 31 Aug 2018.

"Science and Technology in Ancient China." *Crystalinks*, *Ellie Crystal*, crystalinks.com/chinascience.html. Accessed 24 Aug 2018.

"Tacitus on Christ." *Wikipedia*, 8 Aug 2018, *Wikimedia Foundation, Inc.*, en.wikipedia.org/wiki/Tacitus_on_Christ. Accessed 28 Aug. 2018. His works can be found here: en.wikipedia.org/wiki/Tacitus#Works.

"The Garden." *The LDS Endowment. LDSEndowment.org*, ldsendowment.org/garden.html. Accessed 26 Aug 2018.

"The Mormon Temple Endowment Ceremony: Comparison between the pre and post 1990 versions." *LDS-Mormon.com*, lds-mormon.com/compare.shtml. Accessed 26 Aug, 2018.

"The Prairies, Nauvoo, Joe Smith, the Temple, the Mormons &c." *Pittsburg Gazette*, vol. 58, no. 3, 15 Sept. 1843. *Uncle Dale's Readings in Early Mormon History*, sidneyrigdon.com/dbroadhu/PA/penn1842.htm#091543. Accessed 29 Aug 2018.

Aguilar, Francisco de. A Brief Account of the Conquest of New Spain. National Autonomous U of Mexico, 1525.

Arrington, Leonard J. *Brigham Young, American Moses*. Knopf, 1985, pp. 312–13.

Big Love, created by Mark Olsen and Will Scheffer, performance by Bill Paxton, et al., Anima Sola Productions, 2006–11, imdb.com/title/tt0421030/. Accessed 31 Aug 2018.

Burns, David D., M.D. *Feeling Good: The New Mood Therapy*. William Morrow, 1999.

Callinicus, *Life of Saint Hypatius*, 1895.

Chase, Randal S. *Making Precious Things Plain, Vol 1: Book of Mormon Study Guide, Pt. 1:1 Nephi–Mosiah*, Plain and Precious Publishing, 2007, p. 168.

Cheesman, Paul. "An Analysis of the Accounts Relating Joseph Smith's Early Visions." *All Theses and Dissertations*, 1965, scholarsarchive.byu.edu/etd/4590/. Accessed 29 Aug 2018.

Clark, David L. *Of Heaven and Earth: Reconciling Scientific Thought with LDS Theology*. Deseret Book, 1998, p. 203.

Compton, Todd. *In Sacred Loneliness: The Plural Wives of Joseph Smith*. Signature Books, 1997, p. 11.

Dahl, Larry E., and Charles D. Tate, Jr. *The Lectures on Faith, in Historical Perspective*. Bookcraft Pubs, 1990, pp. 3–7.

Deng, Francis M. *Sudan - Civil War and Genocide,* Middle East Quarterly, vol. 8, no. 1, Winter 2001, pp. 13–21, meforum.org/articles/other/sudan-civil-war-and-genocide, Accessed 31 Aug 2018.

Deschner, Karlheinz. *Opus Diaboli*, edited by Reinbek, 1987.

Doctrine and Covenants of the Church of the Latter Day Saints: Carefully Selected from the Revelations of God and Compiled by Joseph Smith Junior. Oliver Cowdery, Sidney Rigdon,

Frederick G. Williams *[Presiding Elders of said Church.] Proprietors.* Kirtland, 1835, *The Joseph Smith Papers,* josephsmithpapers.org/paper-summary/doctrine-and-covenants-1835/9. Accessed 28 Aug 2018.

Ehrman, Bart D. *Jesus, Interrupted: Revealing the Hidden Contradictions in the Bible (And Why We Don't Know About Them).* HarperOne, 2009, pp. 104–12, 263–65.

---. *Misquoting Jesus: The Story Behind Who Changed the Bible and Why.* HarperOne, 2005, pp. 78–81.

Gibbon, Edward. *The History of the Decline and Fall of the Roman Empire.* 1776. Edited by J. B. Bury with an Introduction by W.E.H. Lecky, vol. 1, Fred de Fau and Co.,1906. *Online Library of Liberty,* 2018, *Liberty Fund, Inc.,* oll.libertyfund.org/titles/1365. Accessed 29 Aug 2018.

Gorton, H. Clay. *The Legacy of the Brass Plates of Laban.* Horizon, 1994, p. 84.

Gruss, Edmond C. and Thuet, Lane A. *What Every Mormon (And Non-mormon) Should Know: Examining Mormon History, Doctrines and Claims.* Xulon Press, 2006, pp. 36–48.

Hakeem, Michael. *Holocaust in Christian Russia.* Freethought Today. ffrf.org/legacy/fttoday/back/hakeem/index.html. Accessed 31 Aug 2018.

Hyde, Jesse. "1984 Lafferty case still haunts." *Deseret News,* 24 July 2004, *Deseret News,* deseretnews.com/article/595079489. Accessed 26 Aug 2018.

Inspired Translation, see "Smith, Joseph. *Joseph Smith Translation.*"

Ivins, Anthony W. *Conference Report,* April 1929, p. 15, archive.org/stream/millennialstar9122eng/millennialstar9122eng_djvu.txt. Accessed 31 Aug 2018.

J. E. McCullough, *Home: The Savior of Civilization,* Southern Co-operative League, 1924, p. 42. *Conference Report,* April 1935, p. 116.

Jackson, Kent P., et al., editors. *Joseph Smith's New Translation of the Bible: Original Manuscripts.* Religious Studies Center, Brigham Young University, 2004. *BYU Studies Quarterly,* byustudies.byu.edu/content/joseph-smiths-new-translation-bible-original-manuscripts. Accessed 30 Aug 2018.

Jessee, Dean C. "How Lovely was the Morning." *Dialogue: A Journal of Mormon Thought,* vol. 6, no. 1, p. 87, dialoguejournal.com/wp-content/uploads/sbi/issues/V06N01.pdf. Accessed 29 Aug 2018.

Jordan, Michael. *Dictionary of Gods and Goddesses*. 2nd ed., Checkmark Books, 2005, p. viii.

Kirkham, Francis W. *A New Witness for Christ in America: The Book of Mormon*. Zion's Printing and Publishing Company, 1943, pp. 414–15.

Kirkland, Boyd. "The Development of the Mormon Jehovah Doctrine," *Sunstone*, vol. 36, no. 44, Autumn 1984.

Kouchel, Bernard I. "Mormons Hijack Dead or Alive Jewish Souls." *The Issue of The Mormon Baptisms of Jewish Holocaust Victims and Other Jewish Dead*," 2008. *JewishGen*, jewishgen.org/InfoFiles/ldsagree.html. Accessed 26 Aug 2018.

Krakauer, Jon. *Under the Banner of Heaven: A Story of Violent Faith*, Doubleday, 2003.

Larson, Charles M. *By His Own Hand Upon Papyrus*. Institute for Religious Research, 1985, pp. 173–75.

Larson, Stan. "The Odyssey of Thomas Stuart Ferguson." *Dialogue: A Journal of Mormon Thought*, vol. 23, no. 1, Spring 1990, pp. 53–93.

Latter Day Saints' Messenger and Advocate, vol. 1, no. 3, Dec. 1834, p. 42; vol. 1, no. 5, Feb. 1835, pp. 78–79. *Centerplace.org*, centerplace.org/history/ma/. Accessed 29 Aug 2018.

Lobdell, William. "Bedrock of a Faith is Jolted." *LA Times*, 16 Feb. 2006, articles.latimes.com/2006/feb/16/local/me-mormon16. Accessed 30 Aug 2018.

Longman, Timothy. *Christianity and Genocide in Rwanda*. Cambridge University Press, 2009.

Manchester, William. *A World Lit Only by Fire: The Medieval Mind and The Renaissance-Portrait of an Age*, Back Bay Books, 2009.

McConkie, Bruce R. *Mormon Doctrine*, 2nd ed., Bookcraft, 1979, pp. 369, 389–90, 392, 359, 784.

Moody, Raymond A, with Paul Perry. *The Light Beyond*, Bantam Books, 1988, p. 71.

Moore, Carrie A. "Debate renewed with change in Book of Mormon introduction." *Deseret News*, 8 Nov. 2007, deseretnews.com/article/695226008/Debate-renewed-with-change-in-Book-of-Mormon-introduction.html. Accessed 30 Aug 2018.

Morris, Henry M. *The Biblical Basis for Modern Science*. Master Books, 2002.

Murphy, Thomas W. "Simply Implausible: DNA and a Mesoamerican Setting for the Book of Mormon," *Dialogue: A Journal of Mormon Thought*, vol. 36, no. 109, Winter, 2003, pp. 109–131, papers.ssrn.com/sol3/papers.cfm?abstract_id=2177709. Accessed 30 Aug 2018.

NewsOne Staff. "Mormon Church Apologizes For Baptizing Holocaust Victims." *NewsOne*, 15 February 2012. *Interactive One, LLC*, newsone.com/1875355/mormon-church-apologizes-for-baptizing-holocaust-victims/. Accessed 26 Aug 2018.

Oh, God! Directed by Carl Reiner. Performances by John Denver, George Burns, and Teri Garr. Warner Bros, 1977.

Phelan, John E., Jr. *Essential Eschatology: Our Present and Future Hope*. IVP Academic, 2013, p. 119.

Ramsey, Tom. "How many people have ever lived? Keyfitz's calculation updated." *University of Hawaii at Manoa, Department of Mathematics*, 18 June 1999, math.hawaii.edu/~ramsey/People.html. Accessed 26 Aug 2018.

Rannells, Andrew. "I Believe." *The Book Of Mormon*, Ensemble, Ghostlight Records, 2011.

Roberts, B. H. *Studies of the Book of Mormon*, edited by Brigham D. Madsen, U of Illinois P, 1985, pp. 91–94, 149, 250.

Shakespeare, *Hamlet*, Act 2, Scene 2.

Sister Wives, produced by Tim Gibbons, et al., performance by Meri Brown, et al., Puddle Monkey Productions, 2010–2018, imdb.com/title/tt1721666/. Accessed 30 Aug 2018.

Slick, Matt. "Is Mormonism a cult?" *Christian Apologetics and Research Ministry*, carm.org/is-mormonism-cult. Accessed 12 May 2018.

Smith, Joseph F. *Gospel Doctrine: Selections from The Sermons and Writings of Joseph F. Smith*. 11th ed., Deseret Book, 1959, pp. 365, archive.org/stream/gospeldoctrine009956mbp#page/n383. Accessed 30 Aug 2018.

Smith, Joseph Fielding. *Doctrines of Salvation*, vol 1, pp. 107–20; vol. 2, pp. 58–99, Bookcraft, 1954–56.

Smith, Joseph. *Scriptural Teachings of the Prophet Joseph Smith*. Text selected and arranged by Joseph Fielding Smith, scriptural annotations and introduction by Richard C. Galbraith, Deseret Book, 1993, pp. 162–63; 187; 219; 300–01; 345–47; 353–54,

LDS Scripture Citation Index, scriptures.byu.edu/stpjs.html. Accessed 29 Aug. 2018.

---. *History of the Church of Jesus Christ of Latter-day Saints.* Preface, introduction, and notes by B. H. Roberts, 7 vols., Deseret Book, 1980 (nicknamed *History of the Church*).

 The "King Follett Discourse" is printed in vol. 6, pp. 302–17, *The Joseph Smith Papers*, josephsmithpapers.org/site/accounts-of-the-king-follett-sermon. Accessed 27 Aug. 2018.

 The "Sermon in the Grove" is printed in vol. 6, pp. 473–79, *The Joseph Smith Papers*, Emp.byui.edu/jexj/courses/sermon_in_the_grove.htm. Accessed 27 Aug 2018.

---. *Joseph Smith Translation* (reference throughout this book as *Inspired Translation*). Printed as an Appendix to the Holy Bible. Salt Lake City: Corporation of the President of The Church of Jesus Christ of Latter-day Saints, 1985. (This was originally copyrighted by the RLDS Church [now known as Community of Christ]). Found as the *Inspired Version of the Bible* online at *CenterPlace.org*, centerplace.org/hs/iv/default.htm. Accessed 27 Aug 2018.

---. *Lectures on Faith* (LDS version), found in *The Doctrine and Covenants of the Church of Jesus Christ of Latter Day Saints; Carefully Selected from the Revelations of God. By Joseph Smith, President of Said Church.* 2nd ed. Nauvoo, 1844, pp. 54, 70–71. *The Joseph Smith Papers*, josephsmithpapers.org/paper-summary/doctrine-and-covenants-1844/56. Accessed 25 Aug. 2018.

---. *Teachings of the Prophet Joseph Smith.* Complied by Joseph Fielding Smith, Deseret Book, 1938. *See also* "Smith, Joseph. *Scriptural Teachings.*"

Smith, Lucy. "Lucy Mack Smith, History, 1845." *The Joseph Smith Papers*, handwritten by Howard Coray, pp. 93–94. Intellectual Reserve, Inc., josephsmithpapers.org/paper-summary/lucy-mack-smith-history-1845/100. Accessed August 25, 2018.

 Compare to: Smith, Lucy Mack. *Lucy's Book: Critical Edition of Lucy Mack Smith's Family Memoir*, edited by Lavina Fielding Anderson and Irene M. Bates, Signature Books, p. 357. *Signature Books Library*, signaturebookslibrary.org/lucys-book-03/. Accessed 29 Aug 2018.

This is the portion removed: "About this time their [*sic*] was a great revival in religion and the whole neighborhood was very much aroused to the subject and we among the rest flocked to the meeting house to see if their [*sic*] was a word of comfort for us that might releive [*sic*] our overcharged feelings…"

Snow Smith, Eliza R. *Biography and Family Record of Lorenzo Snow.* Deseret News Company, Printers, 1884, p. 46.

Southerton, Simon G, *Losing a Lost Tribe: Native Americans, DNA and the Mormon Church.* Signature Books, 2004, signaturebooks.com/excerpts/losing.html. Accessed 30 Aug 2018.

Stubbs, Brian D. "Elusive Israel and the Numerical Dynamics of Population Mixing," *FARMS Review*, Maxwell Institute, vol. 15, no. 2, pp. 165–82.

The Book of Mormon—An Account Written by the Hand of Mormon, Upon Plates Taken from the Plates of Nephi. Translated by Joseph Smith, Jun., Palmyra, 1830. The Church of Jesus Christ of Latter-day Saints, 1988.

The Doctrine and Covenants of The Church of Jesus Christ of Latter-day Saints Containing Revelations Given to Joseph Smith, the Prophet, with Some Additions by his Successors in the Presidency of the Church. The Church of Jesus Christ of Latter-day Saints, 1988.

The Holy Bible Containing the Old and New Testaments. Authorized King James Version, The Church of Jesus Christ of Latter-Day Saints, 1988.

The Pearl of Great Price: A Selection from the Revelations, Translations, and Narrations of Joseph Smith, First Prophet, Seer, and Revelator to the Church of Jesus Christ of Latter-day Saints. The Church of Jesus Christ of Latter-day Saints, 1988.

The Qur'an. Translated by M. A .S. Abdel Haleem, Oxford UP, 2005, p. 205. *Internet Archive*, archive.org/details/TheQuranOxfrdWrldClas. Accessed 29 Aug 2018.

Vance, Del. *Beer in the Beehive*: *A History of Brewing in Utah.* 2nd ed., Dream Garden Press, 2008.

Watt, G.D. "Remarks by President Brigham Young, in the Bowery, in G.S.L. City, August 19th, 1866." *Journal of Discourses by President Brigham Young, His Two Counsellors [sic], and the Twelve Apostles*, vol. 11, Liverpool, 1867, p. 272.

Wayment, Thomas A. *The Complete Joseph Smith Translation of the Old Testament*. Deseret Book, 2009.

Wheatcroft, Stephen. "The Scale and Nature of German and Soviet Repression Mass Killings, 1930–1945," *Europe-Asia Studies*, vol. 48, no. 8, 1996, pp. 1319–53.

Whiting, Michael F. "DNA and the Book of Mormon: A Phylogenetic Perspective." *BYU Maxwell Institute*, 2003, pp. 24–35, publications.mi.byu.edu/publications/jbms/12/1/S00003-50be689b951354Whiting.pdf. Accessed 30 Aug 2018.

World Hunger Education Service. "2013 World Hunger and Poverty Facts and Statistics." *Hunger Notes*, worldhunger.org/articles/Learn/old/world%20hunger%20facts%202002_2012version.htm. Accessed 24 Aug. 2018.

Young, Brigham. "Brigham Young Address to Legislature – Feb 5, 1852." *Historian's Office Reports of speeches: Brigham Young, 1852 February 5*, Church History Library, The Church of Jesus Christ of Latter-day Saints, Salt Lake City, 1852, p. 2. *Internet Archive*, archive.org/details/CR100317B0001F0017. Accessed 26 Aug 2018.

Richard Nemelka was born in 1943 in Salt Lake City, Utah to wonderful parents who were devout Mormons. They taught their children to believe in Mormon theology, be active in the Mormon Church, go on missions, and be married in the Mormon temple. Richard did each of these things. He attended West High school and participated in sports and student government. He also attended Brigham Young University, where he earned both a Bachelors and a Masters Degree in Psychology. At BYU, he participated in basketball and baseball and earned various awards and honors. After a short stint playing professional basketball, he attended the University of Utah Law School and was admitted into the Utah State Bar as an attorney in April 1975. He practiced law (primarily in Salt Lake, Davis, and Utah counties) for over 40 years before retiring. He has four fantastic sons and four adorable grandchildren and currently resides in St. George, Utah, where he writes and plays golf.

Cover art by Sara Smith